Multiple-Choice & Topical Review
in Preparation for the
AP Computer Science Principles Examination

FIRST EDITION

by

Leon Schram

John Paul II High School
Plano, Texas

ISBN # 978-1-934780-46-6 / 1-934780-46-4

Preface

This book has been prepared with one purpose in mind: to help students prepare for the Advanced Placement Computer Science Principles Examination. It should be clear from the start that students will have to complete two performance tasks prior to the end-of-course multiple-choice questions on the AP examination. Our focus is on the multiple-choice area. Students of Computer Science frequently get the kind of practice they need in developing algorithms and writing programs through programming assignments during the course of the year, but all too often there is not enough time for teachers to practice multiple-choice questions at the AP Computer Science Examination level. This book seeks to serve that purpose. There are a total of 328 multiple-choice questions, providing a vast array of practice for the examination. Additionally, there is some guidance on the requirements for the Explore Performance Task and the Create Performance Task.

The questions you will find within have been specifically chosen to give students a review experience over the wide range of topics covered on the AP Computer Science Principles Examination. The difficulty level of the questions aims to be as varied and challenging as those on the exam itself, and deliberately more challenging in some areas.

For the teacher of Advanced Placement Computer Science Principles, this book is designed to provide you and your students with additional practice materials. For the student of computer science, I hope this book helps you achieve continued success in an exciting and important field.

All communication concerning this book should be addressed to the publisher and distributor:

D&S Marketing Systems, Inc.
1205 38th Street
Brooklyn, New York 11218

www.dsmarketing.com

Foreword to the 1st Edition

The most important requirement for review materials is that the questions cover the range of topics that will be tested, so that strengths and weaknesses in test preparation can be identified. Another requirement is to gain familiarity with question style. Creating this question book has been very challenging. The topics of the seven Big Ideas in the curriculum are familiar to any experienced computer science teacher. The challenge is to determine the degree of detail that needs to be taught and what needs to be tested.

In creating this first edition I have relied heavily on the College Board's very detailed Course Description for AP Computer Science Principles, the College Board's provided practice exam, workshops I have taught and attended and communication with many teachers who are active with the College Board and AP Computer Science Principles.

The first edition presents a special situation. Any practice exam will simply not be able to provide sample questions in every area shown in the course description. I know from my own experience on the AP Computer Science Test Development Committee that some topics, which we felt were very significant topics, showed up yearly in every test we created. Other, less significant topics were cycled perhaps about every three years. This means that this question book does include questions that are not shown on the current practice exam. However, the topics of these questions are listed in the official course description. Such questions are included with the attitude that these topics may be covered on future AP exams.

Advanced Placement teachers face a classic *no-win situation* as they prepare students for an AP examination. A teacher can give students sample examinations that are very rigorous and hope that students will be relieved that the real exam is not as difficult as the practice test. The problem with this approach is that some students will be discouraged and select not to take the examination. A teacher can also give a relatively easy examination to motivate students and give them a sense of success. This approach also has a problem since it can result in a serious *cold shower* during the real AP examination.

Many teachers prefer a compromise and like to give a practice examination that is neither too hard nor too easy and represents the difficulty level of the actual examination. Such is a lofty goal that is easily mentioned but difficult to attain. Multiple-choice examinations are not released on a yearly basis and the difficulty level of exam questions is hard to predict. We are also at the stage were there exists no released examination yet.

The main purpose of the two sample examinations in this book is to help prepare students for the *real thing*. I have decided to fault on the side of difficulty. Furthermore, students often find questions on the AP examination that are long and time-consuming to read. Normally, students have not received many *full-page* questions during the school year. Students must budget their time wisely as they take difficult, time-controlled tests. The sample examinations in this book intentionally contain some time-consuming questions to alert students to the reality of time budgeting. There are a variety of questions that involve selecting the correct solution for some incomplete procedure. I have noticed with my own students that the biggest problem with such long questions is that students skip them. Students think these questions are too long and too complicated. In reality, the long *complete-the-procedure* style questions are quite manageable, and experience has shown that students handle them very well with sufficient exposure.

Roughly half the questions pertain to programming and algorithms. These questions have very clear definitive answers for students who understand the program code and program logic correctly. Questions on the other big ideas will seem at first to be opinion-style questions. The questions are not mathematical in nature. Yet each question has a single (or sometimes double) correct answer. A question may ask which approach in handling sensitive data is more secure. Well is that not somebody's opinion? In reality, the question can be analyzed and it can be determined that some situations are easier to compromise than others. With practice this style of question becomes more comfortable. The spirit of the topical questions and sample examinations is to give students exposure and prepare them to succeed on the real test. I hope these questions will satisfy that goal.

Leon Schram
Royse City, Texas

Table of Contents

Chapter 1 Review
Selecting a Programming Language
(A chapter mostly for teachers and possible interest to students)

The Reality of the AP Computer Science Principles Curriculum

I have taught AP Computer Science since it started in 1983. Over more than three decades I have seen many changes. These changes were always very clear. We were told what programming language to use. We were told the subset of the language that would be tested. We were told which computer science topics are part of the curriculum. We were told what case study would be used. The challenge always was to learn the new program language, to learn the new case study or to learn the new AP labs and the biggest challenge of all was how to teach this all in less than one year. There was no guesswork about requirements. We knew what to teach.

Well, welcome to AP Computer Science Principles (AP CSP). There is guesswork aplenty. The College Board's provided Course Description is very remarkable in its thorough, systematic explanation of the complex curriculum. Keep in mind that you cannot simply read the course description once and comprehend what is going on.

The curriculum starts with six *Computational Thinking Practices* and then integrates them with the *Seven Big Ideas* that are the major areas of study. There is no guesswork here since the official course description specifies both the practices and the ideas. Now comes the fun, and frankly, it is both the biggest appeal and the biggest challenge of the course. It is the "now what" issue. Teachers have an amazing amount of freedom. Freedom to decide not only how to teach some big idea, but also what to teach. This is exciting, but scary at the same time.

This is a review book meant to assist teachers and students preparing for the AP Computer Science Principles Exam, but this review must start with facing the reality of the unique curriculum of this new course.

The title at the start of this chapter states *Selecting A Programming Language*. Selecting a language requires an appreciation of the scope of the curriculum and a clear understanding how students are evaluated. There are some objective measurements used to determine the final AP score and these measurements are clearly stated in the course description.

Seven Big Ideas

It is easy to provide a curriculum framework, but it is not so easy to determine what to teach and how to distribute time for each topic. There are seven big ideas in the course description, shown in figure 1.1. Perhaps it sounds very simple. Math tells us that the distribution is 1/7 or roughly 14% for each big idea towards the final AP score.

Using 14% sounds simple. but that is not how the course is designed or evaluated. There are two objective measures to determine the weight of topics. First, there is the actual course description, which states very specific percentages that will be used for evaluating students.

Second, there is the College Board provided practice exam. You can count questions in different categories to get a good idea of the practical reality. Between the course description and the practice exam, we should be able to make some accurate conclusions.

Figure 1.1

Big Ideas
Big Idea 1: Creativity
Big Idea 2: Abstraction
Big Idea 3: Data and Information
Big Idea 4: Algorithms
Big Idea 5: Programming
Big Idea 6: The Internet
Big Idea 7: Global Impact

Let us start with the Assessment Overview, shown in figure 1.2. *The Explore Performance Task* (PT) requires that students create a *computational artifact*. Most students will create a movie, some web pages or a still image. Students can do a program, but not many students use that option. So this 16% of the AP score is not in the programming column.

The *Create Performance Task* counts for 24% of the AP score. That is a big chunk. What are the options for the 2nd PT? Is it very flexible like the Explore PT? Yes, it is flexible in what can be shown, but not in format as you will see shortly.

Figure 1.2

AP Computer Science Principles Assessment Overview

The AP Computer Science Principles assessment has two parts. The first is a through-course performance assessment consisting of two performance tasks and the second is an end-of-course AP Exam. All of these components are summative and the scoring results of each will be used to calculate a final AP score using the 1–5 scale, as shown in the table below.

Component	Timing	Percentage of Total AP Score
Explore Performance Task	8 hours	16%
Create Performance Task	12 hours	24%
End-of-Course Exam	2 hours	60%

Sometimes students read the instructions for the first PT and think it is similar for the second PT. It is not. The Create PT requires the creation of a program. Look at the overview from the course description shown in Figure 1.3. It says: In *this performance task, you will be developing a* ***program*** *of your choice.* This is very clear language. That means that at least 24% of your total AP Exam score is based on programming.

Figure 1.3

Performance Task: Create – Applications from Ideas

Overview

Programming is a collaborative and creative process that brings ideas to life through the development of software. Programs can help solve problems, enable innovations, or express personal interests. In this performance task, you will be developing a program of your choice. Your development process should include iteratively designing, implementing, and testing your program. You are strongly encouraged to work with another student in your class.

24% is greater than 14% and that means programming is more than 14% of the AP Score. But there is also the multiple-choice exam. Figure 1.4 shows a table from the course description that assigns percentages to each one of the *big ideas* tested on the exam. Big Idea 5: is 20% of the exam. Now it gets tricky, because many of the big ideas cross over into other categories. Algorithms can be tested with or without programming. It can also be argued that programming is an excellent way to test the accuracy of an algorithm. Designing any meaningful program will include the selection and implementation of algorithms.

Figure 1.4

Big Ideas	Approximate Percentage of Multiple-Choice Questions
Big Idea 1: Creativity	---
Big Idea 2: Abstraction	19%
Big Idea 3: Data and Information	18%
Big Idea 4: Algorithms	20%
Big Idea 5: Programming	20%
Big Idea 6: The Internet	13%
Big Idea 7: Global Impact	10%

Abstraction is also heavily used with programming, but can be shown in many ways without getting programs involved. So let us leave that out. Now do a little math. We have 24% for the *create* performance task. Then there is 20% each for programming and for algorithms on the multiple-choice exam, which is 60% of the total grade. This adds up to 48%. So basically half of the AP Computer Science (Principles) score is based on programming.

We are now ready to look at some other measurements. This is mostly for teachers, but the four styles that follow can be anticipated. Looking at the College Board practice exam of 74 questions closely, the following conclusion can be made.

There are four main styles of programming questions detailed in figure 1.5. They are:

- *Programming questions that use block-based pseudo-code.*

- *Programming questions that use text-based pseudo-code*
  .

- *Programming questions that use a grid to move a robot around using block-based or text-based pseudo-code. There are additional commands just for robot questions.*

- *Programming questions that ask questions about programming logic without using any program code.*

- *Algorithm questions that use logical steps to complete a goal in English.*

Figure 1.5

1. There are programming questions with block-based pseudo-code. The actual program words, like `PROCEDURE` and `REPEAT` are the same in block-based and text-based pseudo-code.	

2. There are programming questions with text-based pseudo-code. The actual program words, like `PROCEDURE` and `REPEAT` are the same in block-based and text-based pseudo-code.	```x ← [15,20,25,30,35,40]
	n ← LENGTH (x) - 1
	k ← 1
	REPEAT n TIMES
	{
	    x[k] ← x[k+1]
	    k ← k + 1
	}```

3. There are programming questions with a robot moving in a grid. The robot, shown by a black triangle, moves along the grid, following commands. These commands are in text-based or block-based pseudo-code. There are also special commands for robot programs only, like `MOVE_FORWARD`.	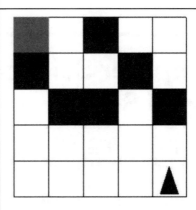
4. There are algorithm questions that look very much like programming.	Consider the algorithm below, which processes two integer variables n1 and n2 and returns variable n3. Step 1: Divide n1 by n2 and assign the remainder to integer variable rem. Step 2: If rem has the value 0, assign the value of n2 to n3 and finish by returning n3. Step 3: If rem does not have the value 0, continue. Step 4: Assign the value of n2 to n1 Step 5: Assign the value of rem to n2. Step 6: Go to Step 1.
5. There are programming questions that ask questions about programming without using any program code.	An algorithm is created to generate a random integer in a specified range. Which of the following programming structures must be added to the existing algorithm to generate a specified quantity of random numbers?

There are exactly 37 questions out of 74 that fall in the categories of the earlier matrix. This is 50% of the multiple-choice AP Exam. This also follows the College Board percentages. With half the end-of-course exam added to the Create Performance task we get 54% for the entire exam. This means that either way one looks at the evaluation process, roughly half the AP Computer Science Principles score revolves around programming.

We are not yet ready to talk about *which programming language* to use. We have looked at the different style of questions that may appear, but not the topics within the language. The AP Exam will present questions in pseudo-code, but those pseudo-code questions are based on a programming subset of commands.

The course description provides a reference guide of programming features that will be tested. It is followed by a set of pseudo-code examples, both block-based and text-based that will be used for actual program code. Figure 1.6 shows the first page of the reference sheet. If you are new to programming this page probably means nothing, but if you are a teacher or a second-year computer science student, you may realize that Object Oriented Programming and all its features are not included.

Figure 1.6

AP Computer Science Principles Exam Reference Sheet

As AP Computer Science Principles does not designate any particular programming language, this reference sheet provides instructions and explanations to help students understand the format and meaning of the questions they will see on the exam. The reference sheet includes two programming formats: text based and block based.

Programming instructions use four data types: numbers, Booleans, strings, and lists.

Instructions from any of the following categories may appear on the exam:

- Assignment, Display, and Input
- Arithmetic Operators and Numeric Procedures
- Relational and Boolean Operators
- Selection
- Iteration
- List Operations
- Procedures
- Robot

No Object Oriented Programming (OOP)? Is that significant? Consider the two program segments in figure 1.7. Both small programs will display **Hello World**. Java is an OOP language. Python can be done without using OOP. Java wants program statements to be inside method containers and then methods need to be inside class containers. All you want to do is say **Hello World** and look at the difference in program code between Java and Python.

Figure 1.7

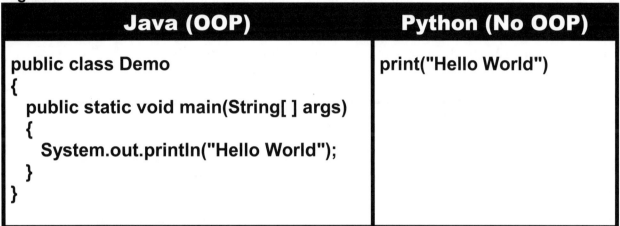

Java (OOP)	Python (No OOP)
```public class Demo { public static void main(String[ ] args) { System.out.println("Hello World"); } }```	```print("Hello World")```

I am intentionally coming out against Java, because I suspect that many teachers, who started as AP Computer Science (A) teachers may feel that Java is their best language. Not best for teaching AP CSP, but they know the language best. For your information Java and C++ are my best languages and I am not suggesting that you use either language.

My point is ... programming is far more important than you might expect by a quick glance at this new computer science curriculum. The course is not program-centric. But it is 50% of the course. Please do realize that there is still another 50% that needs to be taught. The course has many topics and like its AP Computer Science (A) cousin, it is challenging to get the entire curriculum packed into one school year.

For that reason, a language such as Java, with its Object Oriented Programming baggage, should be avoided. There are other languages that can accomplish more in a shorter time. Teachers and students alike may find the banner below rather obvious. Think about it. It is important that you have the proficiency to create a nice computational artifact that demonstrates all the requirements set for this task. You probably want some additional programming features, like graphics. It is not tested on the multiple-choice exam, but it certainly makes you program output more interesting and appealing.

You need to know a programming language to complete the Create Performance Task.

Drop & Drag Programming Languages

On our programming language selection journey we can divide the languages in two categories: *drop & drag languages* and *traditional text languages*. First take a look at three popular drop & drag program languages. Drop & drag programming languages have tremendous appeal for first introduction to programming. Students do not need to be concerned with the exact spelling of program keywords. There are special program blocks, ready to go, that can be selected and placed inside a program. These languages often have special commands to allow rather advanced features to be used. For instance, Lego NXT has a **move** program block that can make a robot car move a certain distance, go at a specified speed and can also be used to make the robot car turn in a circle. You can do quite a lot immediately with very little effort.

Figure 1.8

Scratch	
Scratch allows students to create nice animations by dragging different program features in place. These building blocks are mostly named in a manner that is used by the more traditional text-style language. The program segment shown here demonstrates a two-way selection structure using an **if..else** block.	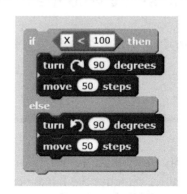
Snap	
Snap is based on Scratch and includes new advanced features. Like Scratch it is a good first-introduction language.	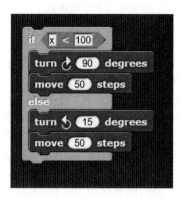
Lego NXT	
The Lego NXT language is designed to interface with its robot program block that can be part of a robot, car or crane. The program blocks use pictures to indicate their purpose. This language is quite different from the pseudo-code that is used by the AP CSP course.	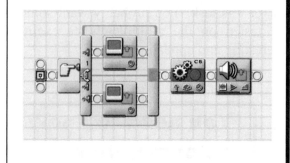

Text-Style Traditional Programming Languages

Text-style traditional languages are the languages used for the majority of programs, especially system programs, such as a computer operating system. These languages do not have the friendly color appearance and quick satisfaction of the drop & drag languages.

Figure 1.8

C++	

C++ is a very popular language in the computer science industry, especially system programming. It has the power to accomplish requirements that are difficult in other languages. This same power can make the language a problem for beginners, who can unknowingly cause problems.	<pre>18 if (sat >= 1100)
	19 {
	20 cout << "Good news applicant" << endl;
	21 cout << "You are admitted" << endl;
	22 }
	23 else
	24 {
	25 cout << "We are sorry applicant" << endl;
	26 cout << "You are not admitted" << endl;
	27 }
	28</pre>

Python	

Python is a language that is very readable and easy to use. It has OOP capabilities, but students can write programs without ever touching any OOP features, including graphics programming.	<pre>14 if (sat >= 1100):
	15 print("Good news applicant")
	16 print("You are admitted.")
	17 else:
	18 print("We are sorry applicant")
	19 print("You are not admitted")
	20</pre>

Java	

Java is a very popular modern language that was designed for Internet use. It is an Object Oriented Programming language with many capabilities.
 	
All programs must satisfy fundamental OOP requirements.
	<pre>18 if (sat >= 1100)
	19 {
	20 System.out.println("Good news applicant");
	21 System.out.println("You are admitted");
	22 }
	23 else
	24 {
	25 System.out.println("We are sorry applicant");
	26 System.out.println("You are not admitted");
	27 }
	28</pre>

It is not my intention in this chapter to explain the virtues and problems of many program languages. The six languages shown were meant more to show the difference between drop & drag and text-style languages. I will conclude this chapter by showing the reasons why I selected Python for my AP CSP students.

Leon Schram's Reasons To Use Python With AP CSP

- All the program language features that are required for the AP CSP course are available in the Python language.

- Python can be taught in a non-OOP procedural style that is simple. Students can quickly reach the point of creating interesting programs.

- Python programming style and appearance is quite similar to the pseudo-code that will be used on the multiple-choice examination.

- The included turtle graphics with Python is easy to use and also provides a great introduction to graphics programming.

- Even though turtle graphics lacks many features of more sophisticated graphics packages, this is easily remedied by an important lab assignment whereby students create their own improved graphics library with turtle graphics. This has the secondary benefit that students now see an excellent example of the use of abstraction with the completion of this assignment. With the aid of the new and improved graphics package, students are well equipped to create interesting graphics programs for the create computational artifact.

- Students may well decide to continue in the field of technology, including computer science and engineering courses. In such courses students will benefit from programming experience with a traditional text-style language, such as Python.

Please keep in mind that you are the teacher of your class. You may already be very familiar with JavaScript and you prefer to use that language. Perhaps you attended a summer workshop where language xyz was promoted for teaching AP CSP and you agreed with the compelling reasons of using language xyz. This chapter has been mostly for the new teachers who likely needs guidance and the opinion of an experienced teacher. Current experienced teachers will have no problems selecting a language. I personally have used Python with my students for several years and I am very pleased with my student feedback and results. I will gladly discuss my Python decision with you if you have questions. Email me at **leonschram@sbcglobal.net**.

Chapter 2 Review
Creativity

Creativity is **Big Idea 1**, but you will not find sample questions in this chapter. There will also not be questions on this topic in the Sample Exams. Figure 2.1 shows a screenshot from the AP CSP Course Description and there is no percentage assigned to *Creativity* for the End-Of-Course Exam. If creativity is part of the curriculum, where is it being tested?

Figure 2.1

Big Ideas	Approximate Percentage of Multiple-Choice Questions
Big Idea 1: Creativity	---
Big Idea 2: Abstraction	19%
Big Idea 3: Data and Information	18%
Big Idea 4: Algorithms	20%
Big Idea 5: Programming	20%
Big Idea 6: The Internet	13%
Big Idea 7: Global Impact	10%

The AP Computer Science Principles Exam Reference Sheet is found in the Reproducibles for Students section and provides programming instructions and explanations to help students understand questions they will see on the AP Exam.

AP Computer Science Principles Course and Exam Description   Return to Table of Contents   84

© 2017 The College Board

There are no multiple-choice questions for the creativity big idea. The End-Of-Course Exam has no such questions, but it is 60% of the total course. Are there creativity points that are earned with the two performance tasks?

For the Explore Performance Task and for the Create Performance Task there exist very specific grading criteria that are binary. Single points are awarded based on a true or false conditions. None of the awarded points appear to be based on any type of creativity, at least not directly.

The AP CSP Course Description has considerable detail on the framework for each big idea. The framework for each big idea includes the Enduring Understandings (EU), Learning Objectives (LO) and the Essential Knowledge (EK). The details of the first page are copied here. Figure 2.2 shows that both the learning objectives and the essential knowledge items heavily discuss creativity in relation to a computational artifact.

Figure 2.2

Big Idea 1: Creativity

Computing is a creative activity. Creativity and computing are prominent forces in innovation; the innovations enabled by computing have had and will continue to have far-reaching impact. At the same time, computing facilitates exploration and the creation of computational artifacts and new knowledge that help people solve personal, societal, and global problems. This course emphasizes the creative aspects of computing. Students in this course use the tools and techniques of computer science to create interesting and relevant artifacts with characteristics that are enhanced by computation.

Essential Questions:

▸ How can a creative development process affect the creation of computational artifacts?

▸ How can computing and the use of computational tools foster creative expression?

▸ How can computing extend traditional forms of human expression and experience?

Enduring Understandings (Students will understand that ...)	Learning Objectives (Students will be able to ...)	Essential Knowledge (Students will know that ...)
EU 1.1 Creative development can be an essential process for creating computational artifacts.	**LO 1.1.1** Apply a creative development process when creating computational artifacts. [P2]	**EK 1.1.1A** A creative process in the development of a computational artifact can include, but is not limited to, employing nontraditional, nonprescribed techniques; the use of novel combinations of artifacts, tools, and techniques; and the exploration of personal curiosities.
		EK 1.1.1B Creating computational artifacts employs an iterative and often exploratory process to translate ideas into tangible form.
EU 1.2 Computing enables people to use creative development processes to create computational artifacts for creative expression or to solve a problem.	**LO 1.2.1** Create a computational artifact for creative expression. [P2]	**EK 1.2.1A** A computational artifact is something created by a human using a computer and can be, but is not limited to, a program, an image, an audio, a video, a presentation, or a Web page file.
		EK 1.2.1B Creating computational artifacts requires understanding of and use of software tools and services.

On the second page of **Big Idea 1**, there are more comments about creativity and then it switches to collaboration. The clear evidence is that creativity is quite heavily emphasized with the two computational artifacts.

Figure 2.2

Enduring Understandings (Students will understand that ...)	Learning Objectives (Students will be able to ...)	Essential Knowledge (Students will know that ...)
EU 1.2 Computing enables people to use creative development processes to create computational artifacts for creative expression or to solve a problem. (continued)	LO 1.2.1 Create a computational artifact for creative expression. [P2] (continued)	EK 1.2.1C Computing tools and techniques are used to create computational artifacts and can include, but are not limited to, programming integrated development environments (IDEs), spreadsheets, three-dimensional (3-D) printers, or text editors.
		EK 1.2.1D A creatively developed computational artifact can be created by using nontraditional, nonprescribed computing techniques.
		EK 1.2.1E Creative expressions in a computational artifact can reflect personal expressions of ideas or interests.
	LO 1.2.2 Create a computational artifact using computing tools and techniques to solve a problem. [P2]	EK 1.2.2A Computing tools and techniques can enhance the process of finding a solution to a problem.
		EK 1.2.2B A creative development process for creating computational artifacts can be used to solve problems when traditional or prescribed computing techniques are not effective.
	LO 1.2.3 Create a new computational artifact by combining or modifying existing artifacts. [P2]	EK 1.2.3A Creating computational artifacts can be done by combining and modifying existing artifacts or by creating new artifacts.
		EK 1.2.3B Computation facilitates the creation and modification of computational artifacts with enhanced detail and precision.
		EK 1.2.3C Combining or modifying existing artifacts can show personal expression of ideas.
	LO 1.2.4 Collaborate in the creation of computational artifacts. [P6]	EK 1.2.4A A collaboratively created computational artifact reflects effort by more than one person.
		EK 1.2.4B Effective collaborative teams consider the use of online collaborative tools.
		EK 1.2.4C Effective collaborative teams practice interpersonal communication, consensus building, conflict resolution, and negotiation.
		EK 1.2.4D Effective collaboration strategies enhance performance.
		EK 1.2.4E Collaboration facilitates the application of multiple perspectives (including sociocultural perspectives) and diverse talents and skills in developing computational artifacts.
		EK 1.2.4F A collaboratively created computational artifact can reflect personal expressions of ideas.

We know that there will be not be any questions on the end-of-course exam about creativity. That is plain and straight out of the course description. We also now know that creativity is connected with the computational artifacts.

In figure 2.3 we look at another College Board document. This is a small corner from the 2018 Explore Performance Tasks Scoring Guide.

The scoring criteria states at the second bullet: *Provides an illustration, representation, or explanation of the computing innovation's intended purpose, function, or effect.*

There it is, but it does not use the word creativity. The simple reality is that you earn this point if the scoring criterion is met with your representation or illustration. To achieve this properly with a limited video time of 1 minute or a single illustration can be done, but it will take considerable creativity to achieve that.

Figure 2.3

Reporting Category	Task	Scoring Criteria
Row 1 Using Development Processes and Tools	COMP. ARTIFACT	The computational artifact: • Identifies the computing innovation. **AND** • Provides an illustration, representation, or explanation of the computing innovation's intended purpose, function, or effect.

It should be clear why there will not be any sample multiple-choice questions following this introduction. More comments will be made about this topic, but that will be in a later chapter on performance tasks.

Chapter 3 Review
Abstraction I, Bits, Bases & Number Systems

It is not that easy to determine to which big idea many questions belong. This chapter will look at questions that involve numbers of different bases and converting between such numbers. All computer data is ultimately stored in binary bits and this storage is hidden from the program user or even the programmer. This is called *data abstraction*. That means that number systems can be part of Big Idea #3 *Data & Information or* Big Idea #2*: Abstraction.*

The good news is that you won't see questions that ask you to identify the big idea. I have decided to place the number system questions in *abstraction*. Sample questions shown by College board publications appear to place such questions in that category. You also need to realize that abstraction is a large topic in computer science. In this chapter the questions are related to the data representation and the understanding of different number systems. This is very different from a later chapter that will focus on other types of abstractions.

The essence of computer information revolves around the bit. Computers store all types of information. It is not only numbers for computation; it is far more. Bits manage to store college essays, email, electronic books and any similar data that is based on strings of characters. The same computers store and manipulate still pictures images, animated videos and all sorts of sound files. Remarkably all that diverse data ultimately starts with the bit and its simple ability to be two states, which are *on* or *off*, *true* or *false*, *1* or *0*, which are the two numbers of base-2 or the *binary* number system.

The starting point of the data story is to first understand how computers handle numbers. This handling of numbers requires converting the base-2 bit into other bases. Why other bases? Dealing with base-2 with its confusing sequence of 1s and 0s was the business of the early, giant computers. It was tedious. It was error-prone and it was very difficult to find errors. There is also another reality. Human beings work with base-10. Nobody wants to drive up to an ATM and withdraw cash and get a prompt to enter the amount in a base-2 number. This means that at a minimum there needs to be some conversion between the base-2 of computer storage and the base-10, *decimal* number system of human interaction.

Furthermore, there are other issues. Handing the storage and access of data requires knowledge of the computer's memory locations where data is stored. These memory locations are not numerical addresses in base-2, but actually use base-16 or *hexadecimal code*, which often is abbreviated to *hex code*. This chapter will show you, and have you practice, a wide variety of conversions between numbers in base 2, base-10 and base-16. Any career in computer science or computer engineering will require a solid knowledge of handling number systems of several bases.

Counting In Number Systems

Counting is something that you will likely take for granted, at least counting in base-10. This mathematical excursion starts by taking a new look at how we count in base-10, and how counting is done in other number systems as well. In base-10 there are ten different single digits from **0** to **9**. Counting in base-10 requires cycling through these ten digits. Every time **9** is reached the counting starts over at **0**.

Using the pattern we observe with base-10 counting, let us set up a set of rules. Keep in mind that there is nothing magic about counting in base-10. Base-10 is only easier for you because you have familiarity. You learned multiplication tables in base-10 and you are constantly surrounded by base-10. However, consider the fact that there are 60 seconds in a minute, 60 minutes in an hour. Not everything is done in base-10. This seems like a good argument, but the truth is that the metric system stays consistently with a single base, base-10 - and it is a base that people are familiar with. Switching from inches to feet, to yards, to miles involves different conversion systems. So what about these number system rules?

Counting Rules For All Bases

The number of single digits is equal to the base value.
Base-10 has 10 single digits
Base-16 has 16 single digits
Base-2 has 2 single digits

The value of the base is expressed as 10.
4 in base-4 is 10
2 in base-2 is 10
16 in base-16 is 10

The largest single digit is one less than the base value.
The largest digit in base-10 is 9
The largest digit is base-5 is 4
The largest digit in base-2 is 1
The largest digit in base-16 is F (base-16 needs digits not used in base-10)

When the largest digit is reached, counting starts over at 0, and the next place holder is incremented by 1.
Base 5: 0 1 2 3 4 10 11 12 13 14 20 21 22 23 24 30
Base 3: 0 1 2 10 11 12 20 21 22 100 101 102 110 111 112 120
Base 2: 0 1 10 11 100 101 110 111 1000 1001 1010 1011 1100

It is easy to keep on talking about how to count. At this stage it is probably simpler to look at several bases and follow the counting scheme of each base as it goes from 0 to 33, at least in base-10 that is. Base-3 and base-2 are shown last. Bases with few digits tend to be confusing because the numbers change so rapidly and so drastically. Look at base-5 and base-8 first to establish the counting pattern, and then check out base-3 and base-2.

Base 10	Base 5	Base 8	Base 3	Base-2
0	0	0	0	0
1	1	1	1	1
2	2	2	2	10
3	3	3	10	11
4	4	4	11	100
5	10	5	12	101
6	11	6	20	110
7	12	7	21	111
8	13	10	22	1000
9	14	11	100	1001
10	20	12	101	1010
11	21	13	102	1011
12	22	14	110	1100
13	23	15	111	1101
14	24	16	112	1110
15	30	17	120	1111
16	31	20	121	10000
17	32	21	122	10001
18	33	22	200	10010
19	34	23	201	10011
20	40	24	202	10100
21	41	25	210	10101
22	42	26	211	10110
23	43	27	212	10111
24	44	30	220	11000
25	100	31	221	11001
26	101	32	222	11010
27	102	33	1000	11011
28	103	34	1001	11100
29	104	35	1002	11101
30	110	36	1010	11110
31	111	37	1011	11111
32	112	40	1012	100000
33	113	41	1020	100001

Counting in Base-16

Counting in base-16 is significant in computer science. You will see that computer memory addresses are displayed in base-16 or hexadecimal. Furthermore, the MAC (Media Access Control) address or physical address of a computer is a base-16 number. There are unique properties between base-2 and base-16 that make base-16 a logical choice for number representation in a computer. In a later section we will investigate these properties. Right now you need to learn how to count in base-16.

Base-16 was intentionally not placed in the previous counting section. Every base in the previous section was smaller than base-10. This was convenient and it insured that you always used some familiar single digit. The story changes with base-16, because now it is necessary to fabricate some new single digit numerals. Base-16 requires the use of 16 single digits. Starting with value 10 base-16 uses letter A and then for 11, 12, 13, 14, and 15 base-16 uses B, C, D, and F respectively. This looks quite bizarre at first, but after a while you get used to it. Check out the table below that counts the first one hundred base-16 numbers.

B-10	B-16	B-10	B-16	B-10	B-16	B-10	B-16	B-10	B-16
1	1	21	15	41	29	61	3d	81	51
2	2	22	16	42	2a	62	3e	82	52
3	3	23	17	43	2b	63	3f	83	53
4	4	24	18	44	2c	64	40	84	54
5	5	25	19	45	2d	65	41	85	55
6	6	26	1a	46	2e	66	42	86	56
7	7	27	1b	47	2f	67	43	87	57
8	8	28	1c	48	30	68	44	88	58
9	9	29	1d	49	31	69	45	89	59
10	a	30	1e	50	32	70	46	90	5a
11	b	31	1f	51	33	71	47	91	5b
12	c	32	20	52	34	72	48	92	5c
13	d	33	21	53	35	73	49	93	5d
14	e	34	22	54	36	74	4a	94	5e
15	f	35	23	55	37	75	4b	95	5f
16	10	36	24	56	38	76	4c	96	60
17	11	37	25	57	39	77	4d	97	61
18	12	38	26	58	3a	78	4e	98	62
19	13	39	27	59	3b	79	4f	99	63
20	14	40	28	60	3c	80	50	100	64

Converting Base-2 to Base-10

There are a variety of algorithms that convert numbers between different bases. We will focus on methods that are more likely to be useful for the conversions that apply to network problems. In this section our concern is converting numbers from any base to base-10. Understanding the conversion process will first require another look at base-10 representation.

Base-10 is limited to 10 different single digits. Values ten, and larger, cannot be represented as a single digit. This problem is handled with special *place holders*. Place holders indicate the true value of a digit, which depends on the position of a digit in a number. The table below shows the place holder values for the base-10 number, 1,234,567. The top row represents the *place holder value*. The second row displays the single digits in their respective position. The bottom row shows the actual value represented by each single digit.

Place Holder	1,000,000	100,000	10,000	1,000	100	10	1
Digit Display	1	2	3	4	5	6	7
Digit Value	1,000,000	200,000	30,000	4,000	500	60	7

The next table is going a step further. This time each place holder will also be shown as a power of base-10. Row-2 will now represent the power of each place holder value. Row-3 will show the base and the appropriate exponent. The next four rows show how the actual value of each place-holding digit is computed. Row-4 computes the place holder value by raising the base 10 to the indicated power for its position. Row-5 is the actual single digit that occupies the position in the number. Row-6 shows how to multiply the digit times the place holder value, and the bottom row shows the actual value of a digit after computation.

Number	1,234,567 base-10						
Power	6	5	4	3	2	1	0
Base^{Power}	10^6	10^5	10^4	10^3	10^2	10^1	10^0
Place Holder	1,000,000	100,000	10,000	1,000	100	10	1
Digit Display	1	2	3	4	5	6	7
Expanded	1×10^6	2×10^5	3×10^4	4×10^3	5×10^2	6×10^1	7×10^0
Digit Value	1,000,000	200,000	30,000	4,000	500	60	7

So far this may seem like a serious *what is the big deal anyway?* The big deal is that all numbers in any base can be expressed in expanded notation, and this expanded notation can be used for conversion between bases.

Consider the following expanded notation for numbers in base-5, base-8, base-16, and base-4.

3214 base-5 $= 3 \times 5^3 + 2 \times 5^2 + 1 \times 5^1 + 4 \times 5^0$

70416 base-8 $= 7 \times 8^4 + 0 \times 8^3 + 4 \times 8^2 + 1 \times 8^1 + 6 \times 8^0$

5a9d base-16 $= 5 \times 16^3 + a \times 16^2 + 9 \times 16^1 + d \times 16^0$

Perhaps you are wondering what is the use of all of this expansion business? Excellent question. With number expansion you can convert a number from any base into a base-10 number. For instance, let us look at **3214 base-5** again, and this time we will do some additional calculations beyond the number expansion.

3214 base-5 $= 3 \times 5^3 + 2 \times 5^2 + 1 \times 5^1 + 4 \times 5^0$

3214 base-5 $= 3 \times 125 + 2 \times 25 + 1 \times 5 + 4 \times 1$

3214 base-5 $= 375 + 50 + 5 + 4$

3214 base-5 $= 434$ base-10

101101 base-2 $= 1 \times 2^5 + 0 \times 2^4 + 1 \times 2^3 + 1 \times 2^2 + 0 \times 2^1 + 1 \times 2^0$

101101 base-2 $= 1 \times 32 + 0 \times 16 + 1 \times 8 + 1 \times 4 + 0 \times 2 + 1 \times 1$

101101 base-2 $= 32 + 0 + 8 + 4 + 0 + 1$

101101 base-2 $= 45$ base-10

It is pretty silly to multiply a number times 1. That made sense with larger base numbers, but in base-2 there is never a multiply issue. It is also convenient to set up a chart of binary numbers. You can start on the right with number 1, and double each number as you move to the left. With such a chart, conversion between base-2 and base-10 becomes easier and more efficient.

101101 base-2 = ??? base-10							
128	64	32	16	8	4	2	1
		1	0	1	1	0	1
		32		8	4		1
32 + 8 + 4 + 1 = 45 base-10							

More Converting Base-2 To Base-10 Examples

1111 base-2 = ??? base-10							
128	64	32	16	8	4	2	1
				1	1	1	1
				8	4	2	1
8 + 4 + 2 + 1 = 15 base-10							

10101 base-2 = ??? base-10							
128	64	32	16	8	4	2	1
			1	0	1	0	1
			16		4		1
16 + 4 + 1 = 21 base-10							

10101010 base-2 = ??? base-10							
128	64	32	16	8	4	2	1
1	0	1	0	1	0	1	0
128		32		8		2	
128 + 32 + 8 + 2 = 170 base-10							

11000000 base-2 = ??? base-10							
128	64	32	16	8	4	2	1
1	1	0	0	0	0	0	0
128	64	0	0	0	0	0	0
128 + 64 = 192 base-10							

11100000 base-2 = ??? base-10							
128	64	32	16	8	4	2	1
1	1	1	0	0	0	0	0
128	64	32	0	0	0	0	0
128 + 64 + 32 = 224 base-10							

Converting Base-10 To Base-2

Converting base-10 to base-2 can use the same logic that was just shown. Create a matrix, like the one shown below. In the event the number is larger than **128**, expand the matrix, making sure to multiply each number times 2. The second matrix may look scary. Arithmetic is not harder with larger numbers it is more tedious. Well relax; it is unlikely you will need to create the second matrix. It is there to show what must be done if the number becomes larger.

100 base-10 = ??? base-2							
128	64	32	16	8	4	2	1

3000 base-10 = ??? base-2														
32768	16384	8192	4096	2048	1024	512	256	128	64	32	16	8	4	2	1

Now back to the problem at hand. Convert **100** base-10 into a base-2 number. You work from left to right. and place a base-2 number in the third row.

Compare **100** & **128**. **100** is smaller. Place **0** in the third row, below **128**. Carry **100** forward.

100 base-10 = ??? base-2							
128	64	32	16	8	4	2	1
0							

Compare **100** & **64**. **100** is larger. Place **1** in the third row, below **64**. Carry **36** forward.

100 base-10 = ??? base-2							
128	64	32	16	8	4	2	1
0	1						

Compare **36** & **32**. **36** is larger. Place a **1** in the third row, below **32**. Carry **4** forward.

100 base-10 = ??? base-2							
128	64	32	16	8	4	2	1
0	1	1	0	0			

Compare **4** with **16** & **8**. **4** is smaller. Place a **0** in the third row below **16** and **8**. Carry **4** forward.

100 base-10 = ??? base-2							
128	64	32	16	8	4	2	1
0	1	1	0	0			

Compare **4** & **4**. They are equal. Place a **1** in the third row below **4**. There is no remainder. Place a **0** in the third row below **2** and **1**.

100 base-10 = ??? base-2							
128	64	32	16	8	4	2	1
0	1	1	0	0	1	0	0
100 base-10 = 01100100 base-2							

More Converting Base-10 To Base-2 Examples

255 base-10 = ??? base-2							
128	64	32	16	8	4	2	1
1	1	1	1	1	1	1	1
255 base-10 = 11111111 base-2							

62 base-10 = ??? base-2							
128	64	32	16	8	4	2	1
0	0	1	1	1	1	1	0
100 base-10 = 00111110 base-2							

251 base-10 = ??? base-2							
128	64	32	16	8	4	2	1
0	1	1	0	0	1	0	0
251 base-10 = 11111011 base-2							

100 base-10 = ??? base-2							
128	64	32	16	8	4	2	1
0	1	1	0	0	1	0	0
100 base-10 = 01100100 base-2							

300 base-10 = ??? base-2								
256	128	64	32	16	8	4	2	1
1	0	0	1	0	1	1	0	0
300 base-10 = 100101100 base-2								

There is a quick and simple way to check your answers. Take the last example. Did you do it correctly? Add up all the values with 1 in the third row and check. Is it **300**? Great, you are correct.

256 + 32 = 288 + 8 = 296 + 4 = 300 !!! Success

Base-2 and Base-16 Properties

Network card addresses are noted in base-16. Computer information that is stored in memory addresses, both RAM and ROM, are indicated by base-16, hexadecimal notation. Soon it may be the case that IP addresses will be computed with base-16. So what is the appeal with base-16? To you it is probably a strange looking number system. After single digit nine, base-16 runs out of conventional single digits and must now use letters to conduct its business. The result is a rather strange looking bunch of numbers. Is there a reason for this choice?

Yes there is. We have nice algorithms for converting between Base 10 and other numbers. This means that converting between base-5 and base-7 requires a double conversion, using base -10 in the middle. This is tedious. There is something special going in between base-2 and base-16 that greatly simplifies our computation.

The base-2 numbers are intentionally shown in groups of four digits, and you will note that leading zeroes are filled in any time that there are not a multiple of four digits used to display the base-2 number.

Binary	Hex	Binary	Hex	Binary	Hex	Binary	Hex
0000	0	0001 0000	10	0010 0000	20	0011 0000	30
0001	1	0001 0001	11	0010 0001	21	0011 0001	31
0010	2	0001 0010	12	0010 0010	22	0011 0010	32
0011	3	0001 0011	13	0010 0011	23	0011 0011	33
0100	4	0001 0100	14	0010 0100	24	0011 0100	34
0101	5	0001 0101	15	0010 0101	25	0011 0101	35
0110	6	0001 0110	16	0010 0110	26	0011 0110	36
0111	7	0001 0111	17	0010 0111	27	0011 0111	37
1000	8	0001 1000	18	0010 1000	28	0011 1000	38
1001	9	0001 1001	19	0010 1001	29	0011 1001	39
1010	a	0001 1010	1a	0010 1010	2a	0011 1010	3a
1011	b	0001 1011	1b	0010 1011	2b	0011 1011	3b
1100	c	0001 1100	1c	0010 1100	2c	0011 1100	3c
1101	d	0001 1101	1d	0010 1101	2d	0011 1101	3d
1110	e	0001 1110	1e	0010 1110	2e	0011 1110	3e
1111	f	0001 1111	1f	0010 1111	2f	0011 1111	3f
						0100 0000	40

Perhaps you noticed the pattern in the base-2 and base-16 counting tables. You need to look closely at the single digits of the base-16 number. You will find that every single base-16 digit corresponds to four base-2 digits. That is right; there is no conversion mathematics involved.

Conversion between base-2 and base-16 requires that base-2 numbers are grouped in sets of four digits, and leading zeroes must be inserted for all digits less than 8. Each one of the sets of four base-2 digits is converted to one of sixteen base-16 single digits. You do need to know the first sixteen base-2 numbers, but after that it becomes a game of substitution. As before, the best approach may be to examine a set of exercises and then try to perform the exercises yourself. Keep in mind that it is wise to spend a little time first to create the following table below for reference:

Base-2	Base-16
0000	0
0001	1
0010	2
0011	3
0100	4
0101	5
0110	6
0111	7
1000	8
1001	9
1010	a
1011	b
1100	c
1101	d
1110	e
1111	f

Converting Base-2 To Base-16

Arithmetic is now not needed. Forget the calculator and any paper arithmetic. You do need to be careful and create groups of four digits from right to left and then fill in leading zeroes. In the matrix below the first step is shown to make **1001001010111** into **0001 0010 0101 0111**. Each group of four digits becomes a single base-16 digit.

1001001010111 base-2 = ??? base-16					
1001001010111 = 0001 0010 0101 0111					
base-2			0001	0010	0101	0111
base-16			1	2	5	7
= 1257 base-16					

Converting Base-2 To Base-16 Examples

111111110010001101 base-2 = ??? base-16					
111111110010001101 = 0111 1111 1100 1000 1101					
base-2		0111	1111	1100	1000	1101
base-16		7	f	c	8	d
= 7fc8d base-16					

110000110010010010011 base-2 = ??? base-16					
110000110010010010011 = 0011 0000 1100 1001 0001 0011					
base-2	0011	0000	1100	1001	0001	0011
base-16	3	0	c	9	1	3
= 30c913 base-16					

101010111100110111101111 base-2 = ??? base-16					
101010111100110111101111 = 1010 1011 1100 1101 1110 1111					
base-2	1010	1011	1100	1101	1110	1111
base-16	a	b	c	d	e	f
= abcdef base-16					

111111111111111111111111 base-2 = ??? base-16					
111111111111111111111111 = 1111 1111 1111 1111 1111 1111					
base-2	1111	1111	1111	1111	1111	1111
base-16	f	f	f	f	f	f
= ffffff base-16					

Converting Base-16 to Base-2

Converting in the opposite direction takes advantage of the same relationship between base-2 and base-16. It is not necessary to provide leading zeroes. Do remember that you use four base-2 zeroes for any single base-16 zero.

7fc0d base-16 = ??? base-2					
base-16		7	f	c	0	d
base-2		0111	1111	1100	0000	1101
= 7fc8d base-16 = 01111111110000001101 base-2					

Number Systems Pitfalls

Concern #1: Arithmetic

Number system questions and conversions involves numbers and arithmetic. Even students who have excellent math skills can easily make arithmetic mistakes. Pay attention, write down intermediate values and on paper (your test) and check what you are doing. Get used to not having a calculator available.

Concern #2: Largest Number and Number Quantity Confusion

The largest number stored in a byte of **8** bits is **255**, but the quantity of numbers in a byte is **256**. At first this may seem confusing, but remember zero. There are **10** single digits in base-10 from **0..9**, but the largest digit is **9**.

Concern #3: Leading zeroes

Every base-16 single digit is equivalent to four base-2 digits. However every base-2 number is not necessarily 4 digit. For instance, take number **435** in base-16. The three digits of **435** in base-2 are: **100**, **11** and **101**. Combining them with a **10011101** base-16 number is wrong.

Each base-16 digit requires leading zeroes if there are not 4 digits, like **0100 0011** and **0101**. So the correct conversion becomes **010000110101**

Chapter 3 Questions
Bits, Bases & Data Abstraction

---

01. The chart below shows ASCII encoding for some characters.

ASCII	CHAR	ASCCII	CHAR	ASCII	CHAR
65	A	97	a	48	0
66	B	98	b	49	1
67	C	99	c	50	2
68	D	100	d	51	3

What binary number is used to store character b ?

(A) 1100010

(B) 0100011

(C) 11000100

(D) 0110010

---

02. The chart below shows ASCII encoding for some characters.

ASCII	CHAR	ASCCII	CHAR	ASCII	CHAR
65	A	97	a	48	0
66	B	98	b	49	1
67	C	99	c	50	2
68	D	100	d	51	3

What ASCII character is represented by the binary number 11110000 ?

(A) z

(B) 8

(C) A non alpha-numeric character

(D) The number is outside the ASCII range

---

03. If decimal number 89 represents ASCII character Y, what binary number is used to store ASCII character Q ?

(A) 1100101

(B) 1010001

(C) 101001

(D) 0101001

---

04. Suppose a computer program needs to sort a list of student records in ascending order according to last name. The program language determines sort order by using the individual ASCII number representations of the characters in each name.

If the initial list contains the following names. Which of the following lists represents the name order after executing the sorting procedure?

["Tom Smith","Joe Schnook","Kathy Bones","Jill Brewer"]

(A) ["Smith Tom","Schnook Joe","Bones Kathy","Brewer Jill"]

(B) ["Joe Schnook","Tom Smith","Jill Brewer","Kathy Bones"]

(C) ["Jill Brewer","Joe Schnook","Kathy Bones","Tom Smith"]

(D) ["Kathy Bones","Jill Brewer","Joe Schnook","Tom Smith"]

05. Consider the following three numbers.

10100 (base-2)   123 (base-10)   d7 (base-16)

Which of the following displays the numbers in ascending order?

(A) d7 (base-16), 123 (base-10), 10100 (base-2)

(B) 10100 (base-2), 123 (base-10), d7 (base-16)

(C) 123 (base-10), 10100 (base-2), d7 (base-16)

(D) d7 (base-17), 10100 (base-2), 123 (base-10)

06. Consider the following four hexadecimal numbers.

7b3d2a   fedcb   11a2b   a7bc26

Which of the following displays the numbers in descending order?

(A) 11a2b, 7b3d2a, a7bc26, fedcb

(B) fedcb, a7bc26, 7b3d2a, 11a2b

(C) 11a2b, fedcb, 7b3d2a, a7bc26

(D) a7bc26, 7b3d2a, fedcb, 11a2b

07. Consider the following four numbers.

101010 (base-2)   43 (base-10)   101100 (base-2)   37 (base-10)

Which of the following displays the numbers in descending order?

(A) 101100 (base-2), 43 (base-10), 101010 (base-2), 37 (base-10)

(B) 37 (base-10), 101010 (base-10), 43 (base-10), 101100 (base-2)

(C) 43 (base-10), 37 (base-10), 101010 (base-2), 101100 (base-2)

(D) 1001010 (base-2), 101100 (base-2), 43 (base-10), 37 (base-10)

---

08. Consider the following four binary numbers.

11100111   10101010   11110000   11001100

Which of the following displays the numbers in ascending order?

(A) 10101010, 11001100, 11100111, 11110000

(B) 11110000, 11100111, 11001100, 10101010

(C) 11100111, 10101010, 11110000, 11001100

(D) 10101010, 11001100, 11110000, 11100111

---

09. A computer program is originally designed to store customer identification using a 5-bit binary sequence. As the number of unique customers grows the program must handle a far greater number of identifications than were originally possible. The new program must handle 10 times the original customer size. Which of the following binary sequences uses the smallest amount of memory and can still handle new requirements?

(A) 7-bit binary sequence

(B) 8-bit binary sequence

(C) 9-bit binary sequence

(D) 10-bit binary sequence

10. A programmer works with an unknown program language. The language provides four different *unsigned* integer data types with the following storage abilities:

`int1` uses 8 bits
`int2` uses 16 bits
`int3` uses 24 bits
`int4` uses 32 bits
`int5` uses 64 bits

An *unsigned* integer uses every bit in the sequence for storage. There is no bit used to indicate a positive or negative number. The `int1` data type has space for 256 unique integers in the [0..255] range. This data type is considered inadequate for the needs of the program. Integers need to store numbers as large as 10,000,000. Which of the following integer data types uses the least memory, but is adequate for the storage requirement?

(A) `int2`

(B) `int3`

(C) `int4`

(D) `int5`

11. Graphics images are stored as two-dimensional arrays of pixels. Many use 24-bits of memory space for each pixel. This is further divided up into three 8-bit sequences that store the RGB (Red, Green, Blue) values of each pixel.

If 24-bits are used for one pixel and this pixel's color is determined by three Red, Green, Blue value, each using 8-bits, how many different color combination exist for a pixel?

(A) 512

(B) 4,096

(C) 262,144

(D) 16,777,216

12. Web pages and computer program have procedures to specify the color of some object. In many cases this follows the 24-bit pixel storage that was explained in question 11. It is common to indicate the RGB values in hexadecimal string notation, where two base-16 digits are used for each color intensity in pixel.

If a program has a command like `setColor("00FF00")` prior to drawing an object. What color will the object be?

(A) A soft shade of purple

(B) An intense shade of green

(C) A soft shade of red

(D) An intense shade of yellow

Chapter 4 Review
Data & Information

Data and Information is one of those very large, general topics that can be multiple courses, an entire degree or field of study. What exactly is data? Google provides us with the following definition. There are several different definitions, including one for computing.

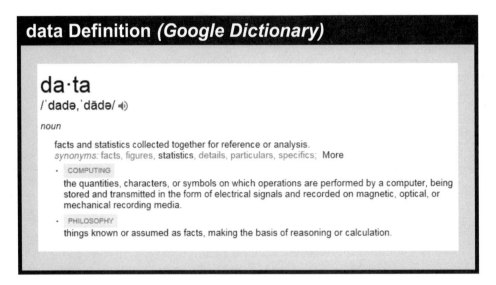

Consider the following sentence: *The information that we gathered from the data indicates that median house prices are increasing at a faster rate than median family incomes.* This sentence implies a connection between *data* and *information*. It also implies that data and information are not synonyms as you might think.

So, what is the difference? In the *median house price* example above, a lot of data is gathered, such as collected by the US Census Bureau. Statisticians look at the median income of millions of people. They also look at the median prices of homes. Data is checked for a range of years, which should be significant enough to show a trend. The analysis of this data provides statisticians with information. Information is fundamentally processed data.

Data and Information

Data and Information are not synonyms. Data by itself does not yet have much meaning. Data needs to be arranged, sorted, analyzed and then conclusions are formed. After this analysis stage, information is available.

Consider information to be processed data.

A major role of a computer is data processing. In an age of terrorism millions of phone calls, emails, text messages, tweets and social media are gathered. By itself this avalanche of data is a gigantic pile of unrelated, seemingly useless, communication. With sophisticated data processing and enormous computer power much useful information can be extracted.

With hindsight we now know the following. Prior to 9/11 a group of middle-eastern men, with temporary visas, were learning to fly in the United States. They wanted to learn to fly an airplane in a limited manner. For instance, they had no interest in learning to land a plane.

Investigations that followed 9/11 stated that intelligence agencies *failed to connect the dots*. It can be stated that *connecting dots* is the results of taking large quantities of data and then come up with useful information. Connecting the dots is data processing, which provides information that shows the big picture from a seemingly large group of unrelated pieces of data

.

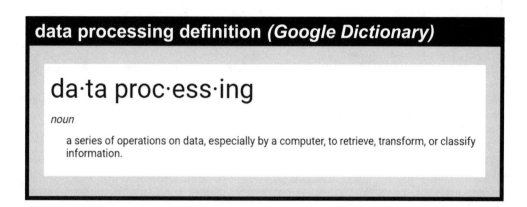

There is data. There is information. There is data processing and then there is also *metadata*. These terms are all related and must be clearly understood. My guess is that the definition below sounds easy enough, but do you really understand what it means?

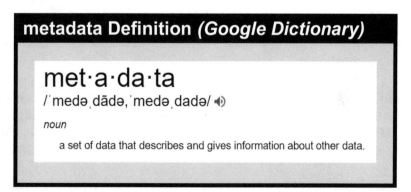

The irony of *metadata* is that, if you work on a computer, you look at metadata each and every day. It is not a complex concept. Look at any folder window, such as the one shown on the next page. It contains a large variety of files. They are intentionally very diverse. Folder content is shown with column information. Usually, you will see the *Name*, the *Date Modified*, the *Type*

and the *Size*. I have added additional columns for *Length*, *Title* and *Artist*. When you look at this window you may not have a clue what *Lara's Theme* is about. You do know that is an MP3 audio file. You can tell that it is 5.8 MB is size and some other information. All the information about the file, but not any of the contents of the file is the *metadata*. It tells you the name, the size, the type, the length, etc.

Name	Date modified	Type	Size	Length	Title	Contributing artists
Blue Danube.mp3	10/9/2017 8:49 AM	MP3 File	13,876 KB	00:07:38	The Blue Danube, Op. 314	André Rieu, Johann ..
C0023.MP4	9/23/2017 7:51 AM	MP4 File	490,464 KB	00:01:13		
C0024.MP4	9/23/2017 7:52 AM	MP4 File	29,573 KB	00:00:04		
Design01.java	6/5/2017 3:15 PM	jGRASP Java file	2 KB			
Design02.java	6/5/2017 3:15 PM	jGRASP Java file	2 KB			
DSC_0040.JPG	9/23/2017 8:25 PM	JPG File	3,565 KB			
DSC_0044.JPG	9/23/2017 8:25 PM	JPG File	4,187 KB			
Go.bat	5/6/2017 7:12 AM	Windows Batc...	1 KB			
Go.command	5/6/2017 7:13 AM	COMMAND File	1 KB			
Graphics01.py	5/6/2017 1:10 PM	PY File	1 KB			
Graphics02.py	5/6/2017 1:11 PM	PY File	1 KB			
Green Berets.mp3	10/9/2017 8:49 AM	MP3 File	4,730 KB	00:02:26	The Ballad Of The Green Berets	SSgt. Barry Sadler
Lab07a.docx	8/12/2017 6:53 AM	Microsoft Wor...	163 KB			
Lara's Theme.mp3	10/9/2017 8:49 AM	MP3 File	5,806 KB	00:03:17	Lara's Theme (From "Doctor ...	The City Of Prague ...
Methods.docx	6/5/2017 2:05 PM	Microsoft Wor...	1,094 KB			
Quiz07.01-05.pptx	6/5/2017 4:55 PM	Microsoft Pow...	131 KB			
Quiz07.06-12.pptx	6/5/2017 4:56 PM	Microsoft Pow...	177 KB			
The Prayer.mp3	10/9/2017 8:49 AM	MP3 File	8,297 KB	00:04:27	The Prayer [feat. Céline Dion]	Andrea Bocelli

Is this metadata useful? It certainly is. Consider the course you are taking, AP Computer Science Principles. You are expected to submit two computational artifacts to the College Board that will be evaluated and become the 40% *free-response* part of your AP Exam score. Look at the paragraph from the Course Description below. It describes the requirements for submitting the computational artifacts. More details about this important requirement come in a later chapter.

> Submit a video, audio, or PDF file. Use computing tools and techniques to create one original computational artifact (a visualization, a graphic, a video, a program, or an audio recording). Acceptable multimedia file types include .mp3, .mp4, .wmv, .avi, .mov, .wav, .aif, or .pdf format. PDF files must not exceed three pages. Video or audio files must not exceed 1 minute in length and must not exceed 30MB in size.

Notice that it states the type of files that are acceptable. It also states that the video must not exceed 1 minute in length and the video may not be larger than 30MB in size. Many items in that paragraph are the metadata requirements of your computational artifact.

Metadata in an Age of Terrorism

We live in an age of tug-of-war. During major terrorist tragedies, such as 9/11, people care only about catching the terrorists. Privacy, convenience and other concerns are secondary. As time passes, memories fade somewhat. Now there is concern that organizations, like the FBI, NSA and CIA are stepping over the bounds of privacy rights as they gather data and try to prevent terrorist actions from happening again.

Much of the data they listen for and look at is not the actual contents of emails and cell phone conversations. That happens later when dots are connected. Our spy agencies have gigantic computers that check the metadata. It is this data that provides information to connect the very important dots. With sufficient metadata a case can be made to get permission to listen to the specific contents of phone calls and email communication.

Databases and Compression

If data and information is such a large field, what does that mean for end-of-course exam preparation? The course description sample questions and the practice exam point to two categories that seem to be quite popular: data compression questions and database questions.

Compression Techniques

There is a technical conflict at work with data. On one side is the desire for extra high-quality images and sound. The amazing quality of today's 4K video and monitors is absolutely stunning and when this is compared to 1950 television, it is hard to believe that people in the Fifties could see what was happening on the screen.

But there is another side. All this data needs to be stored and it needs to be transmitted. Storing data is not free. Right now, October, 2017, RAM on most computers is 4 GB or 8 GB. High-end computers go to 16 GB. The permanent storage on the hard drive has greater space. Typical computers have 500 GB or 1 TB of hard drive storage. High-end computers typically have 2 TB.

Data storage depends on the storage space, which costs money. Likewise, transmission of data depends on the quantity of data that is transmitted per time period. Many individuals and businesses have a data plan for data transmission speed and quantity. Storage is less of an issue than in the past, but with today's Internet, data transmissions and bandwidth are the big concerns. The solution to the conflict of high quality data and the high-expense for large data storage and transmission is data compression. It is possible in some cases to reduce or compress the data file of the original without any loss of quality. That type of compression is known as *lossless compression*. It is also possible to compress data files with a loss of data quality and that is known as *lossy* compression.

Four pictures follow that all started with the original Picture1 of Rome's Trevi fountain. Picture2 is the same picture considerably compressed into a 200 X 200 pixel format. The quality is visibly worse, but perhaps still acceptable for certain applications, such as a small profile picture. In Picture3 you see a close-up of one statue. The zoomed image used Picture1 and the close-up is quite good. Picture4 creates the same close-up using Picture2 and now *pixilation* occurs. *Pixilation* occurs when an image is enlarged to such a degree that individual pixels are visible to the human eye.

Picture1:   2593 X 2593 Pixels Original

Picture2: 200 X 200 Pixels Compressed

Picture3: 2593 X 2593 Original Close-Up

Picture4: 200 X 200 compressed Close-Up

There are two style of data compression:

- *Lossless* **Compression, which compresses data without any loss of data.**

- *Lossy* **Compression, which compresses data with loss of data.**

It may seem not that complicated to use *lossy* compression. A loss of quality is accepted and other factors are more important. Social media pictures, like Facebook, use lossy compression to speed up image transfer and use less space. In most cases the presented pictures still present a perfectly acceptable post.

It is another story in the business world where any loss of quality is not acceptable. Consider an FBI database of finger print images for comparison or a bank's spreadsheet of loans and interest paid. Such data must be 100% accurate and may not lose any of its accuracy with data transmission or storage. Now if *lossless* is a required standard and you must maintain original quality, while at the same time achieve a reduction in data size, how can that be achieved? There are actually many different algorithms to achieve this goal.

Let's consider the following picture. I created this picture, which means it is neither artistic nor sophisticated. The data file that stores the house image has to enter the Internet and may not arrive anywhere with a loss of image quality. This image is 517 X 540 pixels. This means that the bottom row of the roof is close to 500 red pixels.

The next picture shows a section of the roof blown up 800%. The pixilation is easiest to see on the diagonal, black roof outline and the red tiles next to it. Since every pixel of the roof is the same red color, it is difficult to see the individual red pixels. You do realize that there are many rows of tiny red pixels used in the making of the roof.

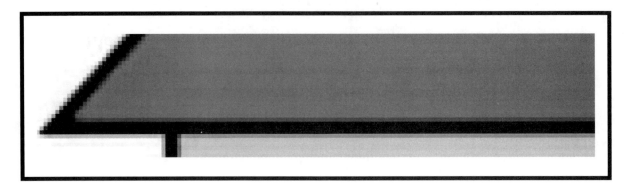

Without any attempts at some compression algorithms, thousands of identical pixels of the same Red, Green, Blue (RGB) values would be stored. That means that one byte is required for each color and at least three bytes are necessary tto store each individual pixel. What if information is stored that states: *The next 500 pixels on this row are color (255,0,0)*. The computer is not so wordy with English so it could be something that is similar to a code like: *+500 (255,0,0)*. That little statement occupies a lot less space than 500 individual pixels. Then, at the receiving end of the Internet transmission trip, the nicely compressed file is able to display the house in its full glory. This technique is not restricted to pixels. The concept is the same for any type of data. Text data may have many spaces. It may have many repeating characters. In an audio file, the same sound may be maintained for a length of time that can easily be compressed. These are just a few, simple examples of compression without loss. There are many sophisticated algorithms that can be used.

Databases

Databases exist in every direction that you look. Businesses store data and that data needs to be organized and retrievable. Database software handles this requirement. At first glance, database software may resemble spreadsheet software. You do see a two-dimensional array of cells. The appearance is the same, but the use and capabilities are quite different.

The primary mission of spreadsheet software is to manage the interaction of values in the cells of the spreadsheet. Formulas are used to handle the calculations between cells to compute sums, interests, payments made, and many other financial or numerical quantifiers.

A database has horizontal rows that are individual records. Each record represents the individual data of a critical unit, such as a *patient record,* a *student record*, or an *employee record.* The record is divided up in separate cells, called fields, for information like *name, age, birthdate*, etc. This arrangement allows information to be seen from the database. One column can provide the information about the number of people over age 50. Another column can show how many companies make a starter motor for a 2013 Chevy Cruze. A hospital database can easily see how many days the average patient stays in the hospital and how many heart operations occur on any given day

The image below represents a partial database created in MS Access of an imaginary Acme Company that sells auto parts. This is a very small database with little information, but it shows the fundamental design. The database has the capability to be sorted according to various criteria in different columns. Individual columns have checkboxes and the user can select not to include certain categories or names in a category.

Part Name	Part Number	Part Cost	In Stock	Car Name	Part Company	Car Year
Alternator	B12341	$100.00	12	Cruze	Bosch	2016
Alternator	B12342	$95.00	7	Camaro	Bosch	2016
Alternator	B12343	$83.00	3	Mustang	Bosch	2017
Alternator	T12341	$134.00	5	Tacoma	Toyota	2015
Alternator	T12342	$134.00	0	Tacoma	Toyota	2016
Alternator	T12343	$140.00	12	Tacoma	Toyota	2017
Alternator	F12341	$175.00	2	F150	Ford	2014
Alternator	F12342	$175.00	5	F150	Ford	2015
Alternator	F12343	$165.00	3	F150	Ford	2016
Alternator	F12344	$200.00	0	F150	Ford	2017
Battery	A12341	$55.00	25	Ram1500	Alstate	2005
Battery	A12342	$50.00	10	Ram1500	Alstate	2006

Data and Information Pitfalls

There are no special concerns in this category. The database questions can be misleading when a lot of information is provided that might confuse you. You need to be alert to the given information. With the provided database information you can draw conclusions. Some conclusions cannot be drawn. You may look at a database that shows someone's personal information. It does not include the value of that person's house. You may decide that this can be based on a person's income. Perhaps this seems valid, but too much information is missing. Two people with the same income can have different priorities. One person prefers to purchase a BMW and live in a modest apartment. The other person prefers a nice house and drives an inexpensive economy car.

01. What is *lossless* data compression?

(A) It is a form of data compression that reduces the data file size without any of loss of data information. It allows the original file to be restored.

(B) It is a form of data compression that reduces the data file size with an acceptable loss of data information. It does not allow the original file to be restored.

(C) It is a form of data compression that reduces the data file size by removing non-essential data. When the file is restored it appears like the original file.

(D) It is a form of data compression that is only used for temporary data files. The file is reduced and stays compressed.

02. What is *lossy* data compression?

(A) It is a form of data compression that reduces the data file size without any of loss of data information. It allows the original file to be restored.

(B) It is a form of data compression that reduces the data file size with an acceptable loss of data information. It does not allow the original file to be restored.

(C) It is a form of data compression that reduces the data file size by removing non-essential data. When the file is restored it appears like the original file.

(D) It is a form of data compression that is only used for temporary data files. The file is reduced and stays compressed.

03. How is it possible to reduce data file in size for compression and then restore it to its original format without any loss of information?

(A) Clever algorithms are used that only remove non-essential "blank" data.

(B) The removed data is stored elsewhere on the Cloud and added later during restoring.

(C) Repetitive data, like a color on an image, can be stored with a formula.

(D) It is not really possible to restore 100%, but the data loss is not noticeable.

04. What is metadata?

(A) It is a name for the data that is lost during data compression.

(B) It is the data that has been analyzed and classified as significant.

(C) It is the name for data that is not compressed.

(D) It is data about data, such as file size, data format, creation date, etc.

05. Consider the adjacent image.
This distorted image is an example of

(A) poor camera filming technique.

(B) pixilation.

(C) too much data compression.

(D) low resolution data storage.

06. Social media companies, like Facebook, lower picture quality of high reslotion images before posting them on the Internet. Why is this an acceptable practice?

(A) Lower quality means smaller files and quicker transmission time.

(B) Lower quality means smaller files and less memory required for storing the image.

(C) Most people will not notice any difference. Social media does not require high resolution quality, such as is needed for printing large pictures or zooming.

(D) All of the above

07. A high resolution picture is taken of an eagle flying in the sky. Is this picture a good candidate for *lossless* data compression or should *lossy* data compression be used?

(A) *Lossy* data compression is fine, because the picture started with high resolution.

(B) This decision cannot be made without knowing the purpose of the image.

(C) This picture is a good candidate for *lossless* data compression. Much of the picture will include sky pixels of the same color that can be stored in a formula and restored to its original image quality.

(D) All still pictures should use *lossless* data compression. Only audio files and video files can manages *lossy* data compression well.

---

08. A school administration program stores information about students. The following student information is stored in the central database. Information can be retrieved by school employees based on their individual access rights.

- Student information about address, birthdate, gender and family
- Student medical records
- Attendance and tardies
- Student grades per course
- Student GPA & class standing
- School club membership
- School athletic team member

Which of the following requests **cannot** be determined using the school's database?

(A) School athlete with the highest GPA

(B) Students who need to take daily medicine at school

(C) Correlation between GPA and scholarship awarded

(D) Correlation between chronic illnesses and attendance

09. The US Army keeps a database of information on all of its current and previous members, which includes:

- Personal information, such as name, birthdate, gender, marital status
- Detailed medical records, including check-ups and all medical procedures.
- Training completed and certificates earned, such as Paratrooper, Ranger, etc.
- Physical Combat Proficiency test records
- History of promotions
- Medals earned
- Observation reports of commanding officer

Which of the following **can** be determined with the database information shown above?

(A) Medals awarded per overseas deployment location

(B) Speed of Army promotion compared to Physical Combat Proficiency test scores

(C) Civilian education compared to Army rank

(D) Combat injuries compared to Army rank

---

10. The National Security Agency (NSA) collects and processes more data than any other US government agency. The enormous data collection raises concern on a regular basis about privacy issues. What can such an agency do to make US citizen more comfortable about their personal and sensitive information?

(A) Make assurances that all data, once looked at for terrorist connections, is removed.

(B) Check only data sources that come from known terrorist individuals or organizations,

(C) Do not collect or store any data from within the United States.

(D) Limit initial data collection to *metadata* until such data triggers security concerns.

11. An auto part store keeps the following database of information about their inventory of thousands of different auto parts. Some customers bring in the auto part, but the majority of customer come in providing information about their needs.

Car Name	Auto Part Company	Part Name	Shelve Location	Part Number	Tool Price	Number in Stock
Chevrolet	Bosch	Alternator	Isle 14, 27	2366576	237.95	19

The database categories need some type of organization and sorting for efficient access. Which of the following will give a fast response to availability of the needed auto part?

(A) Sort first according to *Part Name* and then sort according to *Car Name*.

(B) Sort first according to *Part Number* and then according to *Price*.

(C) Sort first according to *Car Name* and then according to *Part Number*.

(D) Sort first according to *Auto Part Company* and then according to *Part Number*.

---

12. Data files start in many different original formats, like numbers, text, still images, videos and audio sounds. What is true about the storage of all these data files in a computer?

(A) All data files have a different individual system for storing information. Decimal numbers use base-2 bits. Text uses ASCII values. Images use RGB color triples and audio files convert its analog sounds to digital wave length.

(B) All data files, regardless of its original format, are converted into a digital format and at its lowest level become a sequence of binary bits of ones and zeroes that are stored in memory.

(C) All data files start as analog files that are converted to computer digital, decimal files.

(D) All of the above

Chapter 5 Review
Basic Program Features with Pseudo-Code

This is the first of many *programming with pseudo-code* chapters. In the first chapter it was explained that programming is 1 of 7 Big Ideas, but it certainly is not 1/7 of the total evaluation for your AP score. It also needs to be understood very clearly that programming has to be handled in two separate ways that are strongly connected. Learning programming involves writing programs, making mistakes, watching the programs execute on an actual computer. Pseudo-code does not execute. To understand pseudo-code well, you need to understand actual programming with a concrete language, like C++, Java, Python, Scratch, etc.

The design of the AP Computer Science Principles course was intentionally not focused around a specific language. Teachers and students can select the language for programming study and for writing the *Create Performance Task*. But at the same time students needs to understand pseudo-code well, because that is what shows up on the end-of-course multiple-choice AP Exam. The sequence of the programming chapters in this review book follows a sequence that is quite common in most computer science courses. The selection of topics is limited. The course description for AP CSP makes it clear what is tested in the area of programming. The Alert box below shows a capture from the College Board's Course Description. The selection of topics is modest compared to a typical first course for a computer science major, but then the AP CSP course is meant for a broader audience with a broader view of computer science.

Personally, in my classes I teach considerably more than the topics below, but not in the pseudo-code sense. If you are also using the accompany Python programming book you will see that there is a quite an emphasis on graphics and also on mouse and key interaction. None of these topics will be tested on the End-Of-Couse-Exam, but they are very practical topics for the completion of the Create Performance Task. In this book it will be strictly pseudo-code only.

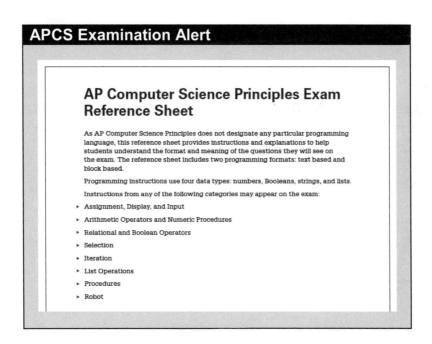

APCS Examination Alert

AP Computer Science Principles Exam Reference Sheet

As AP Computer Science Principles does not designate any particular programming language, this reference sheet provides instructions and explanations to help students understand the format and meaning of the questions they will see on the exam. The reference sheet includes two programming formats: text based and block based.

Programming instructions use four data types: numbers, Booleans, strings, and lists.

Instructions from any of the following categories may appear on the exam:

- Assignment, Display, and Input
- Arithmetic Operators and Numeric Procedures
- Relational and Boolean Operators
- Selection
- Iteration
- List Operations
- Procedures
- Robot

This is not a textbook. It is a review book. The assumption is that students already know one or more actual programming languages. The pseudo-code presented in this review book needs to be compared and taught alongside the selected real programming languages. Eight languages are shown in the matrix below. The top row shows three *drop-and-drag* program languages. They are the most visual and considered the simplest languages to start with. The middle row shows three popular *text-based* program languages. They are the type of languages used to create large commercial programs. The bottom-row shows the two languages selected for the AP CSP course, which are *Block-Based Pseudo-Code* and *Text-Based Pseudo-Code*. Every code image below shows an example of two-way selection. Most text-based languages use *if..else* in the code. You see that Scratch and Snap look different, but *if..else* is visible. Lego NXT has the spirit of two choices, but it is a little harder to see. The pseudo-code examples in the bottom both use identical keywords (always capitalized). The text-based pseudo-code is pretty similar to the language examples from the middle-row.

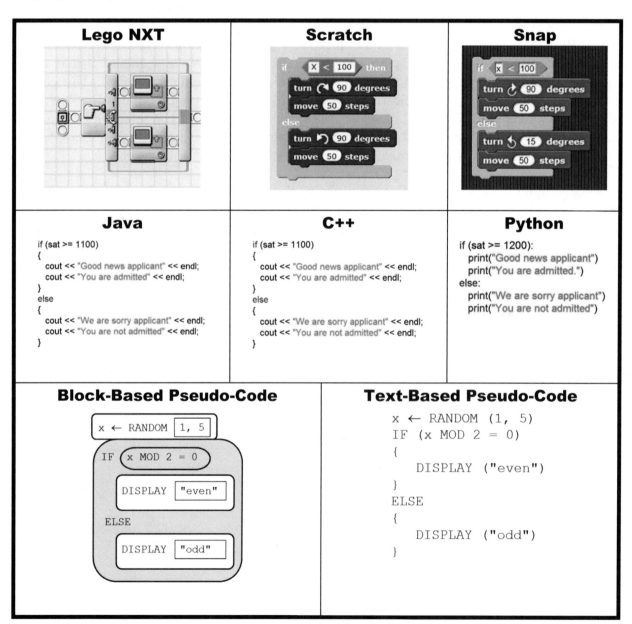

In a sequence of chapters you will review each one of the different pseudo-code program features that are part of the AP CSP curriculum. Understanding the features, such as *Oh, that is a two-way control structure* is the simple part. The logic of the program code is more challenging and will be shown in some of the questions that follow each review chapter. At the End-Of-Course-Exam you will be provide with a reference guide that illustrates each one of the pseudo-code diagrams. It is very wise to become very familiar with this code and not strictly rely on a guide at the AP Exam. In the tables that follow you will see the block-based pseudo-code and text-based pseudo-code side-by-side. The reference guide only shows generic code features. The review chapters will use actual program segments to demonstrate how the pseudo-code appears in a sample short functional program.

Basic Pseudo-Code Program Features

Assignment Operator ←	
First evaluates the expression, if it exists and then assigns the result or the single value to the variable on the left side.	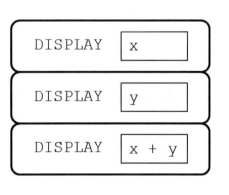
| ```
    x ← 100
    y ← 200
    z ← x + y
``` | |

DISPLAY Command	
First evaluates the expression, if it exists and then displays the result or displays the value of a constant or variable.	DISPLAY x DISPLAY y DISPLAY x + y
| ```
    DISPLAY (x)
    DISPLAY (y)
    DISPLAY (x + y)
``` | |

INPUT Command

Waits for a user-value and assigns it to a variable. The INPUT command should be preceded by a DISPLAY prompt, which clarifies the required user-input.

```
DISPLAY ("Enter Name 1")
n1 ← INPUT ()
DISPLAY ("Enter Name 2")
n2 ← INPUT ()
```

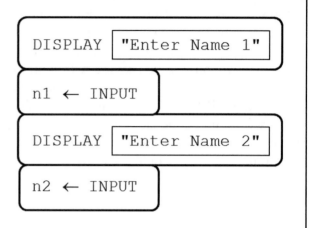

Arithmetic Operators +, -, *, /, MOD

Respectively, these standard operators are used for addition, subtraction, multiplication, division and remainder (modulus) division.

It is possible that additional operators are introduced with a question, such as using the **//** operator for integer division.

```
result1 ← a + b
result2 ← a - b
result3 ← a * b
result4 ← a / b
result5 ← a MOD b
```

result1 ← 3 + 4

result2 ← 3 - 4

result3 ← 3 * 4

result4 ← 3 / 4

result5 ← 3 MOD 4

RANDOM Command

Returns a random integer in the [4..8] range.

```
a ← RANDOM (4, 8)
DISPLAY (a)
```

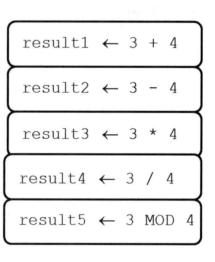

There are some concerns that must be addressed with the *Basic Program Features*. Remember that doing well on an AP Examination not only requires knowledge of the curriculum topics, but it also requires proper test-tasking strategies.

Concern #1: Do Not Underestimate Basic Program Features

This is a big deal with the smart students. They rapidly identify a question as easy. Somehow that means that the question is not worthy of a complete reading nor is it worthy of much attention. In the process unnecessary mistakes are made. Consider the following two questions.

Question01	
Consider the adjacent code segment. What is the output of the program? (A) 100 (B) 200 (C) 300 (D) -100	``` x ← 100 y ← 200 z ← x + y DISPLAY (z) z ← x - y ```
Question02	
Consider the adjacent code segment. What is the value of variable z when the program segment completes execution? (A) 100 (B) 200 (C) 300 (D) -100	``` x ← 100 y ← 200 z ← x + y DISPLAY (z) z ← x - y ```

Both questions use the same identical program segment. Both questions have the same set of four answers. The only difference is that *Question01* asks for the output of the program and *Question02* asks for the value of a variable when the program completes its execution. A surprising number of students miss the second question. Students see the DISPLAY command. They see the simplicity of the code and hardly finish reading the question statement. They select answer (C) and then get a simple question wrong.

Concern #2: Do Not Forget Mathematical Order Of Operations

A surprising number of students get caught with order of operations. Too many students simply perform arithmetic from left to right in the order that the operations occur. That does not work. This is not a review book on arithmetic, but a warning is giving that arithmetic mistakes can be easily made and especially on simple questions.

Question 3	
Consider the adjacent code segment. What is the output of the program? (A) 40 (B) 25 (C) 19 (D) 31	``` a ← 7 b ← 3 c ← 4 d ← a + b * c DISPLAY (d) ```
Question 4	
Consider the adjacent code segment. What is the output of the program? (A) 40 (B) 25 (C) 19 (D) 31	``` a ← 7 b ← 3 c ← 4 d ← (a + b) * c DISPLAY (d) ```

The two questions above are similar. The program code of the second question is slightly different. The question wording and the answers are identical. As you see there are two different correct answers. All too often on *Question01* students will select answer (A).

Concern #3: Watch Out For Random Trickery

The RANDOM command is included with *Basic Program Features*, based on its location in the Reference Guide. The pseudo-code uses the simple version of a RANDOM command. You are not involved with decimal numbers that many languages use. Only be concerned with clean integers. Look at *Question05* and *Question06* below. They appear to be similar.

Question05	
Consider the adjacent code segment. What is the range of possible random integers displayed by the program execution? (A) [1..30] (B) [11..30] (C) [1..20] (D) [0..29]	``` a ← RANDOM (1, 10) b ← RANDOM (11, 20) c ← RANDOM (a, b) DISPLAY (c) ```
Question06	
Consider the adjacent code segment. What is the range of possible random integers displayed by the program execution? (A) [1..30] (B) [11..30] (C) [1..20] (D) [1..10] and [21..30]	``` a ← RANDOM (1, 10) b ← RANDOM (21, 30) c ← RANDOM (a, b) DISPLAY (c) ```

There may be some confusing with *Question06*. Most students recognize that the value of a is in the possible range of [1..10], which means that the smallest number for c is 1. The value for b is in the range of [21..30], which means that the largest number for c is 30. Therefore the possible range for c becomes [1..30]. There is a tendency to believe that numbers [11..20] are not part of the possible outcome. This is wrong.

Concern #4: Do Not Let MOD Confuse You

Modulus division can cause some problems. Program languages usually use the operator **%** or MOD, which is used by the pseudo-code for this course. MOD computes integer division and the result becomes the remainder. This operation can also be called remainder division.

Question 7	
Consider the adjacent code segment. What is the output of the program? (A) 3 (B) 15 (C) 5 (D) 0	``` a ← 50 b ← 15 c ← a MOD b DISPLAY (c) ```
Question 8	
Consider the adjacent code segment. What is the output of the program? (A) 1 (B) 2 (C) 3 (D) 0	``` a ← 75 MOD 15 b ← 30 MOD 7 c ← a MOD b DISPLAY (c) ```

Normally there is no problem with *Question07*. Students who understand remainder division first apply integer division, conclude that 15 divides 3 times into 50 and then the remainder will become 5. No problems.

Question08 is another story. Using the logic of Question07, a becomes 0 (there is no remainder) and then b becomes 2. Now c becomes the remainder of 0 MOD 2. Many students feel that 2 does not divides into 0 and then conclude that 2 is left over. Now think... you are totally broke. You have no cash. Your wallet is empty. You are going to give your friends 1/3 of the cash in your wallet. You keep what is left over. What do your friends get? Nothing. Nothing divided by 3 is still nothing. What is left over? It is not possible to start with nothing and have something left over.

Chapter 5 Questions
Basic Program Features with Pseudo-Code

01.

Consider the adjacent code segment.
What is the output of the program?

    (A) 100

    (B) 200

    (C) 300

    (D) No output

```
x ← 100

y ← 200

sum ← x + y

DISPLAY  sum

sum ← x - y
```

02.

Consider the adjacent code segment.
What is the output of the program?

    (A) 5

    (B) 6

    (C) 12

    (D) 13

```
x ← 10 MOD 4
y ← 25 MOD 7
sum ← x + y
DISPLAY (sum)
```

03.

Consider the adjacent code segment.
What is the output of the program?

(A) 2

(B) 3

(C) 4

(D) 5

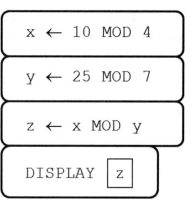

```
x ← 10 MOD 4

y ← 25 MOD 7

z ← x MOD y

DISPLAY  z
```

04.

Consider the adjacent code segment.
What is the output of the program?

(A) 17

(B) 23

(C) 25

(D) 65

```
a ← 10
b ← a - 5
c ← a + 3 * b
DISPLAY (c)
```

05.

Consider the adjacent code segment.
What is the output of the program?

(A) 3.5

(B) 2.0

(C) 1.0

(D) 0.5

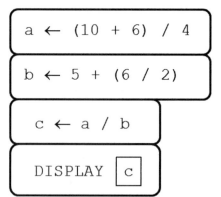

```
a ← (10 + 6) / 4

b ← 5 + (6 / 2)

c ← a / b

DISPLAY  c
```

06.

Consider the adjacent code segment.
What is the output of the program?

(A) 2.0

(B) 2.5

(C) 4.5

(D) No output

```
a ← (12 + 13) / 5
b ← 14 - 5 * 2 + 6
c ← b / a
DISPLAY (c)
```

07.

Consider the adjacent code
segment.
What is the output of the
program?

(A) 6.0

(B) 5.0

(C) 3.0

(D) No output

```
x ← (3 + 6 * 2) MOD (3 * 6 / 2)
DISPLAY x
```

08.

Consider the adjacent code segment.
What is the output of the program?

(A) Not possible to determine

(B) 2, 3 or 5

(C) 1.5

(D) Always displays the value
of x

```
x ← RANDOM (2, 9)
y ← (5 * (x * 3)) / (5 * (x * 2))
DISPLAY (x)
```

09.

Consider the adjacent code segment.
How many different numbers can be
displayed by the execution of the program?

    (A) 3

    (B) 4

    (C) 5

    (D) 6

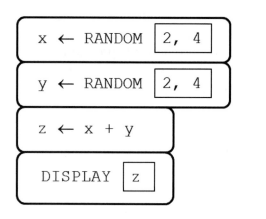

10.

Consider the adjacent code segment.
What is the range of possible random
integers displayed by the program execution?

    (A) [5..200]

    (B) [105..250]

    (C) [5..250]

    (D) [50..100]

```
x ← RANDOM (5, 50)
y ← RANDOM (100, 200)
z ← x + y
DISPLAY (z)
```

11.

Consider the adjacent code segment.
What is the range of possible random
integers displayed by the program execution?

    (A) [5..40]

    (B) [26..60]

    (C) [26..40]

    (D) Cannot be determined

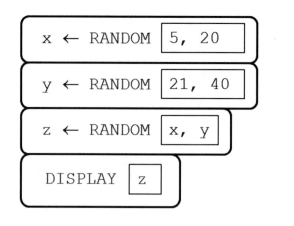

12.

Consider the adjacent code segment.
Which of the following ranges of numbers
are not possible as the result of executing the
program, besides `z < 1` and `z > 40`?

   (A) `[10..21]`

   (B) `[11..20]`

   (C) `[1..40]`

   (D) All numbers in the range `[1..40]`
        are possible.

```
x ← RANDOM (1, 10)
y ← RANDOM (21, 40)
z ← RANDOM (x, y)
DISPLAY (z)
```

13.

Consider the adjacent code segment.
What is the output of the program?

   (A) `300`
        `300`

   (B) `300`
        `100200`

   (C) `100200`
        `300`

   (D) `100200`
        `100200`

```
a ← 100

b ← 200

c ← "100"

d ← "200"

DISPLAY  a + b

DISPLAY  c + d
```

14.	
| Consider the adjacent code segment. What is the output of the program? | ```
a ← 100
b ← 200
c ← "100"
d ← "200"
DISPLAY (a + c)
DISPLAY (b + d)
``` |

(A) 200
   400

(B) 100100
   200200

(C) 200200
   400400

(D) Possible error message
   The provided pseudo-code
   does not address this situation.

15.

Consider the adjacent code segment.
What is the output of the program?

(A) Sue
   Bob
   Sue

(B) Sue
   Bob
   Tom

(C) Tom
   Tom
   Tom

(D) Sue
   Sue
   Sue

```
s1 ← "Tom"

s2 ← "Sue"

s3 ← "Bob"

s1 ← s2

s2 ← s3

s3 ← s1

DISPLAY  s1

DISPLAY  s2

DISPLAY  s3
```
```

16.

Consider the adjacent code segment.
What is the output of the program?

   (A) `Tom  Tom`

   (B) `Sue  Sue`

   (C) `Sue  Tom`

   (D) `Tom  Sue`

```
s1 ← "Tom"
s2 ← "Sue"
t ← s1
s1 ← s2
s2 ← t
DISPLAY (s1, s2)
```

Chapter 6 Review
Control Structures with Pseudo-Code

Types of Control Structures

Program-execution-flow is controlled by three general types of control structures. They are *simple sequence*, *selection* and *repetition*. Program languages provide syntax and special keywords for each one of these three control structures. Before we look at the actual pseudo-code required to implement control structures, let us first take a look at several diagrams that explain each type of control structure.

<u>Simple Sequence</u>

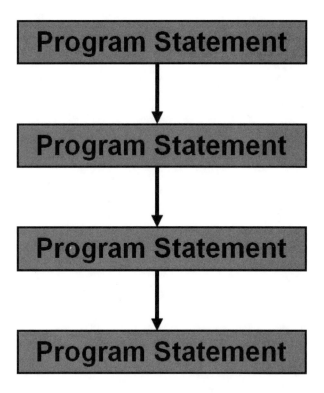

Simple sequence holds no surprises. A series of program statements are executed in the exact sequence that they are written. Altering the program execution logic requires altering the sequence of the program statements.

Selection

Frequently, programs cannot follow a single, simple sequence, path. Decisions need to be made, such as should the applicant be hired or not? Does the employee get overtime pay? Which tax bracket is the deduction to be computed from?

The program flow encounters a special condition. The value of the condition determines if the program flow will "branch off" from the main program sequence. There are three types of selection statements: *one-way*, *two-way* and *multiple-way*. Three diagrams, one for each type of selection, will follow.

One-Way Selection

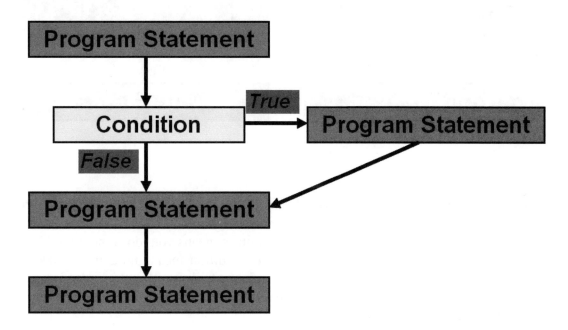

Selection control structures use a special conditional statement. If the condition is **true**, some action is performed, such as branching off to another sequence of program statements. In the case of *one-way selection*, the **true** condition branches off. If the condition is **false**, the program flow continues without change in the program sequence.

Consider the analogy of driving South from Dallas to Austin. Along the way you check if your gas tank is low. If the tank is low, you stop for gas, and then continue to Austin. If the tank is not low you continue to drive south. Keep in mind that regardless of the tank condition, you are heading to Austin.

Two-Way Selection

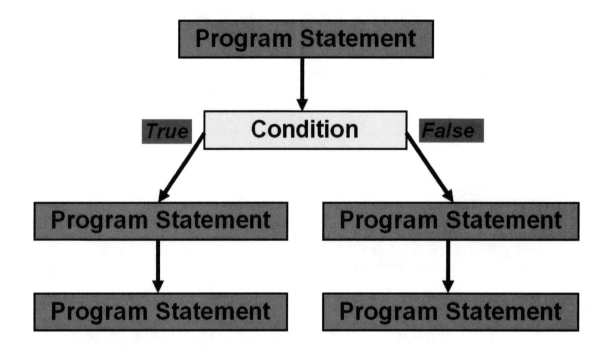

The *two-way* selection control structure also checks to see if some special condition is **true**, but there is a significant difference in how the program flow is handled. With *one-way* selection, the decision is to either do something, or not. A **true** condition means you do something, like get off the road and get gas, before continuing; and a **false** condition means no action is taken. With *two-way* selection, the decision is to either do one thing, or to do another thing. A **true** condition means you do one thing, and a **false** condition means you do the other. Either way, some action will take place.

The *one-way* analogy describes a trip traveling south from Dallas to Austin. Regardless of the gas tank situation, the trip travels to Austin in the same car. Now consider an analogy for *two-way selection*. You are now driving from Austin back to Dallas. The highway you take is I-35 (Interstate 35). When you are about 70 miles from Dallas, shortly after you pass the town of Hillsboro, the highway *forks*. It splits into two roads. You need to decide between going left which means you will take I-35W (Interstate 35 West) to Fort Worth or going right, which means you will take I-35E (Interstate 35 East) to Dallas.

Multi-Way Selection

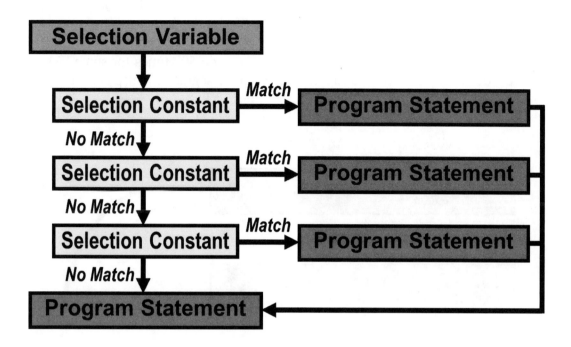

Multiple-way (or *Multi-way*) selection is a little different from one-way and two-way selection. In this control structure the condition is not very explicit. There is a special *selection variable* that is used along with several *selection constants*. The *selection variable* is compared with each *selection constant* until a *match* is found. The *condition* that you do not really see is if the *selection variable* equals a particular *selection constant*. When it finds a match it executes the corresponding program statement.

Multi-way selection is a commonly used control structure that simulates many situations in real life. Many times there are more than 2 things to choose from. For example, do you want chocolate, vanilla, strawberry, pistachio, rocky road, cookies & cream, mint chocolate chip or moo-llennium crunch ice cream for dessert? Do you plan to go to Harvard, Yale, Stanford, Princeton, Texas Tech, UT, OU or some other university? In fact, any time you take a multiple choice test, you are experiencing real life multi-way selection.

The pseudo-code does not provide the type of multi-way selection that is described above. However, it is possible to simulate the same execution result with multiple ELSE..IF conditional program statements.

Python does not have a special control structure for multi-way selection and manages the same logic with multiple ELSE..IF statements like the pseudo-code.

Repetition

Another common application occurs when repetition is required. A grade book program needs to average grades for every student in a class of twenty-five students. A payroll program needs to process paychecks for many employees. Practically everything you can imagine is done multiple times. Nobody is interested in repeating program source code 500 times for some task that is to be performed 500 times. We want to create one program segment, and place this segment in some type of loop control structure that repeats 500 times.

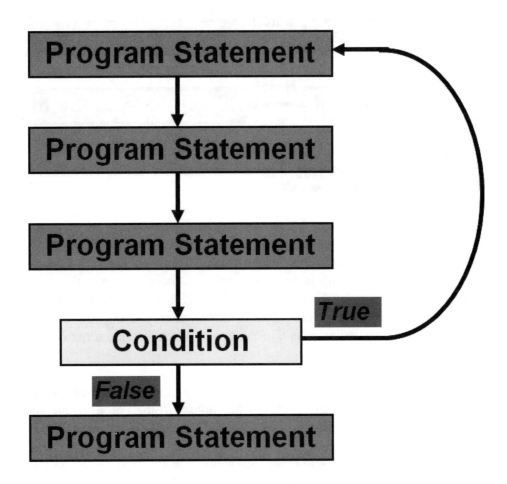

In the diagram above you will notice that the conditional statement is placed after the block of program statements that are repeated. Such a loop control structure is called *post-condition loop*. If the conditional statement precedes the block of repeated statements, then it is called a *pre-condition loop*.

Computer scientists usually call repetition or looping *iteration*. It is not unusual to read a statement like *The loop will iterate 10 times*.

Control Structures with Pseudo-Code

Relational Operators =, ≠, >, <, ≥, ≤

The relational operators are shown here, but in an actual operational program statement. This will make more sense as several program segments are displayed later.

a = b	a equals b
a ≠ b	a does not equal b
a > b	a is greater than b
a < b	a is less than b
a ≥ b	a is greater than or equal to b
a ≤ b	a is less than or equal to b

a = b

a ≠ b

a > b

a < b

a ≥ b

a ≤ b

One-Way Selection with the IF Command

In a one-way selection control structure, the block of one or more statements is executed when the IF condition is true.

```
IF (Sales > 250000)
{
    bonus = bonus + 1000
}
```

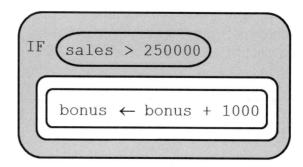

IF sales > 250000

bonus ← bonus + 1000

Two-Way Selection with the IF..ELSE Command

In a two-way selection control structure, the block of one or more statements is executed when the `IF` condition is `true` and the other block is executed if the condition is `false`.

```
IF (sales > 250000)
{
    bonus ← 2000
}
ELSE
{
    bonus ← 1000
}
```

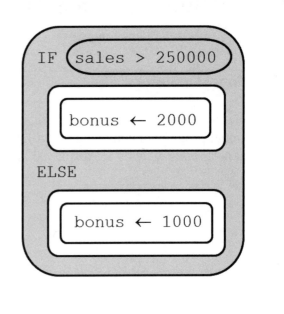

Multi-Way Selection with the ELSE..IF Command

In a multi-way selection control structure, the first block is executed when the `IF` condition is `true`. If the condition is `false` a sequence of conditions is checked until the condition is `true`.

```
IF (score >= 90)
{
    grade ← "A"
}
ELSE IF (score >= 80)
{
    grade ← "B"
}
ELSE IF (score >= 70)
{
    grade ← "C"
}
ELSE IF (score < 70)
{
    grade ← "F"
}
```

Fixed Iteration with the REPEAT n TIMES Command

Repeats displaying a random integer in the [1..9] range 10 times.

```
REPEAT 10 TIMES
{
    DISPLAY (RANDOM (1, 9))
}
```

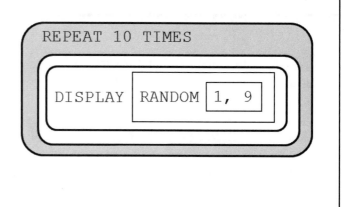

Conditional Iteration with the REPEAT UNTIL Command

Repeats an unknown number of times until the condition of (pin = 1234) is true based on user input.

```
REPEAT UNTIL (pin = 1234)
{
    DISPLAY ("Enter PIN")
    pin ← INPUT ()
}
```

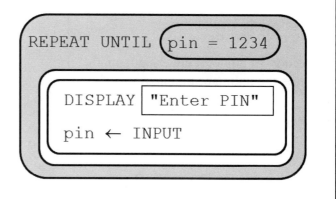

Control structures are straight forward, but you do need to pay close attention because small changes in the conditional statements can make considerable differences in program execution.

Concern #1: Watch Out For OBOBs (Off By One Bugs)

The OBOB is a common error for the fast test-taking student who does not pay close attention. Such a student may well select answer (A) for Question 1. Question 2 is only slightly different with a change from using *greater than* to *greater than or equal to*. That small difference changes the answer.

Question 1	

Consider the adjacent code segment. What is the output of the program?
 	
    (A) Good Job
 	
    (B) 2500
 	
### (C) Sorry, no bonus 	
 	
    (D) 0
	<pre>sales ← 500000
	IF (sales > 500000)
	{
	    DISPLAY ("Good Job")
	    bonus ← 2500
	}
	ELSE
	{
	    DISPLAY ("Sorry, no bonus")
	}</pre>

Question 2	

Consider the adjacent code segment. What is the output of the program?
 	
### (A) Good Job 	
 	
    (B) 2500
 	
    (C) Sorry, no bonus
 	
    (D) 0
	<pre>sales ← 500000
	IF (sales ≥ 500000)
	{
	    DISPLAY ("Good Job")
	    bonus ← 2500
	}
	ELSE
	{
	    DISPLAY ("Sorry, no bonus")
	}</pre>

Two questions and for the fast test-taker the program code may seem identical. Occasionally, I have on a quiz or a test given such a sequence of questions. Often students speak up stating that both questions are the same. Of course speaking up during a test is a big no-no, but some students are eager to point out teacher mistakes.

Concern #2: Program Sequence Matters

Questions that involve loops start with a first priority. How many times does the loop structure repeat or iterate? Then you proceed at observe the statements that are repeated. Look at *Question 3* and *Question 4*. Do you see the difference?

Question 3	

Consider the adjacent code segment. What is the last output of the program?
 	
 (A) 9
 	
 ### (B) 10
 	
 (C) 11
 	
 (D) No output
	```count ← 0```
	 ```REPEAT 10 TIMES```
	 ```{```
	
	 ``` count ← count + 1```
	 ``` DISPLAY (count)```
	 ```}```

Question 4	

Consider the adjacent code segment. What is the last output of the program?
 	
 ### (A) 9
 	
 (B) 10
 	
 (C) 11
 	
 (D) No output
	```count ← 0```
	 ```REPEAT 10 TIMES```
	 ```{```
	
	 ``` DISPLAY (count)```
	 ``` count ← count + 1```
	 ```}```

The two questions above are similar. Both questions actually have the same program statements, but *Question 4* displays before the count variable increases. The result is that *Question 3* displays numbers from 1 to 10 and *Question 4* displays numbers from 0 to 9.

Concern #3: Confusion Between Assignment and Equality

In many languages, such as Java and Python a single **=** means assignment, like `x = a + b;` One **=** operator does not mean equality. The equality operator requires two **==**, like you see in the statement `if (pin == 1234)`. With the College Board pseudo-code that same `if` statement is similar, but not exactly the same and looks like `IF (pin = 1234)`.

Chapter 6 Questions
Control Structures with Pseudo-Code

01.

Consider the adjacent code segment. What is the output of the program?

(A) `1000.0`

(B) `Extra Bonus`
    `2500.0`

(C) `Extra Bonus`
    `3500.0`

(D) No output

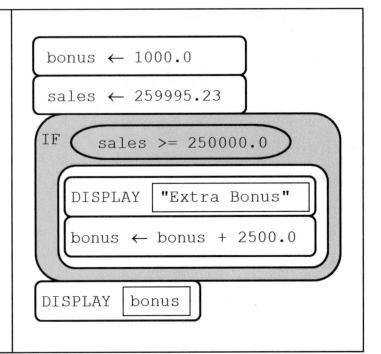

02.

Consider the adjacent code segment. If this program is executed 10,000 times, which of the following is the expected odd/even number output?

(A) Roughly 50% even and 50% odd

(B) More odd than even

(C) More even than odd

(D) It will be totally random

```
x ← RANDOM (1, 5)
IF (x MOD 2 = 0)
{
    DISPLAY ("even")
}
ELSE
{
    DISPLAY ("odd")
}
```

03.

Consider the adjacent code segment.
What is the output of the program?

    (A) A

    (B) B

    (C) C

    (D) F

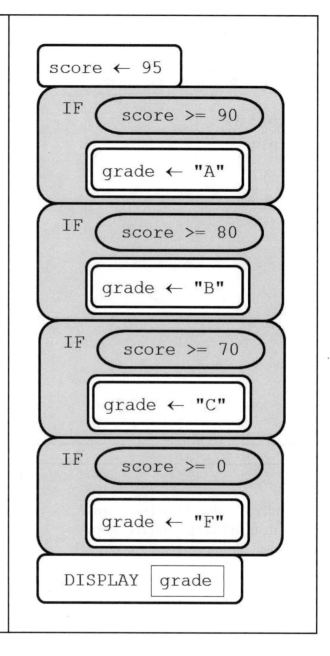

04.

Consider the adjacent code segment. What is the output of the program?

(A) A

(B) B

(C) C

(D) F

```
score ← 85
IF (score >= 90)
{
    grade ← "A"
}
ELSE IF (score >= 80)
{
    grade ← "B"
}
ELSE IF (score >= 70)
{
    grade ← "C"
}
ELSE
{
    grade ← "F"
}
DISPLAY (grade)
```

05.

Consider the adjacent code segment. How many different numbers can be displayed during program execution?

(A) 4

(B) 5

(C) 6

(D) 8

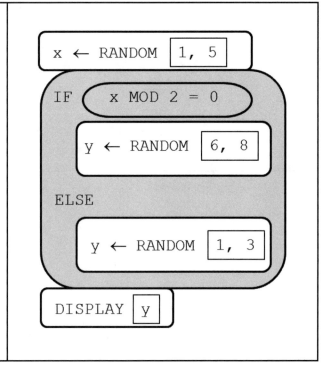

06.

Consider the adjacent code segment. What is the output of the program?

(A) 100

(B) 200

(C) 300

(D) Cannot be determined

```
x ← <unknown integer>
n ← 0
IF (x > 500)
{
    IF (x < 300)
    {
        n ← 100
    }
    ELSE
    {
        n ← 200
    }
}
ELSE
{
    IF (x > 700)
    {
        n ← 300
    }
    ELSE
    {
        n ← 200
    }
}
DISPLAY (n)
```

07.

Consider the adjacent code segment. What is the output of the program?

(A) 32

(B) 8

(C) 4

(D) 0

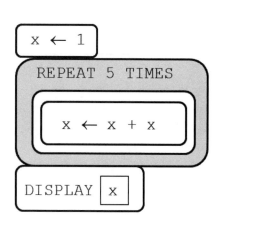

Consider the adjacent code segment.
What is the output of the program?

(A) 100

(B) 70

(C) 28

(D) 15

```
k ← 1
sum ← 0
REPEAT 5 TIMES
{
    k ← k + 1
    sum ← sum + (k * 5)
}
DISPLAY (g)
```

Consider the adjacent code segment.
What is the output of the program?

(A) 7

(B) 8

(C) 9

(D) 10

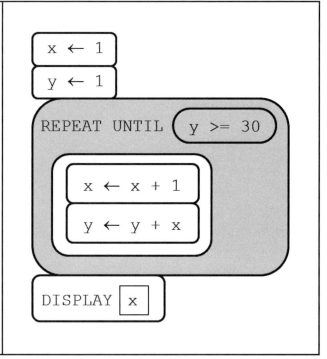

10.

Consider the adjacent code segment.
What is the output of the program?

   (A) 1

   (B) 228

   (C) 12

   (D) 1080

```
n1 ← 120
n2 ← 108
r ← 1
g ← 1
REPEAT UNTIL (r = 0)
{
    r ← n1 MOD n2
    if (r = 0)
    {
        g ← n2
    }
    ELSE
    {
        n1 ← n2
        n2 ← r
    }
}
DISPLAY (g)
```

11.

Consider the adjacent code segment. What is the output of the program?

(A) 13

(B) 9

(C) 7

(D) 4

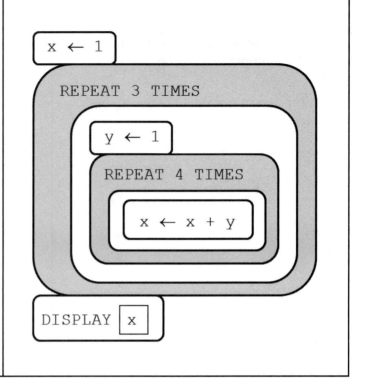

```
x ← 1
REPEAT 3 TIMES
    y ← 1
    REPEAT 4 TIMES
        x ← x + y
DISPLAY x
```

12.

Consider the adjacent code segment. What is the output of the program?

(A) 16

(B) 14

(C) 12

(D) 8

```
x ← 0
REPEAT 2 TIMES
{
    x ← x + 1
    REPEAT 2 TIMES
    {
        x ← x + 1
        REPEAT 2 TIMES
        {
            x ← x + 1
        }
    }
}
DISPLAY (x)
```

Chapter 7 Review
Boolean Logic & Logic Gates

In this chapter we will review Boolean logic. The rules of Boolean operators can be conveniently displayed in a *truth table*. This is a table, which shows all of the possible combinations of Boolean statements and indicates the value of each one. Remember that a Boolean statement is either `true` or `false`.

In the truth tables that follow, a single letter indicates a single, simple Boolean condition. Such a condition is either `true` or `false`. Boolean statement A is `true` or `false`. Likewise Boolean statement B is `true` or `false`. The truth tables will show the results of Boolean statements that use both A and B with a variety of Boolean operators. Employment requirements will be used to explain the logic of each truth table. In each case imagine that an accountant needs to be hired. Condition A determines if the applicant has a `Degree` and condition B determines if the applicant has at least five years of work experience.

Boolean OR Operator

The or Operator		
A	B	A **or** B
T	T	T
T	F	T
F	T	T
F	F	F

Notice that two conditions have four possible combinations. It is important that you know the results for each type of combination. In this case the employment analogy requires a **Degree OR Experience**. This requirement is quite relaxed. You have a Degree, fine. You have Experience, that's also fine. You have both, definitely fine. You have neither, that's not fine and causes a no hire situation.

Boolean AND Operator

The **and** Operator		
A	B	A **and** B
T	T	T
T	F	F
F	T	F
F	F	F

Now employment requires a **Degree AND Experience**. This requirement is much more demanding than the OR operator. You have a Degree, fine, provided you also have Experience. Having only one of the qualifications is not good enough.

Boolean XOR Operator

The **xor** Operator		
A	B	A **xor** B
T	T	F
T	F	T
F	T	T
F	F	F

English, uses both the OR operator, as well as the AND operator in communication. The use of XOR is another story. A peek at the truth table shows if conditions A and B are both true, the compound result is false. I will try to explain this by using the "cheap boss" analogy. A manager wants to hire somebody and not pay much money. The advertisement states that a degree or experience is required.

Candidate X walks in and the boss says: "I'll hire you, but your pay will be low. You see, you have a degree, but you have no experience at all."

Candidate Y walks in and the boss says: "I'll hire you, but your pay will be low. You see, you have experience but you have no degree."

Candidate Z walks in and the boss says: "I'm sorry I cannot hire you. You are over qualified since you have a degree and also experience."

You will not see the XOR logic operator in the pseudo-code reference guide. The AP Examination is a strange creature. There is an exact course description and that description outlines the curriculum and what may be tested. Imagine that the course description outlines 27 program language commands. Fine, you certainly want to know those commands, but you also need to be prepared for some commands that may show up on the test. In such a case the new commands will be explained inside the question and you are tested on both your ability to comprehend a new concept and how to use it. I feel better if you know the XOR operator.

Boolean NOT

The **not** Operator	
A	**not** A
T	F
F	T

This section will finish with the simplest Boolean operator, NOT. This operator takes the condition that follows and changes true to false or false to true. There are special rules that need to be followed when a complex Boolean statement is used with not. Such rules will be explained later in the chapter. Right now we want to understand the simple truth table shown above. In English we need to use "double negative" sentences to create an appropriate analogy. I can say "It is NOT true that Tom Smith is valedictorian." This statement results in Tom not being Valedictorian. On the other hand, if I say "It is NOT true that Tom Smith is NOT the Valedictorian." Now Tom is the Valedictorian.

Make Sure You Know DeMorgan's Law

not(A or B) = not A and not B   same as   ~(A + B) = ~A * ~B

not(A and B) = not A or not B   same as   ~(A * B) = ~A + ~B

De Morgan's Law is very important in programming.
Failure to use this law properly causes many logic errors in programs.

Boolean Logic with Pseudo-Code

Logical Operator OR

This program segment demonstrates a compound condition with a logical OR. The truth table of OR shows that there are three possible combinations that will result in true or hiring.

```
IF (exp ≥ 5 OR edu ≥ 16)
{
    DISPLAY ("You're hired")
}
ELSE
{
    DISPLAY (You're not hired")
}
```

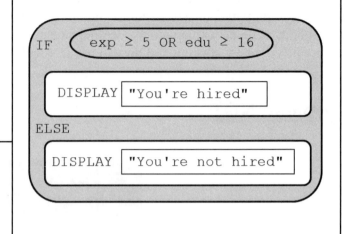

Logical Operator AND

This program segment demonstrates a compound condition with a logical AND. The truth table of AND shows that there is only one possible combinations that will result in true or hiring.

```
IF (exp ≥ 5 AND edu ≥ 16)
{
    DISPLAY ("You're hired")
}
ELSE
{
    DISPLAY (You're not hired")
}
```

IF (exp ≥ 5 AND edu ≥ 16)
DISPLAY "You're hired"
ELSE
DISPLAY "You're not hired"

Logical Operator NOT

The logical NOT operator is quite simple. It results in the negation of whatever condition follows.

```
boolean ← true
DISPLAY (boolean)
boolean ← NOT (boolean)
DISPLAY (boolean)
```

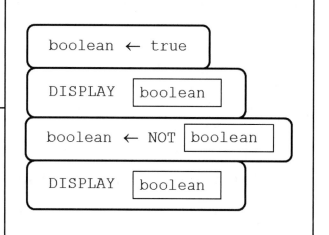

Using Logic Gates

What you see here is neither an example of block-based pseudo-code nor text-based pseudo-code. It is a drawing of logic gates, which are hardware related.

You are not responsible for knowing the actual symbols that indicate different types of logic gates. Still on the AP Exam you will likely see one or more logic gate questions. The adjacent diagram shows two logic gates, which both have two Boolean inputs and one Boolean output. The type of operator is shown inside the rectangle.

Later in this chapter you will see four questions that use this type of format.

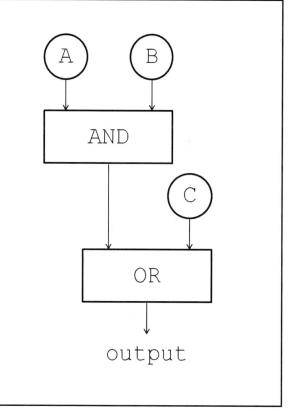

Boolean logic is quite straight-forward with simple compound conditions, meaning two conditions with one operator, like *if you (get good grades and keep your room clean) you can go on the spring ski trip.* The tricky part happens when the expression is no longer a single logic operator. When Boolean expressions get longer they become tedious. It is very unlikely that you will encounter anything that is long, but there are two areas of concern that may show up.

Concern #1: Questions that use De Morgan's Law

Question 1	

Consider the adjacent code segment. Which of these three statements are logically equivalent?
 	
    (A) a1 and a2 only
 	
### (B) a1 and a3 only 	
 	
    (C) a2 and a3 only
 	
    (D) a1, a2 and a3
	``` a1 ← NOT (x AND y) a2 ← NOT (x) AND NOT (y) a3 ← NOT (x) OR NOT (y) ```

Question 2	

Consider the adjacent code segment. Which of these three statements are logically equivalent?
 	
    (A) a1 and a2 only
 	
### (B) a1 and a3 only 	
 	
    (C) a2 and a3 only
 	
    (D) a1, a2 and a3
	``` a1 ← NOT (x OR y) a2 ← NOT (x) OR NOT (y) a3 ← NOT (x) AND NOT (y) ```

Both questions involve the use of De Morgan's law, which was shown earlier. Students who are used to high school Algebra I and their good friend the *Distributive Property*, may be very much inclined to select answer (A) for both questions. But Boolean logic has its own set of rules one important rule is De Morgan's Law.

Concern #2: Watch for Short-Circuiting

Boolean expressions can appear quite complex. Question 3 and Question 4 below both have Boolean expressions with four Boolean variables. In normal situations this could require truth tables that have 16 different possible combinations. In special situations it is not necessary to evaluate the entire complex expression.

Question 3	

Consider the adjacent code segment. What is the output of the program?
 	
### (A) `true` 	
 	
    (B) `false`
 	
    (C) `false` only if d equals `false`
 	
    (D) Cannot be determined
	`a ← true`
	`b ← false`
	`c ← true`
	`d ← < Unknown Boolean value >`
	`x ← a OR ((a AND b) OR (c OR d))`
	`DISPLAY (x)`

Question 4	

Consider the adjacent code segment. What is the output of the program?
 	
    (A) `true`
 	
### (B) `false` 	
 	
    (C) `true` only if d equals `true`
 	
    (D) Cannot be determined
	`a ← false`
	`b ← true`
	`c ← true`
	`d ← < Unknown Boolean value >`
	`x ← a OR ((a AND b) OR (c OR d))`
	`DISPLAY (x)`

Both questions involve a complex Boolean expression with four variables. And both expressions are quick and easy to solve using *short circuiting*. In *Question 3* it is known that a equals `true`. You are done. You need nothing else. With an OR operation `true` OR anything equals `true`.

Question 4 shows a similar story. It is known that a equals `false`. Again you are done. With an AND operation `false` AND anything equals `false`.

01.

Consider the adjacent code segment. What is the output of the program?

(A) 1200

(B) false

(C) true

(D) admitted

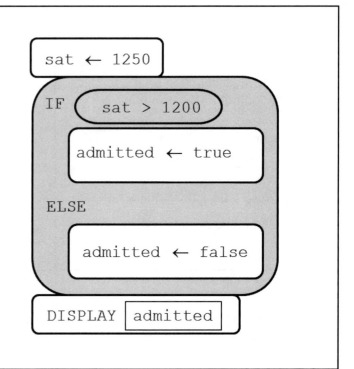

02.

Consider the adjacent code segment.
What is the output of the program?

(A) You're Hired

(B) You're Not Hired

(C) true

(D) false

```
education ← 13
experience ← 5
IF (education >= 16 OR experience >= 5)
{
    DISPLAY ("You're Hired")
}
ELSE
{
    DISPLAY ("You're Not Hired")
}
```

03.

Consider the adjacent code segment. What is the output of the program?

(A) `true false`

(B) `false true`

(C) `true true`
      `or`
   `false false`

(D) `true true`

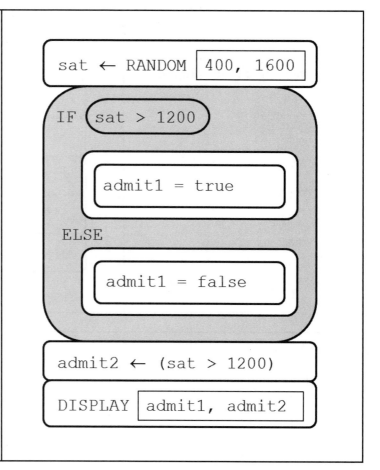

```
sat ← RANDOM  400, 1600

IF  (sat > 1200)

        admit1 = true

ELSE

        admit1 = false


admit2 ← (sat > 1200)

DISPLAY  admit1, admit2
```

04.

Consider the adjacent code segment.
What is the output of the program?

(A) `false false`

(B) `true true`

(C) `true false`

(D) `false true`

```
n1 ← RANDOM (400, 500)
n2 ← RANDOM (450, 550)
result1 ← (n1 >= 400 AND n2 <= 550)
result2 ← (n2 >= 550 OR n2 <= 550)
DISPLAY (result1, result2)
```

05.

Consider the adjacent code segment. What is the output of the program?

(A) true
   true

(B) false
   false

(C) true
   false

(D) x3 will always equal x4

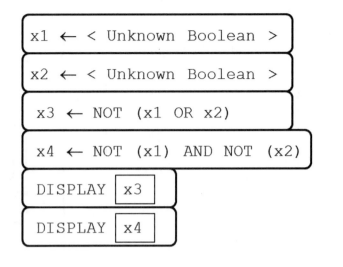

```
x1 ← < Unknown Boolean >

x2 ← < Unknown Boolean >

x3 ← NOT (x1 OR x2)

x4 ← NOT (x1) AND NOT (x2)

DISPLAY  x3

DISPLAY  x4
```

06.

Consider the adjacent code segment. What is the output of the program?

(A) true
   true

(B) false
   false

(C) true
   false

(D) x3 will always equal x4

```
x1 ← <Unknown Boolean >
x2 ← <Unknown Boolean >
x3 ← NOT (x1 AND x2)
x4 ← NOT (x1) OR NOT (x2)
DISPLAY (x3)
DISPLAY (x4)
```

07.

Consider the adjacent code segment.
What is the output of the program?

(A) true or false

(B) false

(C) true

(D) Memory overflow error

```
a ← true
b ← < Unknown Boolean Value >
c ← < Unknown Boolean Value >
d ← a OR ((a AND b) OR (b AND c))
DISPLAY  d
```

08.

Consider the adjacent code segment.
What is the output of the program?

(A) true or false

(B) false

(C) true

(D) Memory overflow error

```
a ← false
b ← < Unknown Boolean Value >
c ← < Unknown Boolean Value >
d ← a AND ((a AND b) OR (b AND c))
DISPLAY (d)
```

09.

Consider the adjacent code segment.
A equals `true`.
B equals `false`.
C equals `true`.

What will be the value of `output`?

   (A) `true`

   (B) `false`

   (C) Cannot be determined

   (D) OR gate cannot have double input

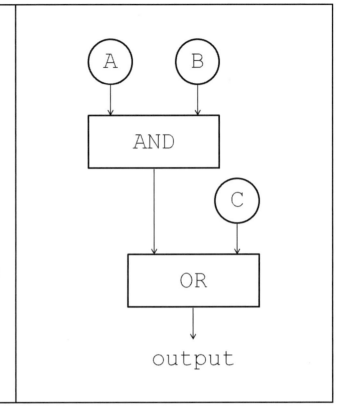

10.

Consider the adjacent code segment.
A equals `true`.
B equals `false`.
C equals `true`.

If the output must equal true, what is the required value for C?

   (A) Cannot be determined

   (B) Does not matter
       Can be `true` or `false`

   (C) Must be `false`

   (D) Must be `true`

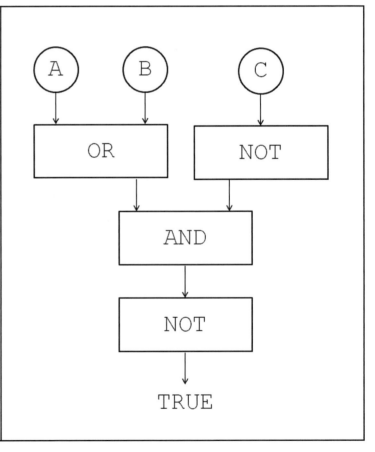

11.

Consider the adjacent code segment.
A equals `true`.
B equals `false`.
C equals `true`.
D is unknown.

If the output must equal true, what is the required value for D?

    (A) Cannot be determined

    (B) Does not matter
        Can be `true` or `false`

    (C) Must be `false`

    (D) Must be `true`

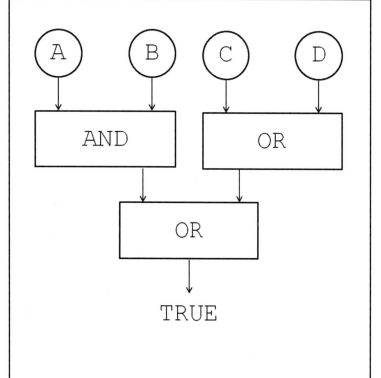

12.

Consider the adjacent code segment.
A is unknown.
B equals `false`.
C equals `true`.
D equals `false`.

If the output must equal true, what is the required value for A?

    (A) Cannot be determined

    (B) Does not matter
        Can be `true` or `false`

    (C) Must be `false`

    (D) Must be `true`

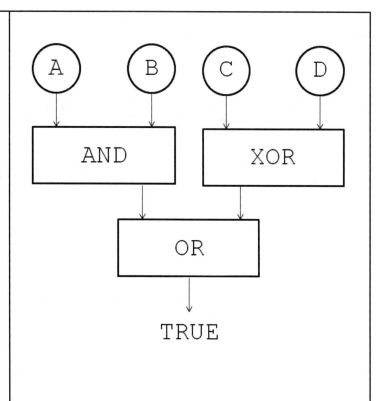

Chapter 8 Review
List Processing with Pseudo-Code

Computer program languages use variables to store and access program values. This is done in mathematics and in science with equations and formulas. Computer Science uses the same approach. Variables can store single values, such as an integer, a real number, a character or a Boolean value. Computer languages also have data structures that can store more than one variable or record.

For the AP CSP course there is a single data structure, called a *list*. The use and implementation in pseudo-code makes this list resemble the traditional static array from languages like FORTRAN, BASIC, Pascal, C++ and Java. A static array is a data structure that stores a fixed number of elements of the same data type. Individual elements can be accessed using an array index which specifies the address for the element in the array. It is similar to a street address. A street has an array of homes. Individual homes are indicated by a street number. The street address analogy works well in another area also. There is a difference between the location of the home and the occupants at that location. We are not confused at all with homes. Street numbers and people are very different. The problem with arrays is that an array, which uses consecutive integer values for its index locators, may also store integers at the array locations.

The pseudo-code provided for this course uses the term *list*, which works very well. I do believe the *list* is meant to be a data structure with elements of the same type. The nature of the AP CSP course is not to get overly excited about very small distinctions. The program language Python, which is used by many schools for AP CSP, has several data structures and one of them is a list. In practice it will seem very similar to those teachers and students who are familiar with arrays.

APCS Examination Alert

There is a considerable number of list-specific procedures available for the list, including **INSERT**, **APPEND**, **REMOVE** and **LENGTH**. You may not see examples of questions in the Course Description or the practice exam for all of these list operations.

Be warned that a singular exam, whether a practice exam or a released exam can never thoroughly cover every possible topic and feature that is listed in the course decription as part of the curriculum. Teach and prepare for the material posted in the Course Description. Do not try to guess what might or might not be tested.

List Operations Pseudo-Code Program Features

As you look at the pseudo-code that is used for list processing, make sure not to get confused. A *list* is a data structure that can store one or more elements. The word *list* was used in the last sentence in the manner that we use *list* in English, such as a shopping list. It is also common that the variable name of a *list* data structure is `list` as you see with the very first pseudo-code example below.

Using the list Index Operator

Lists can have many elements and access to a specific element is done with the index operator. In many program languages the index operator is a set of square brackets `[ ]` like the ones you see below with the text-based pseudo-code. The number inside the index operator is the location of the element. Block-based pseudo-code uses a box for index access.

```
DISPLAY (list[1])
DISPLAY (list[5])
DISPLAY (list[8])
```

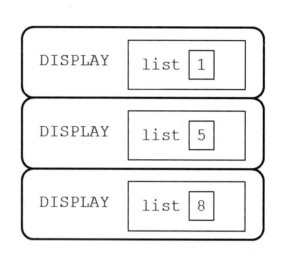

Single Element List Assignment

Assignment to a list element is done with the ← assignment operator. The two examples shown here are three times assigning a single element to a single location.

```
list[1] ← 11
list[5] ← 25
list1[8] ← list2[1]
```

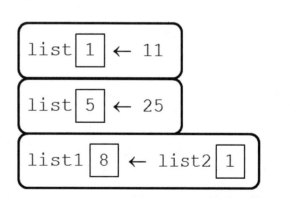

Multi-Element List Assignment

This example shows multi-element assignment. It is also called an *initializer list*. This type of assignment is used to declare a new data structure with a group of initial elements.

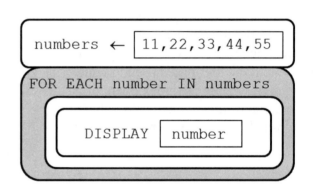

```
list1 ← [11,22,33,44,55]
list2 ← [val1,val2,val3]
```

FOR EACH..IN Loop with a List

The FOR EACH..IN loop only works with a data structure, like a list. Keep in mind that specific elements cannot be accessed nor can they be altered.

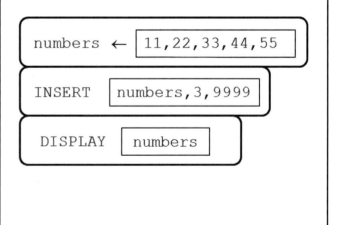

```
numbers ← [11,22,33,44,55]
FOR EACH number IN numbers
{
    DISPLAY (number)
}
```

INSERT Command with a List

In this example, the INSERT command inserts a new element, 9999, at index 3 of the numbers list. The current element at index 3 is not replaced, but shifted to index 4 along with all the elements that follow, who also shift to the next index.

```
numbers ← [11,22,33,44,55]
INSERT (numbers, 3, 9999)
DISPLAY (numbers)
```

APPEND Command with a List

The APPEND command adds an additional element at the end of the list. In the example 9999 follows 55 in the numbers list.

```
numbers ← [11,22,33,44,55]
APPEND (numbers,9999)
DISPLAY (numbers)
```

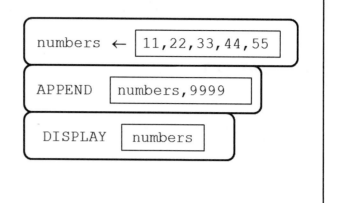

REMOVE Command with a List

The REMOVE command removes the element of the numbers list at index 2.

```
numbers ← [11,22,33,44,55]
REMOVE (numbers, 2)
DISPLAY (numbers)
```

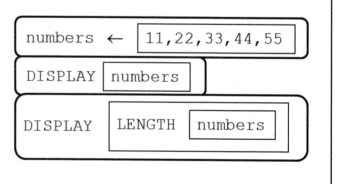

LENGTH Command with a List

The LENGTH command returns the number of elements in the numbers list. This is the same value as the largest index of numbers.

```
numbers ← [11,22,33,44,55]
DISPLAY (numbers)
DISPLAY (LENGTH (numbers))
```

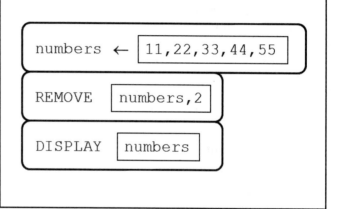

Basic Program Features Pitfalls

Concern #1: Index Confusion

Simple or primitive data types like integers, real numbers, characters and Booleans have a single value. Data structures like an array or list have multiple elements. Access to these elements is done with an index value. Any attempt to access an element with an index value that does not exists result in an *index out of range error*.

Question 1	

Consider the adjacent code segment. What is the output of the program?
 	
(A) 11 55
 	
(B) 11 44
 	
(C) 99 99
 	
(D) Index out of range error message
	``
	x ← [11,22,33,44,55]
	index ← 0
	n ← LENGTH (numbers)
	REPEAT n TIMES
	{
	    x[index] ← 99
	    index ← index + 1
	}
	DISPLAY (x[0])
	DISPLAY (x[n-1])
	``

Question 2	

Consider the adjacent code segment. What is the output of the program?
 	
(A) 11 55
 	
(B) 11 44
 	
(C) 99 99
 	
(D) Index out of range error message
	``
	x ← [11,22,33,44,55]
	index ← 1
	n ← LENGTH (numbers)
	REPEAT n TIMES
	{
	    x[index] ← 99
	    index ← index + 1
	}
	DISPLAY (x[1])
	DISPLAY (x[n])
	``

Program languages, like C++, Java and Python start array and list indexes at **0**. The largest index elements in such data structures is **n-1**, where n is the length of the structure. The pseudo-code used the AP Exam uses index **1** for the first index. Question 1 works fine for conventional program languages, but gives an error for pseudo-code. Question 2 provides code that is meant for the AP Exam pseudo-code.

Concern #2: Aliasing

Aliasing occurs when two or more data structures references the same memory location. In Question 1, **list1** get memory space for its elements, but **list2** does not get its own memory. It references or shares the same memory location as **list1**. This has the side effect that any change in **list1** will become a change in **list2**. This style question may not show up on the AP Exam, but it could well show up in your Create Performance Task program. Be warned.

Question 3	
| Consider the adjacent code segment. Note that the `NEXTLINE` procedure executes a *Carriage Return, Line Feed* (CRLF) after the previous output. What is the output of the program? <br><br> (A) 11 22 99 44 99 <br>     11 22 99 44 99 <br><br> (B) 11 22 33 44 99 <br>     11 22 99 44 55 <br><br> (C) 11 22 99 44 55 <br>     11 22 33 44 99 <br><br> (D) 11 22 33 44 55 <br>     11 22 33 44 55 | ```
list1 ← [11,22,33,44,55]
list2 ← list1
list2[3] ← 99
list1[5] ← 99
index ← 1
REPEAT 5 TIMES
{
    DISPLAY (list1[index])
    NEXTLINE ()
    DISPLAY (list2[index])
}
``` |
| The adjacent code solves the aliasing problem. The second data structure, list2 is first initialized as an empty list. Then in a loop, each element of list1 is appended to list2. The end result is that both data structures have their own memory for its elements. | ```
list1 ← [11,22,33,44,55]
list2 ← []
n = LENGTH (list1)
FOR EACH item IN list1
{
    APPEND(list2,item)
}
``` |

01.

Consider the adjacent code segment.
What is the output of the program?

    (A) 15 25 35

    (B) 10 20 30 40

    (C) 10 15 20 25 30 35 40

    (D) Index Out Of Range error
        message

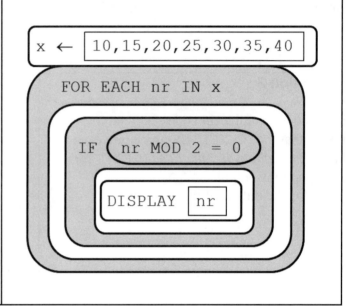

02.

Consider the adjacent code segment.
What is the output of the program?

    (A) 15 25 35

    (B) 10 20 30 40

    (C) 10 15 20 25 30 35 40

    (D) Index Out Of Range error
        message

```
numbers ← [10,15,20,25,30,35,40]
n ← LENGTH (numbers)
k ← 1
REPEAT n TIMES
{
    IF (k MOD 2 = 0)
    {
        DISPLAY (numbers[k])
    }
    k ← k + 1
}
```

03.

Consider the adjacent code segment. What values are stored in the x list at the conclusion of running the program?

(A) [40,15,20,25,30,35]

(B) [40,40,40,40,40,40]

(C) [15,15,20,20,25,25]

(D) [15,15,15,15,15,15]

```
x ← 15,20,25,30,35,40

n ← LENGTH (x) - 1

k ← 2

REPEAT n TIMES
{
    x k ← x k-1
    k ← k + 1
}
```

04.

Consider the adjacent code segment. What values are stored in the x list at the conclusion of running the program?

(A) [20,25,30,35,40,40]

(B) [20,20,25,30,35,40]

(C) [15,20,30,35,40,40]

(D) [15,15,20,25,30,35]

```
x ← [15,20,25,30,35,40]
n ← LENGTH (x) - 1
k ← 1
REPEAT n TIMES
{
    x[k] ← x[k+1]
    k ← k + 1
}
```

05.

Consider the adjacent code segment. What values are stored in `list` at the conclusion of running the program?

(A) `[33,66,22,44,55,11]`

(B) `[11,33,22,44,55,66]`

(C) `[11,66,22,44,55,33]`

(D) `[11,33,22,66,55,44]`

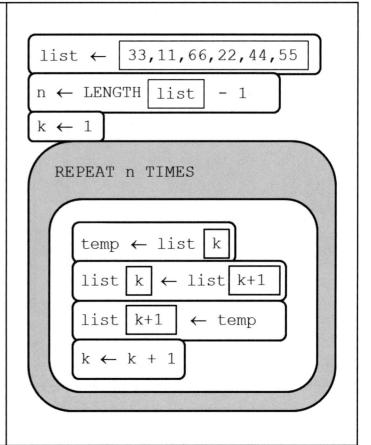

06.

Consider the adjacent code segment. How are the values arranged after running the program segment?

(A) The largest number is located at the end of `list`.

(B) The smallest number is located at the end of `list`.

(C) `list` is sorted in ascending order.

(D) `list` is sorted in descending order.

```
list ← <unknown integers>
n ← LENGTH (list) - 1
k ← 1
REPEAT n TIMES
{
    IF (list[k] > list[k+1])
    {
        temp ← list[k]
        list[k] ← list[k+1]
        list[k+1] ← temp
    }
    k ← k + 1
}
```

07.

Consider the adjacent code segment. For this program assume that the **//** operator computes integer division. What is the output of the program?

(A) 1 22 33 44 55

(B) 11 11 11 11 11

(C) 1 1 1 1 1

(D) 1 2 3 4 5

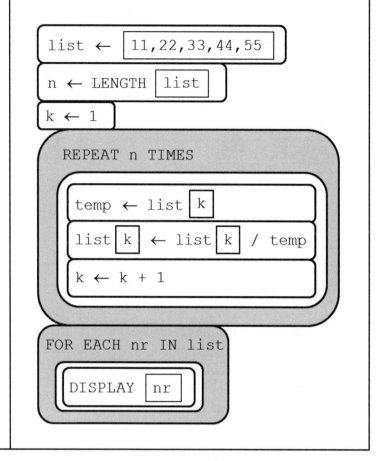

```
list ← 11,22,33,44,55

n ← LENGTH list

k ← 1

REPEAT n TIMES

    temp ← list k

    list k ← list k / temp

    k ← k + 1

FOR EACH nr IN list

    DISPLAY nr
```

08.

Consider the adjacent code segment. For this program assume that the **//** operator computes integer division. What is the output of the program?

(A) 1 22 33 44 55

(B) 11 11 11 11 11

(C) 1 1 1 1 1

(D) 1 2 3 4 5

```
list ← [11,22,33,44,55]
n ← LENGTH (list)
k ← 1
REPEAT n TIMES
{
    list[k] ← list[k] // list[1]
    k ← k + 1
}
FOR EACH item IN list
{
    DISPLAY (item)
}
```

09.

Consider the adjacent code segment.
What is the output of the program?

(A) 11 22 33 44 55

(B) 99 99 99 99 99

(C) 110 121 132 143 154

(D) Index Out Of Range error message

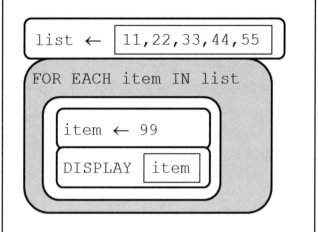

```
list ← 11,22,33,44,55

FOR EACH item IN list

    item ← 99

    DISPLAY  item
```

10.

Consider the adjacent code segment.
Note that the NEXTLINE procedure
executes a *Carriage Return, Line Feed*
(CRLF) after the previous output.
What is the output of the program?

(A) 11 22 33 44 55
    11 22 33 44 55

(B) 99 99 99 99 99
    99 99 99 99 99

(C) 99 99 99 99 99
    11 22 33 44 55

(D) 11 22 33 44 55
    99 99 99 99 99

```
list ← [11,22,33,44,55]
FOR EACH item IN list
{
    item ← 99
    DISPLAY (item)
}
NEXTLINE()
FOR EACH item IN list
{
    DISPLAY (item)
}
```

11.

Consider the adjacent code segment. Note that the NEXTLINE procedure executes a *Carriage Return, Line Feed* (CRLF) after the previous output. What is the output of the program?

(A) 11 33 44 55
    11 33 55

(B) 11 22 44 55
    11 22 44

(C) 11 33 44 55
    11 44 55

(D) 11 22 44 55
    11 22 55

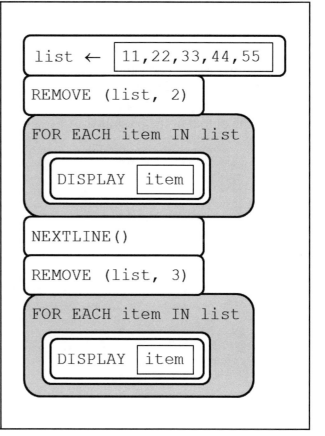

```
list ←  11,22,33,44,55

REMOVE (list, 2)

FOR EACH item IN list

    DISPLAY  item

NEXTLINE()

REMOVE (list, 3)

FOR EACH item IN list

    DISPLAY  item
```

12.

Consider the adjacent code segment. What is the output of the program?

(A) 11 33 55

(B) 22 44 66

(C) 11 44 33 55

(D) 11 22 44 33 66 55

```
list ← [11,22,44,33,66,55]
k ← 1
REPEAT UNTIL (k > LENGTH (list))
{
    IF (list[k] MOD 2 = 0)
    {
        REMOVE(list,k)
    }
    k ← k + 1
}
FOR EACH item IN list
{
    DISPLAY (item)
}
```

13.

Consider the adjacent code segment. Note that the NEXTLINE procedure executes a *Carriage Return, Line Feed* (CRLF) after the previous output. What is the output of the program?

(A) 11 22 33 44 66
    11 22 33 40

(B) 66 11 22 33 44 55
    40 66 11 22 33 44 55

(C) 11 22 33 44 55 66
    11 22 33 40 44 55 66

(D) 11 22 33 44 55 66
    11 22 33 44 55 66 40

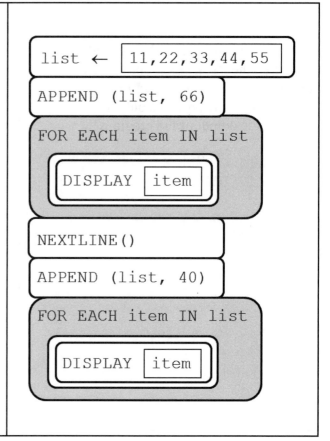

14.

Consider the adjacent code segment. What is the output of the program?

(A) 55 44 33 22 11 11 22 33 44 55

(B) 11 22 33 44 55 55 44 33 22 11

(C) 55 44 33 22 11 22 33 44 55

(D) 11 22 33 44 55 44 33 22 11

```
list1 ← [11,22,33,44,55]
list2 ← [55,44,33,22,11]
FOR EACH item IN list1
{
    APPEND (list2, item)
}
FOR EACH item IN list2
{
    DISPLAY (list2)
}
```

15.

Consider the adjacent code segment.
What is the output of the program?

    (A) 11 30 40 22 33 44 55

    (B) 11 22 30 40 33 44 55

    (C) 11 30 40 44 55

    (D) 11 22 30 40 55

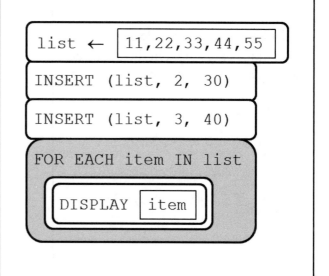

```
list ←  11,22,33,44,55

INSERT (list, 2, 30)

INSERT (list, 3, 40)

FOR EACH item IN list

    DISPLAY  item
```

16.

Consider the adjacent code segment.
What is the output of the program?

(A) 55 44 33 22 11 11 22 33 44 55

(B) 11 22 33 44 55 55 44 33 22 11

(C) 11 22 33 44 55

(D) 11 22 33 44 55 44 33 22 11

```
list1 ← [11,22,33,44,55]
list2 ← [55,44,33,22,11]
k ← 1
n = LENGTH (list1))
REPEAT n TIMES
{
    INSERT (list2, k, list1[k])
    k ← k + 1
}
FOR EACH item IN list2
{
    DISPLAY (list2)
}
```

17.

Consider the adjacent code segment. What values are stored in the `list` at the conclusion of running the program?

    (A) `[22,66,33,55,44]`

    (B) `[66,55,44,33,22]`

    (C) `[22,33,44,55,66]`

    (D) `[66,44,22,55,33]`

```
list ← [66,44,22,55,33]
n ← LENGTH (list) - 1
REPEAT n TIMES
{
    q ← 1
    REPEAT UNTIL (q = n)
    {
        if (list[q] > list[q+1])
        {
            temp = list[q]
            list[q] = list[q+1]
            list[q+1] = temp
        }
        q ← q + 1
    }
}
```

18.

Consider the adjacent code segment. What values are stored in the `list` at the conclusion of running the program?

    (A) `[22,66,33,55,44]`

    (B) `[66,55,44,33,22]`

    (C) `[22,33,44,55,66]`

    (D) `[66,44,22,55,33]`

```
list ← [66,44,22,55,33]
n ← LENGTH (list) - 1
REPEAT n TIMES
{
    q ← 1
    REPEAT UNTIL (q = n)
    {
        if (list[q] < list[q+1])
        {
            temp = list[q]
            list[q] = list[q+1]
            list[q+1] = temp
        }
        q ← q + 1
    }
}
```

19.

Consider the adjacent code segment. Note that the NEXTLINE procedure executes a *Carriage Return, Line Feed* (CRLF) after the previous output.
What is the output of the program?

(A) 1 2 3 4 5 6 7 8 9

(B) 9 8 7 6 5 4 3 2 1

(C) 1 4 7
   2 5 8
   3 6 9

(D) 1 2 3
   4 5 6
   7 8 9

```
matrix ← [[1,2,3],[4,5,6],[7,8,9]]
row ← 1
REPEAT 3 TIMES
{
    col ← 1
    REPEAT 3 TIMES
    {
        DISPLAY (matrix[row][col])
        col ← col + 1
    }
    NEXTLINE()
    row ← row + 1
}
```

20.

Consider the adjacent code segment.
What is the output of the program?

(A) 18

(B) 16

(C) 14

(D) 12

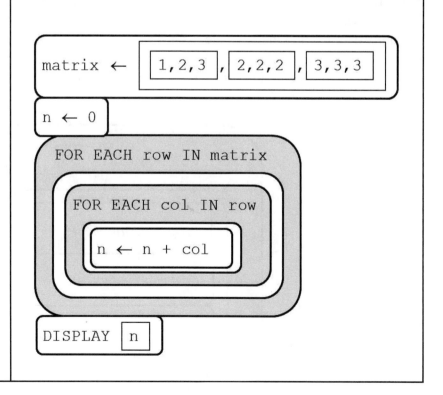

Chapter 9 Review
Procedures with Pseudo-Code

If a group of program statements performs a practical purpose, a purpose that may well be repeated in a program, then it should not be necessary to repeatedly write this same program code. In early program languages this set of program statements would be placed in a module called a subroutine. The subroutine was called by the line number of the module or by the name used in the heading of the subroutine to execute its statements.

Over time names have changed. Special subroutines that returned a value were called *functions*, just as it happens in mathematics with a square root function. Subroutines that did not return a value were called *procedures*. Later modules became methods. It is not the intention of this course to explain the precise difference between some of these program module names.

For the AP Computer Science Principles course the curriculum uses the name procedures and that is it. You will see that there are two types of procedures. There are procedures that use RETURN statements and procedures that have no RETURN statements.

Working with regular program languages or with pseudo-code program languages makes no difference. There is a group of program statements that compute a value or display a circle or do something that is useful in a program. This set of program statements are placed inside a *block*. Many languages use curly braces **{ }** to identify the block. Some languages use indentation and some use visual block shapes. With the pseudo-code, the block-based language uses a rounded rectangle as a block. One example is shown below. You will see a heading with PROCEDURE, followed by the procedure name what and then the set of parameter values, p1 and p2 that will be used by the procedure to execute the program statements.

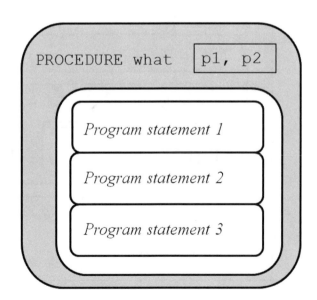

The text-based pseudo-code that follows uses a similar approach that is closer to the text-based program languages, like Java and Python. Be especially aware of the curly braces. In real program languages beginning programmers frequently forget to close a "block" of program statements with a curly brace. You may also have noticed, in a previous chapter, that the control structures use blocks as well that are created in the same manner as procedures.

```
PROCEDURE what (p1, p2)
{
        Program statement 1
        Program statement 2
        Program statement 3
}
```

Procedures that return values should be very familiar to students. You have seen these modules as functions in mathematics. In math courses you worked with functions that returned a value, such as y = sqrt(x). In that example x is the parameter or argument of the function. The value of x is used to compute the square root and that value is returned and assigned to variable y. The two images below are similar to the previous ones, but both examples add a RETURN statement.

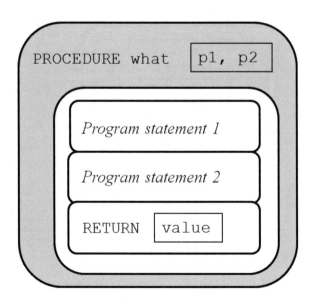

```
PROCEDURE what (p1, p2)
{
        Program statement 1
        Program statement 2
        RETURN value
}
```

PROCEDURE without RETURN

This procedure has a heading with the keyword PROCEDURE, a name that is used to call the procedure, hello, and a parameter list str1 and str2.

Below the heading is a block of program statements that are executed when the procedure is called.

```
PROCEDURE hello (str1, str2)
{
    DISPLAY ("Hello")
    DISPLAY (str1)
    DISPLAY (str2)
}
```

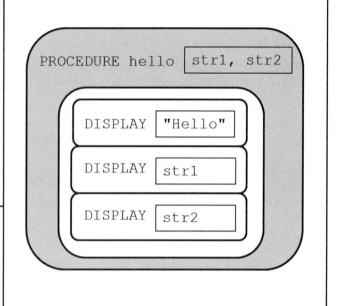

RETURN PROCEDURE

The RETURN procedure has the same heading and block of program statements as a regular procedure, but the program statements include a RETURN statement that returns a value to the program location where the procedure was called.

```
PROCEDURE add (n1, n2)
{
    sum = n1 + n2
    RETURN sum
}
```

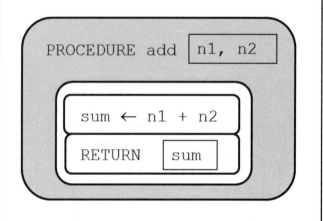

Procedure Pitfalls

Procedures are very practical modules that make programs more efficient, more reliable and more readable. There are not many pitfalls. There certainly can be very tricky procedures, but the trick is in the program code within the procedure and not with the procedure itself.

Concern #1: Matching Parameter Count

Question 1	
Consider the adjacent procedure and code segment. What is the output as a result of executing the code segment? (A) 30 (B) 10 (C) 20 (D) Error message	```PROCEDURE what (n1, n2)` `{` ` if (n1 > n2)` ` {` ` RETURN n1` ` }` ` ELSE` ` {` ` RETURN n2` ` }` `}`  `x ← what (10, 20, 30)` `DISPLAY (x)```
Question 2	
Consider the adjacent procedure and code segment. What is the output as a result of executing the code segment? (A) 30 (B) 10 (C) 20 (D) Error message	```PROCEDURE what (n1, n2)` `{` ` if (n1 > n2)` ` {` ` RETURN n1` ` }` ` ELSE` ` {` ` RETURN n2` ` }` `}`  `x ← what (10, 20)` `DISPLAY (x)```

Both questions use the same procedure. Question 1 calls the procedure using 3 parameters and Question 2 uses 2 parameters. Question 1 will get an error message because the parameters of the calling program statement --- `x ← what (10, 20, 30)` --- does not match the parameters in the procedure heading --- `PROCEDURE what (n1, n2)`.

Concern #2: Calling a return procedure incorrectly

Question 3	

Consider the adjacent procedure and code segment. What is the output as a result of executing the code segment?
 	
(A) 30
 	
(B) 10
 	
(C) 20
 	
(D) Error message
	``
	PROCEDURE what (n1, n2)
	{
	    if (n1 > n2)
	    {
	        RETURN n1
	    }
	    ELSE
	    {
	        RETURN n2
	    }
	}
	
	what (10, 20)
	DISPLAY (x)
	``

Question 4	

Consider the adjacent procedure and code segment. What is the output as a result of executing the code segment?
 	
(A) 30
 	
(B) 10
 	
(C) 20
 	
(D) Error message
	``
	PROCEDURE what (n1, n2)
	{
	    if (n1 > n2)
	    {
	        RETURN n1
	    }
	    ELSE
	    {
	        RETURN n2
	    }
	}
	
	x ← what (10, 20)
	DISPLAY (x)
	``

Both questions use the same procedure. Question 3 calls procedure what in the manner that is correct for a *no return procedure*. This means that variable x does not get a value. Question 4 handles the procedure call correctly.

Concern #3: The order of parameters is important

Question 5	

Consider the adjacent procedure and code segment. What is the output as a result of executing the code segment?
 	
(A) -10
 	
(B) 10
 	
(C) 20
 	
(D) Error message
	``
	PROCEDURE subtract (n1, n2)
	{
	    difference ← n1 - n2
	    RETURN difference
	}
	
	diff ← subtract (10, 20)
	DISPLAY (diff)
	``

Question 6	

Consider the adjacent procedure and code segment. What is the output as a result of executing the code segment?
 	
(A) 30
 	
(B) 10
 	
(C) 20
 	
(D) Error message
	``
	PROCEDURE subtract (n1, n2)
	{
	    difference ← n1 - n2
	    RETURN difference
	}
	
	diff ← subtract (20, 10)
	DISPLAY (diff)
	``

Once again both procedures are identical. This time the values of the calling parameters are different. In some cases it does not matter. For instance, in an add procedure or a multiply procedure the order of parameters makes no difference.

Chapter 9 Questions
Procedures with Pseudo-Code

01. Consider the adjacent procedure. What is the result of calling the procedure? *(Parameter x is a list of integers.)*

    (A) mystery returns the sum of the elements in list x.

    (B) mystery displays every element in list x.

    (C) mystery returns the first element in list x only.

    (D) mystery returns the last element in list x only.

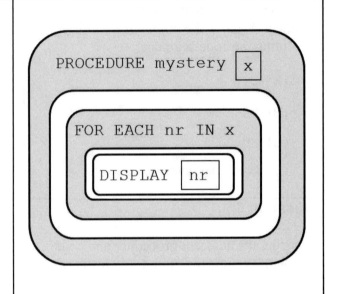

02. Consider the adjacent procedure. What is the result of calling the procedure? *(Parameter a is an integer and parameter b is a list of integers.)*

    (A) mystery returns every multiple of a in list b

    (B) mystery returns every factor of a in list b

    (C) mystery displays every multiple of a in list b

    (D) mystery displays every remainder of a in list b

```
PROCEDURE mystery (a, b)
{
    n ← LENGTH (b)
    k ← 1
    REPEAT n TIMES
    {
        if (b[k] MOD a = 0)
        {
            DISPLAY (b[k])
        }
        k ← k + 1
    }
}
```

03. Consider the adjacent procedure. What is the result of calling the procedure? *(Parameter x is a list of integers.)*

(A) `mystery` displays every element in list x in reverse order.

(B) `mystery` displays every element in list x from front to end.

(C) `mystery` displays the first element in list x only.

(D) `mystery` displays the last element in list x only.

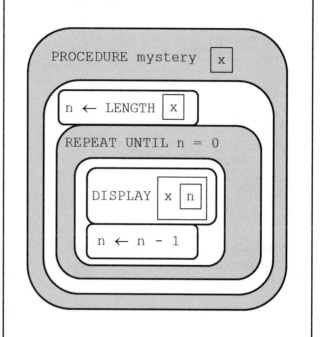

04. Consider the adjacent procedure. What is the result of calling the procedure? *(Parameter x is a list of integers.)*

(A) `mystery` places the largest element at the end of list x.

(B) `mystery` places the smallest element at the end of list x.

(C) `mystery` places the first element at the end of list x.

(D) `mystery` places the last element at the end of list x.

```
PROCEDURE mystery (x)
{
    n ← LENGTH (x)
    index ← 1
    REPEAT UNTIL (index = n)
    {
        if (x[index] > x[index+1])
        {
            temp ← x[index]
            x[index] ← x[index+1]
            x[index+1] ← temp
        }
        index ← index + 1
    }
}
```

05. Consider the adjacent procedure. What is the result of calling the procedure? *(Parameters a, b, c are integers.)*

(A) `mystery` returns the largest parameter.

(B) `mystery` returns the smallest parameter.

(C) `mystery` displays the largest parameter.

(B) `mystery` displays the smallest parameter.

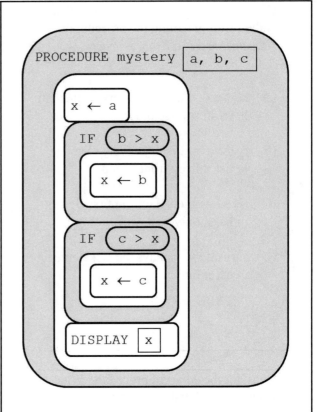

06. Consider the adjacent procedure. What is the result of calling the procedure? *(Parameters a, b, c are integers.)*

(A) `mystery` returns the largest parameter.

(B) `mystery` returns the smallest parameter.

(C) `mystery` displays the largest parameter.

(B) `mystery` displays the smallest parameter.

```
PROCEDURE mystery (a, b, c)
{
    x ← a
    if (b > x)
    {
        x ← b
    }
    if (c > x)
    {
        x ← c
    }
    RETURN (x)
}
```

07. Consider the adjacent procedure. What is the result of calling the procedure? *(Parameters a, b are integers.)*

(A) mystery returns a / b.

(B) mystery returns a * b.

(C) mystery returns b^a.

(D) mystery returns a^b.

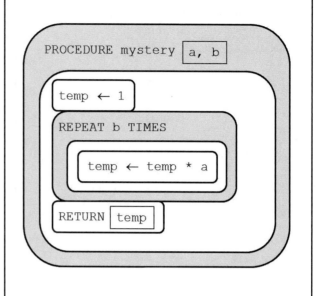

```
PROCEDURE mystery  a, b

    temp ← 1
    REPEAT b TIMES
        temp ← temp * a
    RETURN  temp
```

08. Consider the adjacent procedure. What is the result of calling the procedure? *(Parameters a, b are integers.)*

(A) mystery returns a / b.

(B) mystery returns a * b.

(C) mystery returns b^a.

(D) mystery returns a^b.

```
PROCEDURE mystery (a, b)
{
    temp ← 0
    REPEAT b TIMES
    {
        temp ← temp + a
    }
    RETURN temp
}
```

09. Consider the adjacent procedure. What is the result of calling the procedure? *(Parameter n is an integer.)*

(A) `mystery` returns `n / a`.

(B) `mystery` returns `n * a`.

(C) `mystery` returns a^n.

(D) `mystery` returns `n!` (factorial).

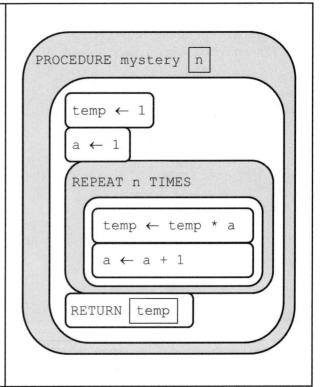

```
PROCEDURE mystery  n

    temp ← 1
    a ← 1

    REPEAT n TIMES

        temp ← temp * a
        a ← a + 1

    RETURN  temp
```

---

10. Consider the adjacent procedure. What is the result of calling the procedure? *(Parameters n1, n2 are integers.)*

(A) `mystery` returns the remainder of `n1 / n2`.

(B) `mystery` returns the GCF of `n1` and `n2`.

(C) `mystery` returns the LCM of `n1` and `n2`.

(D) `mystery` returns $n1^{n2}$.

```
PROCEDURE mystery (n1, n2)
{
    rem ← 1
    REPEAT UNTIL (rem = 0)
    {
        rem ← n1 MOD n2
        IF (REM = 0)
        {
            g ← n2
        }
        ELSE
        {
            n1 ← n2
            n2 ← rem
        }
    }
    RETURN (g)
}
```

11. Consider the adjacent procedure. What is the result of calling the procedure? *(Parameter x is a list of integers.)*

(A) mystery returns the largest integer element in list x.

(B) mystery returns the smallest integer element in list x.

(C) mystery returns the median element in list x.

(D) mystery returns the mean value of list x.

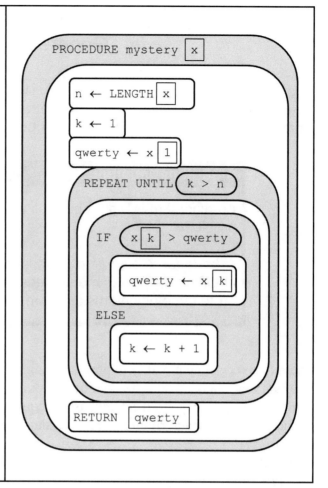

12. Consider the adjacent procedure. What is the result of calling the procedure? *(Parameter x is a list of integers.)*

(A) mystery returns the largest integer element in list x.

(B) mystery returns the smallest integer element in list x.

(C) mystery returns the median element in list x.

(D) mystery returns the mean value of list x.

```
PROCEDURE mystery (x)
{
    n ← LENGTH (x)
    sum ← 0
    FOR EACH item in x
    {
        sum ← sum + item
    }
    RETURN sum / n
}
```

Chapter 10 Review
General Algorithms

Algorithms are not limited to computer science. Algorithms are everywhere and everybody uses them. The name algorithm has a mathematical feel to it, but this is not always true. A well-written recipe for a special desert is an algorithm. Look at the definition below.

Algorithm Definition

An algorithm is a step-by-step sequence of instructions to solve a problem.

A *brute-force algorithm* is unconcerned with the efficiency of the algorithm and uses many steps to reach a stated goal. Typically, brute force algorithms are primarily used by computers.

There is a very simple reality in programming. The best programmer in the world cannot write a program that plays chess is he/she does not know how to play chess. This means you must have some algorithm in your head that is a sequence of steps in English or some other human language. Then the algorithm must be translated to a program language.

This course is not program-language specific, so you will see the brute-force algorithm right next to a program language implementation that is the text-based pseudo-code used in this course. You will observe that program languages are usually more concise than human languages.

Brute Force GCF Algorithm in Text-Based Pseudo-Code	Brute Force GCF Algorithm in English
``` PROCEDURE getGCF (n1, n2) { gcf ← 1 k ← 2 REPEAT UNTIL (k = n1) { IF (n1 MOD k = 0 AND n2 MOD k = 0) { gcf ← k } k ← k + 1 } RETURN gcf } ```	01. Let n1 be the 1st number. 02. Let n2 be the 2nd number. 03. Start GCF with 1. 04. Start count with 2. 05. Check if count is a factor of n1. 06. Check if count is a factor of n2. 07. If 05 & 06 are true GCF becomes count. 08. Increase count by 1. 09. If count is less than or equal to n1 goto 05. 10. GCF is the Greatest Common Factor.

It is not the goal of most computer scientists to create brute-force algorithms. They much prefer to design a very nice *elegant algorithm*. Elegance is harder to define than brute force. It is certainly somewhat in the eye of the beholder, but think of elegant describing an algorithm that is concise with a few steps and also efficient in execution. Is there an elegant algorithm for the GCF? You will be pleased to realize that our good Greek philosopher, Euclid, of Euclidean Geometry fame, created a very nice algorithm for computing the GCF more than 200 years ago. The English steps and the pseudo-code program will be shown below again side-by-side.

Euclid's GCF Algorithm in Text-Based Pseudo-Code	Euclid's GCF Algorithm in English

``
PROCEDURE getGCF (n1, n2)
{
  gcf ← 1
  rem ← 1
  REPEAT UNTIL (rem = 0)
  {
    rem ← n1 MOD n2
    IF (rem = 0)
    {
      gcf ← n2
    }
    else
    {
        n1 ← n2
        n2 ← rem
    }
  }
  RETURN gcf
}
``
	01. Let n1 be the 1st number.
	
	02. Let n2 be the 2nd number.
	
	03. Start GCF with 1.
	
	04. Start remainder with 1.
	
	05. Do integer division with n1 and n2 and determine the remainder.
	
	06. If the remainder equals 0 the GCF is n2 otherwise
	n1 becomes n2
	and n2 becomes the remainder
	
	07. Goto 05.

In the case of the Greatest Common Factor there are many algorithms. You have seen two algorithms and you have seen program code that implements the algorithms. The brute force approach is usually meant for a computer. Be aware that brute force is an issue with security.

There is a finite number of PINs (Personal Identification Number). It would not be that difficult to write a computer program that systematically tries every possible 4 digit number. Such programs pretty much fail, because only a limited number of tries are allowed before the account is locked.

Another example of brute force is finding somebody on a long street and pushing the bell at each house until the person you are looking for answers. It can quickly become unmanageable if you only know the town the person lives in and then try every address. At that stage you consider different algorithms, such as places of work, visiting favorite restaurant, checking social media, placing an ad on television, etc.

The example of an algorithm for finding a friend without an address in a large town brings up another issue with algorithms. It is not always possible to succeed with a regular algorithm or it may take too long. In such a case the best approach might be to try a *heuristic*. This is not a common vocabulary word. A decent synonym is *trial and error*.

Consider the program output by a student, called John Smith. This is a test of understanding graphics commands in the language Java and it also requires an understanding of Coordinate Geometry. Many students get stuck with the triangle. They try to recall how to use the *midpoint* formula and other mathematical theorems and rules. Yet many students complete that assignment very quickly by approximating the requirements and making adjustments after each attempt. That is using *trial-and-error* or a *heuristic* approach.

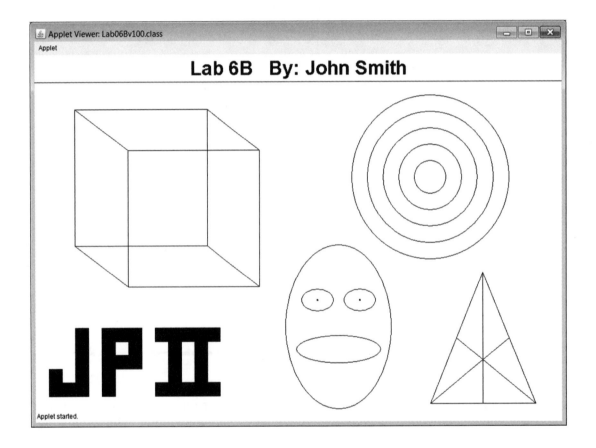

You can also do something that is somewhat like a heuristic. Perhaps it may be between an algorithm and a heuristic. You can apply a set of rules in a step-by-step manner and repeatedly apply the rules to improve the result, even if the result is not 100 % correct.

It may sound strange, but consider computing the value of mathematical pi. This value can be computed many ways. For the purpose for this chapter the emphasis is on algorithms and mathematics that is comfortable to all students. To follow the next example you need to understand some basic Geometry and also know the *Theorem of Pythagoras*.

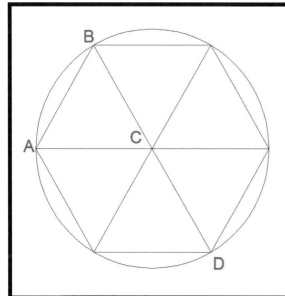

If **AB** = **BC** = **X** then it follows that

Diameter **BD** = **2X** and the

Hexagon Perimeter = **6X**

With Perimeter as *Circumference*

PI = 6X / 2X = 3

Approximating PI Algorithm Stage 1

The picture you see here shows a regular hexagon, which by definition has six equal sides. The 6 triangles in this regular hexagon are *equilateral* and they are also *congruent* to each other. The algorithm we will study and the one that you will need to finish starts from these mathematical facts.

We know that both **AC** and **BC** are radii and all the lines starting from the center to the circle at the hexagon vertices are also radii, which are equal in length. Now with this knowledge we can then conclude that the perimeter of the regular hexagon is six times the length of the radius. Remember that each side of the hexagon is one side of an equilateral triangle.

Now imagine that we use the perimeter of this regular hexagon as a rough approximation of the length of the circumference of the circle that circumscribes the hexagon. If we say that the radius of the circle, like **BC** is **1 inch** or we say **X** then we get the values that are itemized to the left.

Approximating PI Algorithm Stage 2

Are you impressed by our computation that computed **PI = 3**? Probably not, but we are not finished. I threw this ball; you have to catch it and now go further on the PI algorithm train. Now consider the 12-sided polygon on the right.

Does the 12-Sided polygon appear to be a much better approximation of a circle than the 6-sided polygon? You can visually see the difference and see that this is an improvement.

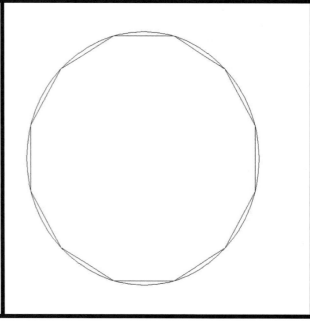

Approximating PI Algorithm Stage 3

This means that a 24-sided polygon and a 48-sided polygon keep getting closer to the value of PI. You may now have the pleasure to finish this algorithm in a lab activity that involves an algorithm to compute the perimeter of a many-sided polygon and then continue to write a program that follows your algorithm.

You know that if the radius of a regular hexagon equals 1 unit then the perimeter equals 6 units and PI equals 3. Look at the drawing on the right. Do you know the length of 12-sided polygon using **AE** and can you continue and compute the lengths of a regular polygon with an ever increasing number of sides? This is the mission of the algorithm.

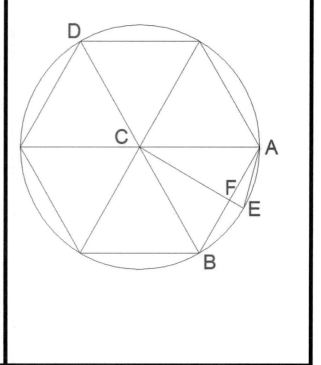

Algorithm Pitfalls

Algorithms use sequence, selection and iteration. This is exactly what is used for the execution control of a program. Concerns with control structures are similar to concerns with algorithms. When an algorithm repeats, it checks some condition to see if the loop is finished. Whether you use an algorithm in English or write an algorithm in a program language, it is easy to be off by one repetition. There are also conditions used with selection that may involve Boolean logic. In other words, pitfalls with algorithms do not bring many new concerns.

More will be stated about algorithms in a later chapter. Computer programs use searching and sorting algorithms frequently. An entire chapter will be devoted to those specialty algorithms.

Questions about algorithms may have a sequence of steps, written in English, which explain how to solve a given problem. You may also see actual program code used for algorithm questions, which for this course will be the text-based and block-based pseudo-code.

Chapter 10 Questions
General Algorithms

---

01. Use the algorithm steps below for questions 01-02. Consider the steps below for an unspecified algorithm, which uses two integer variables: `n1` and `n2` to compute `qwerty`.

Step 1: Divide `n1` by `n2` using integer division and determine the `remainder`.

Step 2: If the `remainder` equals zero, `qwerty` equals `n2`. The algorithm is finished.

Step 3: `n1` becomes `n2`

Step 4: `n2` becomes `remainder`

Step 5: Go to Step 1.

If the algorithm is used to compute `qwerty` with `n1` = 30 and `n2` = 42, which of the following becomes the value of `qwerty` when the algorithm is finished?

(A) 12   (B) 8   (C) 6   (D) 3

---

02. Consider the adjacent code segment, which is intended to implement the algorithm shown in Question 01. Is the code segment a correct implementation of the algorithm?

(A) Yes, it is a faithful step-by-step implementation.

(B) Yes, it is correct and will compute *qwerty* with the same logic, but not all the steps are 100% identical.

(C) No, the pseudo-code will not compute the same result.

(D) No, the pseudo-code will only compute the same result if `n1` is greater than `n2`.

```
n1 ← 30
n2 ← 42
rem ← 1
qwerty ← 1
REPEAT UNTIL (rem = 0)
{
    rem = n1 MOD n2
    if (rem = 0)
    {
        qwerty ← n2
    }
    ELSE
    {
        n1 ← n2
        nr ← rem
    }
}
```

03. The *Least Common Multiple* (LCM) is a practical value in arithmetic that is used with fraction addition and fraction subtraction. For Question 03 you may assume that the procedure `getGCF(n1,n2)` can be used, which returns the GCF of n1 and n2.

Which of the following procedures will correctly return the LCM of n1 and n2 ?

(A)
```
PROCEDURE getLCM (n1, n2)
{
    gcf ← getGCF (n1, n2)
    lcm ← n1 / gcf * n2
    RETURN lcm
}
```

(B)
```
PROCEDURE getLCM (n1, n2)
{
    gcf ← getGCF (n1, n2)
    lcm ← (n1 + n2) / gcf
    RETURN lcm
}
```

(C)
```
PROCEDURE getLCM (n1, n2)
{
    gcf ← getGCF (n1, n2)
    lcm ← (n1 + n2) * gcf
    RETURN lcm
}
```

(D)
```
PROCEDURE getLCM (n1, n2)
{
    gcf ← getGCF (n1, n2)
    temp ← (n1 + n2) / 2
    RETURN temp * gcf
}
```

04. Consider the adjacent procedure. What values are displayed by executing the following three statements?

```
PRINT (isPerfect(6))
PRINT (isPerfect(10))
```

(A) true true

(B) true false

(C) false true

(B) false false

```
PROCEDURE isPerfect (n)
{
    k ← 2
    sum ← 1
    REPEAT UNTIL (k = n)
    {
        if (n MOD k = 0)
        {
            sum ← sum + k
        }
        k ← k + 1
    }
    RETURN sum = n
}
```

05. Assume that `list` contains one or more integers placed in random order. Which one of the following code segments correctly assigns the largest integer to `max`?

(A)
```
list ← <positive integers>
FOR EACH item IN list
{
    if (item > max)
    {
        max ← item
    }
}
```

(B)
```
list ← <positive integers>
max ← -1
FOR EACH item IN list
{
    if (item > max)
    {
        item ←  max
    }
}
```

(C)
```
list ← <positive integers>
max ← -1
FOR EACH item IN list
{
    if (item > max)
    {
        max ← item
    }
}
```

(D)
```
list ← <positive integers>
FOR EACH item IN list
{
    max ← -1
    if (item > max)
    {
        max ←  item
    }
}
```

06. Programs and algorithms have similar goals, such as using a sequence of steps to reach a specified goal. What is a difference between a program and an algorithm?

(A) Programs are shorter than algorithms.

(B) Programs are written in a human language.
    Algorithms are written in a computer language like Java, C++ or Python.

(C) Programs are written in machine language.
    Algorithms are written in a computer language like Java, C++ or Python.

(D) Programs are written in a computer language like Java, C++ or Python.
    Algorithms are written in a human language

07. Consider the adjacent incomplete procedure, which is meant to return the `mean` value of the numbers in `list`. Which the following code segments must replace `<missing code>` for the procedure to execute correctly?

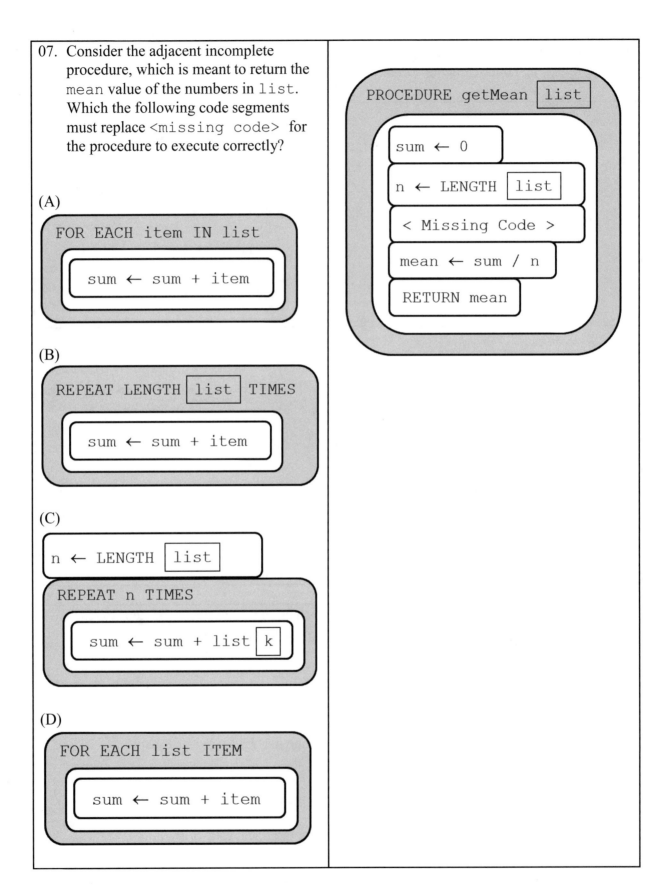

PROCEDURE getMean `list`

sum ← 0

n ← LENGTH `list`

< Missing Code >

mean ← sum / n

RETURN mean

(A)

FOR EACH item IN list

sum ← sum + item

(B)

REPEAT LENGTH `list` TIMES

sum ← sum + item

(C)

n ← LENGTH `list`

REPEAT n TIMES

sum ← sum + list `k`

(D)

FOR EACH list ITEM

sum ← sum + item

08. Consider the adjacent `mystery` procedure and the code segment below the procedure.

Note: for this problem assume that `//` is integer division and `/` is real number division.

What is the output as a result of executing the code segment?

(A) `38.5 33`

(B) `33 38.5`

(C) `38 33`

(D) `33 38`

```
PROCEDURE mystery (list)
{
    n ← LENGTH (list)
    IF (n MOD 2 = 0)
    {
        mid ← n // 2
        x ← (list[mid] + list[mid+1]) / 2
    }
    ELSE
    {
        mid ← (n + 1) // 2
        x ← list[mid]
    }
    RETURN x
}


list1 ← (11,22,33,44,55)
DISPLAY (mystery(list1))
list2 ← (11,22,33,44,55,66)
DISPLAY (mystery(list2))
```

09. Consider the adjacent procedure. What is the result of calling the procedure? *(Parameters a, b are integers.)*

(A) `mystery` returns `a / b`.

(B) `mystery` returns `a * b`.

(C) `mystery` returns b^a.

(D) `mystery` returns a^b.

```
PROCEDURE mystery (a, b)
{
    temp ← 0
    REPEAT b TIMES
    {
        temp ← temp + a
    }
    RETURN temp
}
```

10. Consider the adjacent procedure. What is the result of calling the procedure? *(Parameter n is an integer.)*

(A) `mystery` returns `n / a`.

(B) `mystery` returns `n * a`.

(C) `mystery` returns a^n.

(D) `mystery` returns `n!` (factorial).

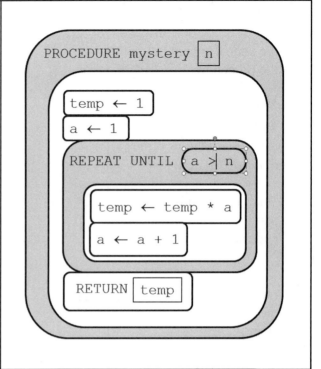

```
PROCEDURE mystery  n

    temp ← 1
    a ← 1

    REPEAT UNTIL  a > n

        temp ← temp * a
        a ← a + 1

    RETURN  temp
```

11. Consider the adjacent `reverse` procedure. The intention of the procedure is to `reverse` the elements in `list`. What is the result for `list` after procedure `reverse` is executed?

(A) All the elements in `list` are reversed.

(B) Only the first half of the elements in `list` are reversed.

(C) Only the second half of the elements in `list` are reversed.

(D) First, all the elements in `list` are reversed, but as the procedure continues the elements are exchanged again until the original `list` remains.

```
PROCEDURE reverse (list)
{
    n ← LENGTH (list)
    a ← 1
    b ← n
    REPEAT n TIMES
    {
        temp ← list[a]
        list[a] ← list[b]
        list[b] ← temp
        a ← a + 1
        b ← b - 1
    }
}
```

12. Consider the adjacent isSorted procedure. The intention of the procedure is to return true if the numbers in list are sorted and false otherwise.
Will this procedure execute as desired for a sorted list?

(A) Yes it will for list that can be sorted in any order.

(B) Yes it will, provided list is sorted in descending order.

(C) Yes it will, provided list is sorted in ascending order.

(D) No it will not determine if list is sorted in any order.

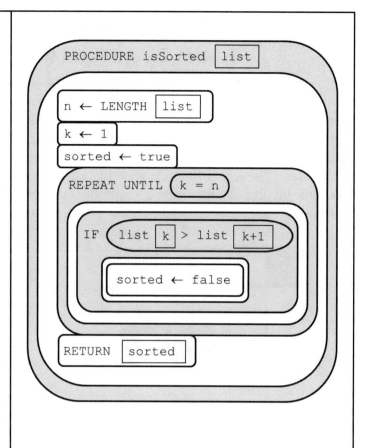

Chapter 11 Review
Robot Operations with Pseudo-Code

There are two styles of pseudo-code in the AP CSP Exam, text-based and block-based. It may seem that there is a third style, called robot-based. This is not true. The robot questions are distinctly different, but the program code used for the questions will be either text-based or block-based. The key difference with the other questions is the output appearance. The robot questions involve a grid with a robot busily moving around the grid. Other programming questions, if they involve output, display text. Two sample robot grids are shown below.

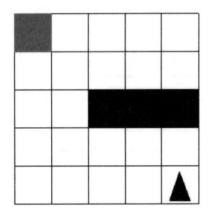
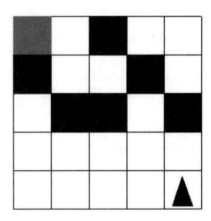

Many grids will use a matrix of five rows and five columns. This is not a requirement. The grid can show up in various sizes. One consistent pattern is that the robot is represented by a black triangle and the robot can face in four directions: up, down, left and right. The grid may be empty, except for the robot, but there may also be other cells that are shaded. Solid black cells indicate obstacles. A robot can only move into a white cell or a gray cell, but not a black cell. The gray cell is often used as the destination cell.

Questions will likely be in two categories:

1. You are provided with a grid and a robot in a starting position. You are also provided with program code and this code can be text-based or block-based. You must then select from four different grids that show the final position of the robot.

2. You are provided with a grid that shows the robot in a starting position and the robot needs to end up at a specified cell, which may be a gray cell. You then need to select from different program segments that will achieve the desired goal.

Robot Pseudo-Code Commands

The robot uses any of the pseudo-code commands that are shown in the reference guide of the AP CSP Course Description. What follows are a set of program commands that are unique to robot programs only. You will see in some of the examples that the robot commands work together with the existing pseudo-code commands.

MOVE_FORWARD Command	
The robot moves one cell, in the grid, forward in the direction that it is facing.	`MOVE_FORWARD`
`MOVE_FORWARD ()`	

ROTATE_LEFT Command	
The robot rotates inside its cell 90 degrees to the left (counter-clockwise).	`ROTATE_LEFT`
`ROTATE_LEFT ()`	

ROTATE_RIGHT Command	
The robot rotates inside its cell 90 degrees to the right (clockwise).	`ROTATE_RIGHT`
`ROTATE_RIGHT ()`	

CAN_MOVE Command

This command is used with black squares and other obstacles, like borders. Procedure CAN_MOVE returns `true` if there is an open square in the direction relative to where the robot is facing; otherwise it returns `false`.

The direction can be (`left`, `right`, `forward` or `backward`)

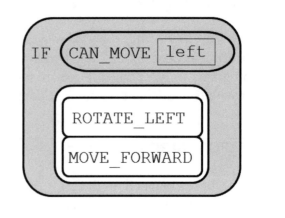

```
IF (CAN_MOVE (left))
{
    ROTATE_LEFT ()
    MOVE_FORWARD ()
}
```

Robot Pitfalls

Concern #1: Watch for robot commands that are not part of the reference guide.

You do need to know all the commands in the reference guide, but you must also expect to encounter commands that are explained directly in the question. It can happen anywhere in the exam and it does not have to be limited to the robot questions. It is more likely to be the case with robot code and the course description shows some examples. It is not a problem. Just do not get flustered, take a breath and carefully read the specifications of the new command.

APCS Examination Alert

Expect New Pseudo-Code Commands

The AP Exam will very likely include commands that are not part of the provided reference guide. The commands are explained within the context of the question.

Goal_Reached Command

The GOAL_REACHED command is very practical for robot programs. The robot does not always move 20 times or 10 times, but makes moves until the job is done. In most cases this means that the robot has entered the gray cell. The screenshot below is from the AP CSP Course Description sample exam questions. You will note that the command is explained within the question. This command is very practical and may well show up on your exam.

8. The code segment below is intended to move a robot in a grid to a gray square. The program segment uses the procedure GoalReached, which evaluates to true if the robot is in the gray square and evaluates to false otherwise. The robot in each grid is represented as a triangle and is initially facing left. The robot can move into a white or gray square but cannot move into a black region.

```
REPEAT UNTIL (GoalReached ())
{
    IF (CAN_MOVE (forward))
    {
        MOVE_FORWARD ()
    }
```

MoveAndTurn Command

The MoveAndTurn command is the name of a procedure, which is shown below. The concept is similar to the GoalReached command but the explanation is different. With Goal_Reached the purpose and functionality of the command was explained. In the case of MoveAndTurn, the actual procedure logic is shown by providing the program code of the procedure. This means that you must first comprehend what the intent of the procedure is and then apply the command logic to the question. This screenshot below is also from the AP CSP Course Description sample exam questions.

Consider the procedure MoveAndTurn below.

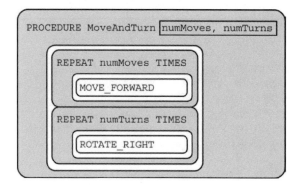

Which of the following code segments will move the robot to the gray square?

Concern #2: Count the robot moves correctly.

The robot has many paths it can take to reach a goal. Suppose that a robot starts in the top-left corner, facing right. This is shown in the adjacent grid image.

How many moves does it take for the robot to get back to the starting position while moving along the perimeter of the grid?

It is a small thing, but you may quickly count the number of cells visited and be done. The problem here is that sometimes two moves are made in one square when the robot needs to turn.

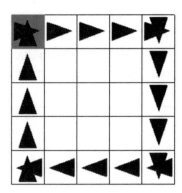

Concern #3: Watch out for black cells.

There are questions where a grid is provided, such as the adjacent one shown, and the object is to move the robot from the starting position to the gray cell.

You must look at four programs segments and select two segments that will get the robot to its goal.

Be careful that you remember that the robot cannot enter a black cell or move through a black cell.

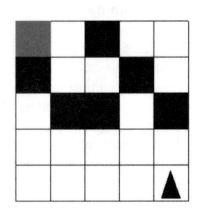

Chapter 11 Questions
Robot Operation with Pseudo-Code

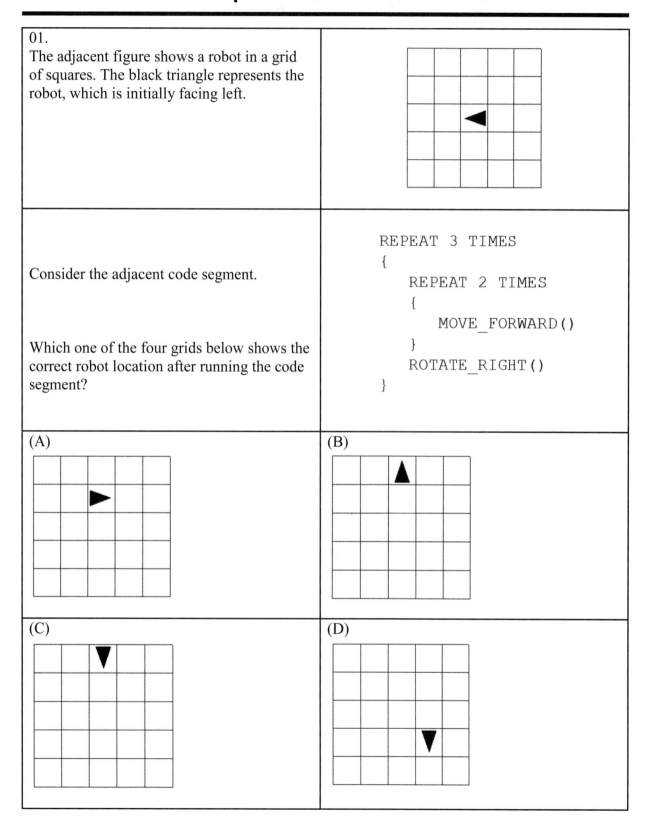

01.
The adjacent figure shows a robot in a grid of squares. The black triangle represents the robot, which is initially facing left.

Consider the adjacent code segment.

Which one of the four grids below shows the correct robot location after running the code segment?

```
REPEAT 3 TIMES
{
    REPEAT 2 TIMES
    {
        MOVE_FORWARD()
    }
    ROTATE_RIGHT()
}
```

(A)

(B)

(C)

(D)

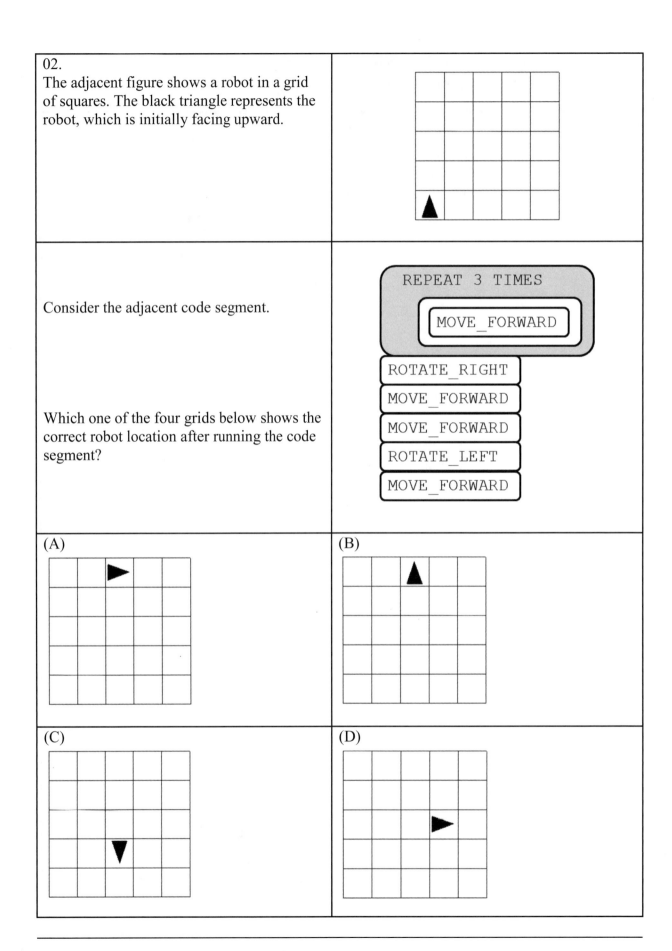

02.
The adjacent figure shows a robot in a grid of squares. The black triangle represents the robot, which is initially facing upward.

Consider the adjacent code segment.

REPEAT 3 TIMES

MOVE_FORWARD

ROTATE_RIGHT

MOVE_FORWARD

MOVE_FORWARD

ROTATE_LEFT

MOVE_FORWARD

Which one of the four grids below shows the correct robot location after running the code segment?

(A)

(B)

(C)

(D)

03.
The figure below shows a robot in a grid of squares. The black triangle represents the robot, which is initially facing downward.

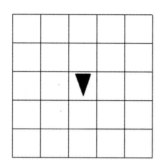

Consider the adjacent code segment.

Which one of the four grids below shows the correct robot location after running the code segment?

```
k ← 0
REPEAT UNTIL (k = 5)
{
    MOVE_FORWARD()
    IF (k MOD 2 = 0)
    {
        ROTATE_RIGHT()
    }
    ELSE
    {
        ROTATE_LEFT()
        ROTATE_LEFT()
        MOVE_FORWARD()
    }
    MOVE_FORWARD()
    k ← k + 1
}
```

(A)

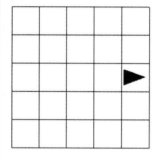

(B)

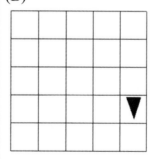

(C)

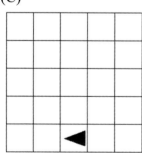

(D)

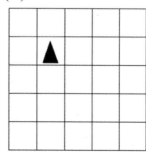

04.
The figure below shows a robot in a grid of squares. The black triangle represents the robot, which is initially facing upward.

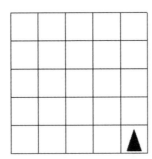

Consider the adjacent code segment.

Which one of the four grids below shows a robot location that is not possible after running the code segment?

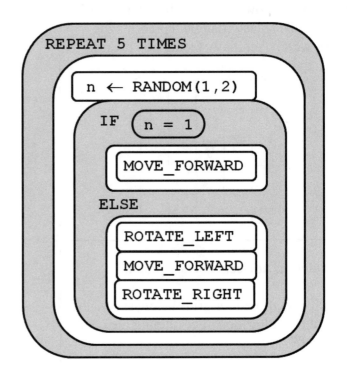

```
REPEAT 5 TIMES
    n ← RANDOM(1,2)
    IF  n = 1
        MOVE_FORWARD
    ELSE
        ROTATE_LEFT
        MOVE_FORWARD
        ROTATE_RIGHT
```

(A)

(B)

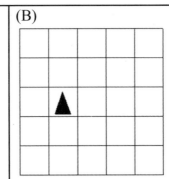

(C)

(D)

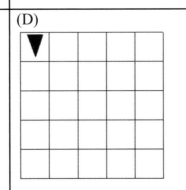

05.
The adjacent figure shows a robot in a grid of squares. The black triangle represents the robot, which is initially facing left.

Consider the adjacent code segment.

Which one of the four grids below shows the correct robot location after running the code segment?

```
REPEAT 2 TIMES
{
    REPEAT 2 TIMES
    {
        MOVE_FORWARD()
        ROTATE_RIGHT()
        MOVE_FORWARD()
        ROTATE_LEFT()
    }
}
```

(A)

(B)

(C)

(D)

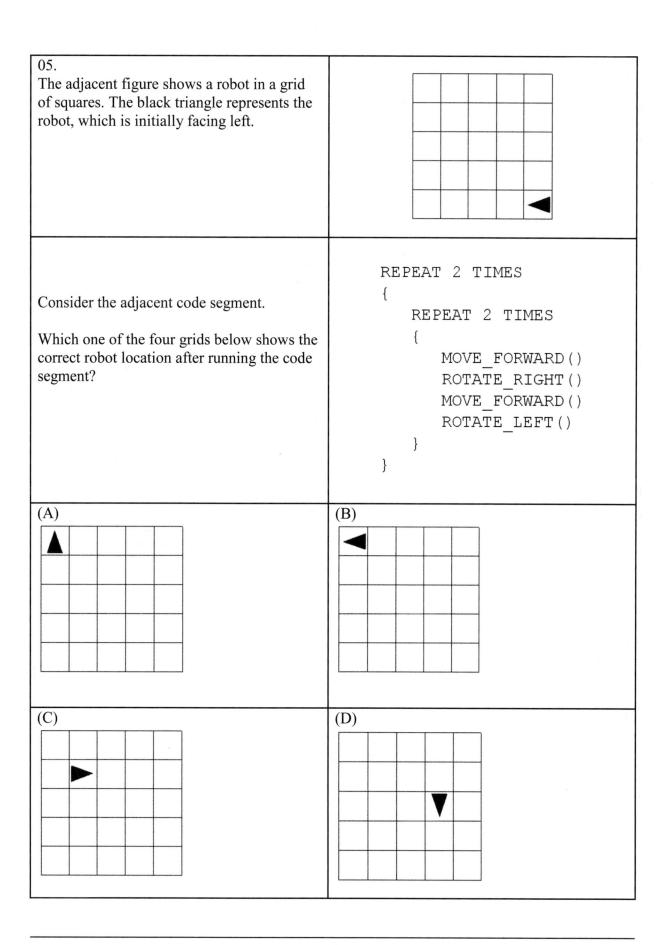

06. The adjacent figure shows a robot in a grid of squares. The black triangle represents the robot, which is initially facing right.	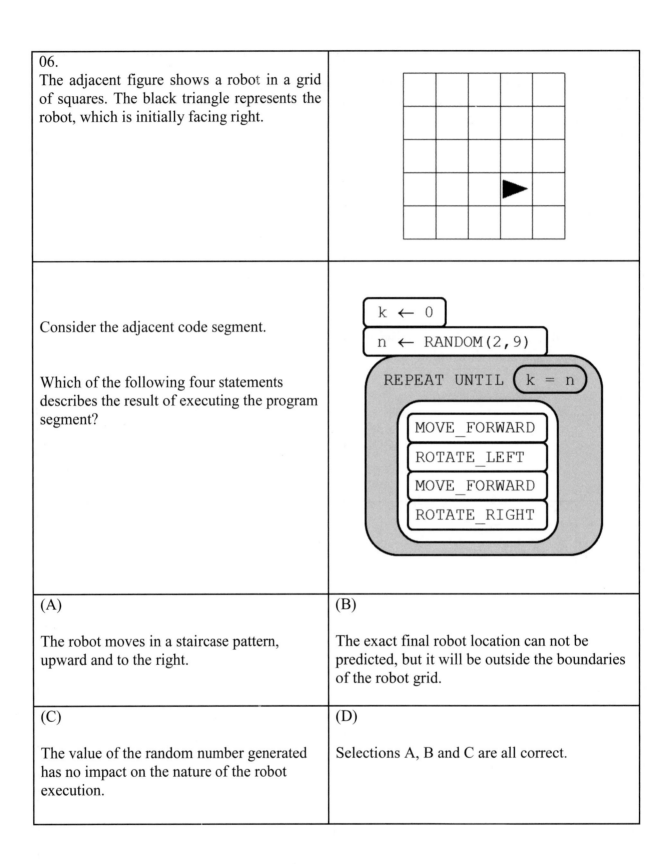
Consider the adjacent code segment. Which of the following four statements describes the result of executing the program segment?	

(A) The robot moves in a staircase pattern, upward and to the right.	(B) The exact final robot location can not be predicted, but it will be outside the boundaries of the robot grid.
(C) The value of the random number generated has no impact on the nature of the robot execution.	(D) Selections A, B and C are all correct.

07.
The two figures below each show a robot in a grid of squares. The black triangle represents the robot, which is initially facing right. The left figure represents the robot location at the start of program execution. The right figure represents the location at end of program execution.

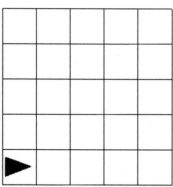

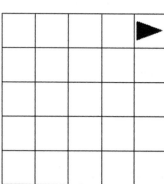

Which of the following code segments will move the robot to the required square?

(A)

```
REPEAT 4 TIMES
{
    MOVE_FORWARD ()
    ROTATE_RIGHT ()
    MOVE_FORWARD ()
    ROTATE_LEFT ()
}
```

(B)

```
REPEAT 4 TIMES
{
    MOVE_FORWARD ()
    MOVE_FORWARD ()
    ROTATE_LEFT ()
    ROTATE_RIGHT ()
}
```

(C)

```
REPEAT 4 TIMES
{
    MOVE_FORWARD ()
    ROTATE_LEFT ()
    MOVE_FORWARD ()
    ROTATE_RIGHT ()
}
```

(D)

```
REPEAT 4 TIMES
{
    MOVE_FORWARD ()
    ROTATE_LEFT ()
    MOVE_FORWARD ()
}
```

08.
The adjacent figure shows a robot in a grid of squares.
The black triangle represents the robot, which is initially
facing right, starting in the gray square. The grid shows
the complete path taken by a robot during its execution.
The robot ends in the square where it started and displays
every square along its path. Which of the program
segments below will execute the required path? Keep in
mind that it is not sufficient to start and end in the gray
square. The path, as shown, must be followed.

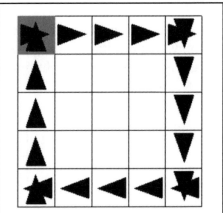

(A)

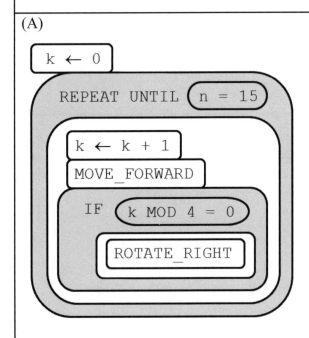

(B)

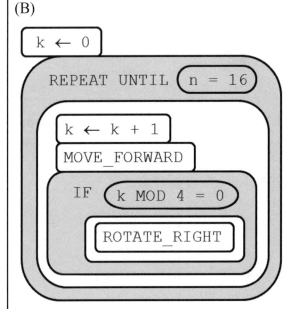

(C)

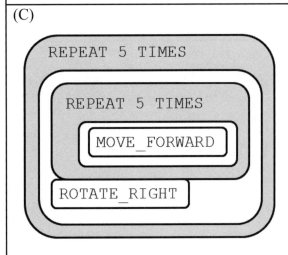

(D)

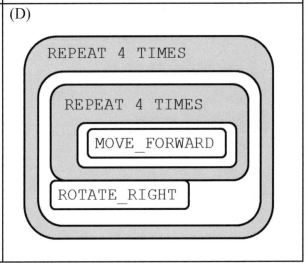

09.
The adjacent figure shows a robot in a grid of squares. The black triangle represents the robot, which is initially facing left. The robot can move into a white or grey square, but cannot move into a black square.

Which of the following program segments will finish with the robot inside the gray square?

The program may only use 1 MOVE_FORWARD, 1 ROTATE_RIGHT and 1 ROTATE_LEFT command.

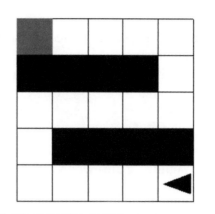

(A)
```
k ← 1
REPEAT UNTIL (k = 18)
{
    MOVE_FORWARD ()
    IF (k = 5 OR k = 7)
    {
        ROTATE_RIGHT ()
    }
    IF (k = 11 OR k = 13)
    {
        ROTATE_LEFT()
    }
    k ← k + 1
}
```

(B)
```
k ← 1
REPEAT UNTIL (k = 17)
{
    MOVE_FORWARD ()
    IF (k = 4 OR k = 6)
    {
        ROTATE_RIGHT ()
    }
    IF (k = 10 OR k = 12)
    {
        ROTATE_LEFT()
    }
    k ← k + 1
}
```

(C)
```
k ← 1
REPEAT UNTIL (k = 9)
{
    MOVE_FORWARD ()
    IF (k = 4)
    {
        ROTATE_RIGHT ()
    }
    k ← k + 1
}
```

(D)
It is not possible to get to the grey square without duplicating some robot commands in the code segment.

10.
The adjacent figure shows a robot in a grid of squares. The black triangle represents the robot, which is initially facing upward. The robot can move into a white or grey square, but cannot move into a black square.

For this question you may use a procedure that is not in the reference guide, called GOAL_REACHED, which returns true when the robot enters a gray square and false otherwise.

Now consider the program code below that is meant to move the robot to the gray square during execution. Which of the following statements in the bottom-right cell is true about the execution of the code?

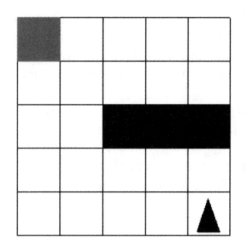

```
REPEAT UNTIL (GOAL_REACHED())
{
    IF (CAN_MOVE ("forward"))
    {
        MOVE_FORWARD()
    }
    ELSE IF (CAN_MOVE ("right"))
    {
        ROTATE_RIGHT ()
        MOVE_FORWARD ()
    }
    ELSE IF (CAN_MOVE ("backward"))
    {
        ROTATE_RIGHT ()
        ROTATE_RIGHT ()
    }
    ELSE IF (CAN_MOVE ("left"))
    {
        ROTATE_LEFT ()
        MOVE_FORWARD ()
    }
}
```

(A)
This code will work correctly for the provided grid.

(B)
The code will not necessarily work for all grid configurations.

(C)
The code will work for any type of grid configuration.

(D)
Choices (A) and (B) only

11.
The adjacent figure shows a robot in a grid of squares. The black triangle represents the robot, which is initially facing upward. The robot can move into a white or grey square, but cannot move into a black square.

For this question you may use a procedure that is not in the reference guide, called GOAL_REACHED, which returns true when the robot enters a gray square and false otherwise.

Now consider the program code below that is meant to move the robot to the gray square during execution. The code is identical to Question 10. Which of the following statements in the bottom-right cell is true about the execution of the code?

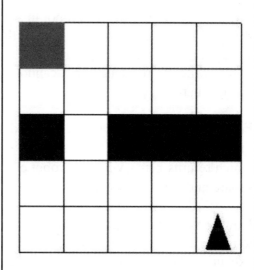

```
REPEAT UNTIL (GOAL_REACHED())
{
    IF (CAN_MOVE ("forward"))
    {
        MOVE_FORWARD()
    }
    ELSE IF (CAN_MOVE ("right"))
    {
        ROTATE_RIGHT ()
        MOVE_FORWARD ()
    }
    ELSE IF (CAN_MOVE ("backward"))
    {
        ROTATE_RIGHT ()
        ROTATE_RIGHT ()
    }
    ELSE IF (CAN_MOVE ("left"))
    {
        ROTATE_LEFT ()
        MOVE_FORWARD ()
    }
}
```

(A)
This code will work correctly for the provided grid.

(B)
The code will not work correctly for the provided grid.

(C)
The code will work for any type of grid configuration.

(D)
The code will not work for any type of grid configuration.

12.
The adjacent figure shows a robot in a grid of squares. The black triangle represents the robot, which is initially facing upward. The robot can move into a white or grey square, but cannot move into a black square.

For this question you may use a procedure that is not in the reference guide, called GOAL_REACHED, which returns true when the robot enters a gray square and false otherwise.

Now consider the program code below that is meant to move the robot to the gray square during execution. Which of the following statements in the bottom-right cell is true about the execution of the code?

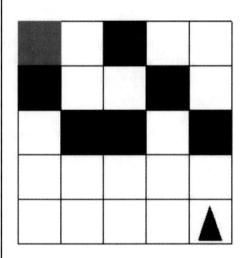

```
REPEAT UNTIL (GOAL_REACHED())
{
    IF (CAN_MOVE ("forward"))
    {
        n ← RANDOM (1, 3)
        if (n = 1)
        {
            MOVE_FORWARD()
        }
        ELSE IF (n = 2)
        {
            ROTATE_RIGHT ()
        }
        ELSE IF (n = 3)
        {
            ROTATE_RIGHT ()
            MOVE_FORWARD ()
        ELSE
        {
            ROTATE_LEFT ()
            MOVE_FORWARD ()
        }
    }
}
```

(A)
This code will work correctly for the provided grid.

(B)
The code will not work correctly for the provided grid.

(C)
The code will work for any type of grid configuration.

(D)
The code will not work for any type of grid configuration.

Chapter 12 Review
String Processing with Pseudo-Code

A major percentage of computer operations involve string processing. A string is a list or an array of characters. The most popular example of a computer program that processes strings is a word processor. In such a program words are constantly added, altered, deleted and corrected. Most program languages have many procedures to simplify string processing with program code.

The most common string operation is *concatenation*. In many program languages this operation uses the same addition + operator that is used for numeric addition. It resembles addition, but in a string sense. Two strings are added by placing the second string at the end of the first string as shown below.

Addition & Concatenation

100 + 200 = 300 (addition)

"100" + 200" = "100200" (concatenation)

Concatenation example with pseudo-code

```
s1  ←  "Tom"
s2  ←  "Jones"
s3  ←  s2 + ", " + s1
```

s3 stores "Jones, Tom"

Keep in mind that a blank space is also a string character.

Concatenation is an operation, which is different from a procedure. There exist many string procedures that manage string processing. This chapter will focus on the SUBSTRING procedure, shown on the next page. Using the provided pseudo-code style shown earlier, SUBSTRING ("AARDVARK", 4, 7) becomes VAR or DVA.

This chapter will provide sample questions that will focus on both string concatenation operations, substring procedures and user-defined string procedures.

The SUBSTRING Procedure

The Course Description reference guide does not include a `substring` procedure.
The substring procedure is used in this chapter as it is found in various languages, like Java.

SUBSTRING example with pseudo-code

```
str ← "AARDVARK"
sub ← SUBSTRING (str, 4, 7)
DISPLAY (sub)
```

Parameter **4** is the index of first character in the substring and parameter **7** is the index of the finish boundary.

This means that the program segment will display `VAR` in a language, like Java.

Since the reference guide indicates that the first element in a pseudo-code list starts with index 1, the same can be assumed about any string question in this chapter. In that case the program segment will display `DVA`.

Do not assume certain processes, based on other known languages. Follow the actual instructions of the reference guide and the AP Exam questions.

Feel assured that any procedure used on the end-of-course exam that is not detailed in the reference guide, will be explained with the question where it is introduced. This approach gives the College Board two testing advantages.

- Questions can have greater variety by testing additional programming features that are explained during the actual exam.

- Students are tested of their ability to comprehend and utilize new programming features that they have not used in any prior practice.

It is tough to say what to expect with string processing. It was mentioned earlier that the best indications are to use the course description and released exams. There are no released exams yet, but there is a practice exam that is available from the College Board for teachers who have completed the AP Audit process.

The sample questions in the course description and the practice exam show no evidence of string processing questions. In the course description, there is an itemized list of program features that students can expect to see on the AP Exam. It does not mention strings processing, explicitly. However, it does include *List Operations* and a string is a list of characters.

Further investigation in the Course Description is shown below. The screen shot shown has patched some pieces together to focus only on the string issue. It does say that Strings and string operations, including concatenation and some form of substring, are common.

Figure 13.3

Enduring Understandings (Students will understand that ...)	Learning Objectives (Students will be able to ...)	Essential Knowledge (Students will know that ...)
EU 5.3 Programming is facilitated by appropriate abstractions.	LO 5.3.1 Use abstraction to manage complexity in programs. [P3]	
		EK 5.3.1I Strings and string operations, including concatenation and some form of substring, are common in many programs.

s Course and Exam Description

Return to Table of Contents   28

© 2017 The College Board

So what can you expect? Probably not a whole bunch of string questions, especially if the practice exam and course description sample questions are any indication. But we need to be careful and be prepared. There are two realities about AP Computer Science Exams that must be understood and remembered.

1. Practice exams and released exams will not be able to test every possible feature, which is part of the curriculum, on a single exam.

2. The AP Test Development Committee can always create questions that use features, not found in the course description and perhaps not shown in a practice or released exam, but explained in the question. In the provided sample questions there is a robot question that introduces the `GoalReached` procedure, specifically meant for that question. This `GoalReached` procedure is not part of the reference guide robot commands.

The second point is very important. The option to introduce any new material on a test, as long as its intention is clearly explained, is fair game on any test. This is an important testing skill to see how quickly students can handle a new concept that was not taught or explained prior to the AP Examination.

It may be the case that there are no string questions at all. A question that tests knowledge about the difference between numerical addition and string concatenation seems very reasonable. Beyond that, string questions may appear that include explanations about new procedures used for one or more questions. The bottom line is to be prepared. It is better to assume inclusion and be prepared than to assume exclusion and be surprised.

String Pitfalls

The first pitfall is a repeat of a problem mentioned in the list problems chapter. Students will work with actual program languages to prepare their Create Performance Task. Such programs may well include arrays, lists, strings and other data structures that use an index to access individual elements of the data structure. In many languages the index of the first element is 0. The pseudo-code on your exam uses a list that starts with index 1. This can cause some confusion.

Another pitfall with substrings is that many students think that the index parameters are values of the first index and last index of the substring. This is not true. The last substring character is at an index that is one less than the parameter as you see in the example below.

String Question Concerns

The pseudo-code tested on the AP Exam uses a list where the first element is at index [1].

Substring parameters can be confusing. In the program segment below, the substring that is returned starts at index 4 and ends at index 6.

```
str ← "AARDVARK"
sub ← SUBSTRING (str, 4, 7)
DISPLAY (sub)
```

01.

Consider the adjacent code segment. Note that the NEXTLINE() procedure executes a *Carriage Return, Line Feed* (CRLF) after the previous output. What is the output of the program?

(A) Kathy Jones
    Kathy Jones

(B) Jones Kathy
    Jones Kathy

(C) Kathy Jones
    Jones Kathy

(D) Jones Kathy
    Kathy Jones

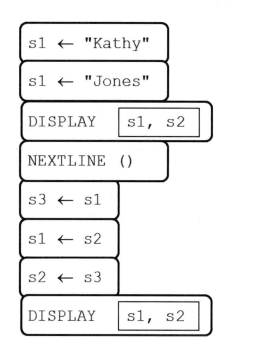

```
s1 ← "Kathy"

s1 ← "Jones"

DISPLAY    s1, s2

NEXTLINE ()

s3 ← s1

s1 ← s2

s2 ← s3

DISPLAY    s1, s2
```

02.

Consider the adjacent code segment. Note that the NEXTLINE procedure executes a *Carriage Return, Line Feed* (CRLF) after the previous output. What is the output of the program?

(A) Kathy Jones
    Jones Jones

(B) Jones Kathy
    Jones Kathy

(C) Kathy Jones
    Kathy Kathy

(D) Jones Kathy
    Jones Jones

```
s1 ← "Kathy"
s2 ← "Jones"
DISPLAY (s1, s2)
NEXTLINE ()
s1 ← s2
s2 ← s1
DISPLAY (s1, s2)
```

03.

Consider the adjacent code segment.
What is the output of the program?

(A) dv

(B) va

(C) d

(D) v

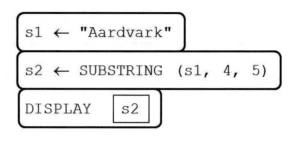

```
s1 ← "Aardvark"

s2 ← SUBSTRING (s1, 4, 5)

DISPLAY    s2
```

04.

Consider the adjacent code segment.
What is the output of the program?

(A) CARC RAC

(B) RACE CARC

(C) CAR RACE

(D) RACE CAR

```
str ← "RACECAR"
n ← LENGTH (str)
s1 ← SUBSTRING (str, 5, n+1)
s2 ← SUBSTRING (str, 1, 5)
DISPLAY (s1, s2)
```

05.

Consider the adjacent code segment.
What is the output of the program?

(A) Q Q Q Q Q Q

(B) Q W E R T Y

(C) Q Q W Q E Q R Q T Q Y Q

(D) Q W E R T Y Q Q Q Q Q Q

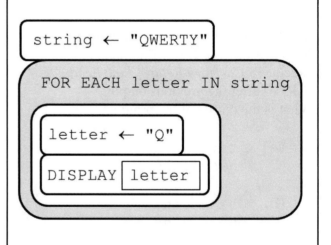

```
string ← "QWERTY"

FOR EACH letter IN string

    letter ← "Q"

    DISPLAY  letter
```

06.

Consider the adjacent incomplete procedure reverse. Procedure `reverse` returns `string2` as the reverse of the `string1` parameter. For instance, if `string1` equals "Tornado" then `string2` returns "odanroT".

Which one of the statements below, when replacing `<missing code>`, will make procedure `reverse` execute properly?

```
PROCEDURE reverse (string1)
{
    string2 = ""
    n ← LENGTH (string1)
    REPEAT UNTIL (n = 0)
    {
        < Missing Code >
        n ← n - 1
    }
    RETURN string2
```

(A) `string2 ← string1[n]`

(B) `string2 ← string2 + string1[n]`

(C) `string2[n] ← string1[n]`

(D) `string2[n] ← string2[n] + string1[n]`

07.

Consider the adjacent code segment. What is the output of the program?

(A) Q Q Q Q Q Q

(B) Q W E R T Y

(C) Q Q W Q E Q R Q T Q Y Q

(D) Q W E R T Y Q Q Q Q Q Q

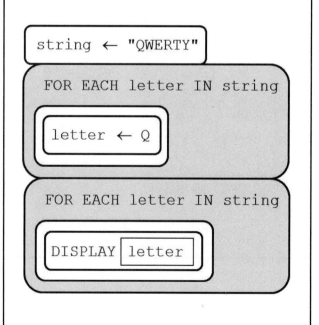

```
string ← "QWERTY"

FOR EACH letter IN string
    letter ← Q

FOR EACH letter IN string
    DISPLAY letter
```

08.

Consider procedure `vowels` below.
What string values are displayed by after executing the following two program statements?

```
DISPLAY (vowels ("500 Orleans Court"))
DISPLAY (vowels ("THE LAZY QUICK BROWN FOX JUMPS")
```

(A) AEIOU
   AEIOU

(B) OEAOU
   EAUIOOU

(C) Oeaou
   EAUIOOU

(D) O
   EAUIOOU

```
PROCEDURE vowels (s1)
{
    s2 = ""
    FOR EACH c IN s1
    {
        if (c="A" OR c="E" OR c="I" OR c="O" OR c="U")
        {
            s2 ← s2 + c
        }
    }
    RETURN s2
}
```

09.

Consider the adjacent `mystery` procedure. What Boolean values are displayed after executing the following two program statements?

```
DISPLAY (mystery("ABCDEFG"))
DISPLAY (mystery("RACECAR"))
```

    (A) `true`
        `true`

    (B) `true`
        `false`

    (C) `false`
        `true`

    (D) `false`
        `false`

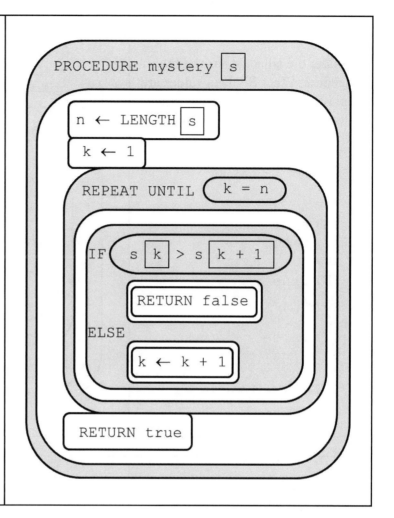

```
PROCEDURE mystery  s

    n ← LENGTH  s
    k ← 1

    REPEAT UNTIL  k = n

        IF  s k  > s k + 1
            RETURN false
        ELSE
            k ← k + 1

    RETURN true
```

10.

Return to procedure `mystery` shown above in question 09.
Assume that a pre-condition of calling the procedure is that parameters consist of upper-case letters only. Which of the following describes the purpose of procedure `mystery`?

    (A) Procedure `mystery` checks if all the characters are upper-case letters.

    (B) Procedure `mystery` determines if all characters in the parameter are alpha-numeric characters.

    (C) Procedure `mystery` determines if the letters of the parameter string are in an alphabetical ascending order.

    (D) Procedure `mystery` determines if the letters of the parameter string are in an alphabetical descending order.

11.

Consider the adjacent `mystery` procedure. What Boolean values are displayed after executing the following two program statements?

```
DISPLAY (mystery("RACECAR"))
DISPLAY (mystery("AARDVARK"))
```

(A) true
    true

(B) true
    false

(C) false
    true

(D) false
    false

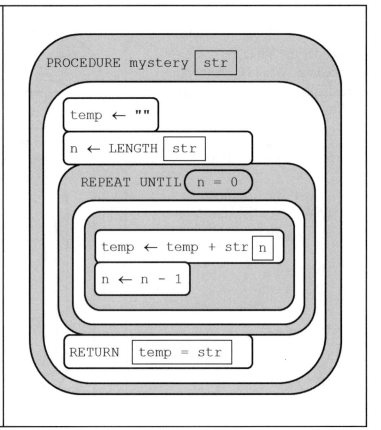

12.

Consider the adjacent `mystery` procedure. What Boolean values are displayed after executing the following two program statements?

```
DISPLAY (mystery("Madam"))
DISPLAY (mystery("1234321"))
```

(A) true
    true

(B) true
    false

(C) false
    true

(D) false
    false

```
PROCEDURE mystery (str)
{
    palindrome ← true
    start ← 1
    end ← LENGTH (str)
    REPEAT UNTIL (start > end)
    {
        if (str[start] ≠ str[end])
        {
            palindrome ← false
        }
        start ← start + 1
        end ← end - 1
    }
    return palindrome
```

Chapter 13 Review
Sorting & Searching Algorithms

The AP CSP Course Description mentions searching in its Algorithm section. Both the *linear search* and the *binary search* are mentioned by name and it states that the *binary search* can only be used when the list is sorted. It is possible sorting will not be tested, but I believe in the *better be prepared than surprised* philosophy, mentioned earlier. Even if a sort algorithm and its code may never be tested, it is still a good exercise to look at sorting logic in understanding algorithmic logic. You will also get more experience working with the pseudo-code that will be used on the AP Exam.

One sort be presented in this chapter. It is the *bubble sort*, which is a rather simple sort in terms of program code and one of the easier sorts to comprehend. Both the algorithmic logic and the program code will be presented.

The *Bubble Sort* gets its name because data *bubbles* to the top. Consider the following small list of five numbers, shown in the table below, which shows the **1st Comparison Pass**. It will be used to demonstrate the logic of the *Bubble Sort* step-by-step. At every stage, adjacent numbers are compared, and if two adjacent numbers are not in the correct order, they are swapped. Each pass through the number list places the largest number at the end or "top" of the list. It has *bubbled* to the surface. The illustrations show how numbers will be sorted from smallest to largest. The smallest number will end up in the left-most list location, and the largest number will end up in the right-most location.

1st Comparison Pass

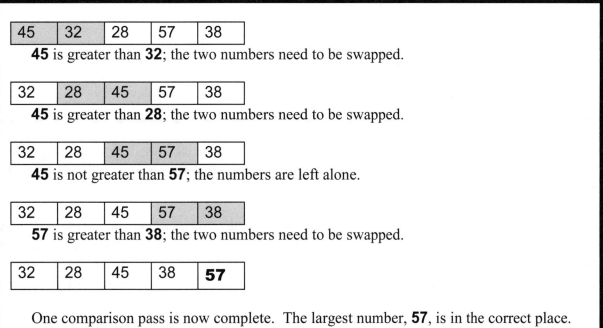

2nd Comparison Pass

The 2nd Comparison Pass uses the same *compare-and-swap* logic as the first pass.

| 32 | 28 | 45 | 38 | **57** |

32 is greater than **28**; the two numbers need to be swapped.

| 28 | 32 | 45 | 38 | **57** |

32 is not greater than **45**; the numbers are left alone.

| 28 | 32 | 45 | 38 | **57** |

45 is greater than **38**; the two numbers need to be swapped.

| 28 | 32 | 38 | **45** | **57** |

We can visually see that the list is now sorted.
It is not necessary to compare **45** and **57**, but the computer may not realize that.
The second comparison pass is complete, and **45** is in the correct place.

3rd Comparison Pass

| 28 | 32 | 38 | **45** | **57** |

28 is not greater than **32**; the numbers are left alone.

| 28 | 32 | 38 | **45** | **57** |

32 is not greater than **38**; the numbers are left alone.

| 28 | 32 | **38** | **45** | **57** |

The third pass is complete, and **38** is "known" to be in the correct place.

Visually you now see a list of [23,32,38,45,57], which is sorted in ascending order. Technically, following our algorithm, the computer does not realize this and we need to go one more pass. Why one and not two?

You have seen that one *compare-and-swap* pass places one number in the correct place. It may seem that you then need 5 *compare-and-pass* executions to get all five numbers in the correct place. The reality is that you are finished with one less pass. Any time when you have n numbers and you have placed n-1 numbers in the correct location, the last number will be placed correctly at well.

4th Comparison Pass

28	32	**38**	**45**	**57**

28 is not greater than 32; the numbers are left alone.

28	**32**	**38**	**45**	**57**

The fourth pass is complete, and **32** is "known" to be in the correct place.
A fifth pass is not necessary. **28** is the only number left.

With **5** numbers there will be **4** comparison passes.
With **n** numbers there will be **n-1** comparison passes.

You have seen the logic of the *bubble sort* algorithm. Now how do you translate such an algorithm into program language code? Why not start with the code for the *partial sort* shown next. It is an incomplete *bubble sort* that only places one element - the largest - in the correct location. If we can understand this step, then it will be easier to see how the entire sort works.

Partial Sort Pseudo-Code

The `partialSort` procedure below is a direct translation of a single comparison pass from the earlier algorithm steps into text-based pseudo-code.

```
PROCEDURE partialSort (numbers)
{
    n ← LENGTH (numbers)
    q ← 1
    REPEAT n-1 TIMES
    {
        IF (numbers[q] > nummbers[q+1])
        {
            temp ← numbers[q]
            number[q] ← numbers[q+1]
            numbers[q+1] ← temp
        }
        q ← q + 1
    }
}
```

Complete Bubble Sort Pseudo-Code

The code within the box outline is the earlier *partialSort* procedure, which only placed one element in the right location. The partialSort code must be executed once for each element in the list, except the final element. This is what is shown below.

```
PROCEDURE bubbleSort (numbers)
{
    n ← LENGTH (numbers)
    REPEAT n-1 TIMES
    {

        q ← 1
        REPEAT n-1 TIMES
        {
            IF (numbers[q] > nummbers[q+1])
            {
                temp ← numbers[q]
                number[q] ← numbers[q+1]
                numbers[q+1] ← temp
            }
            q ← q + 1
        }

    }
}
```

Many people like organization, but fundamentally the biggest justification for sorting is searching. Long before there were computers; file folders, library index cards, and books of all types were positioned in a sequence, sorted numerically or alphabetically.

The first search we look at is the *linear search,* which is also known as the *sequential search.* It is a very simple algorithm. Take a list of elements, start with the first element and check each element in the list in sequence until you have found the element.

The procedure that follows returns the index of the target element or it returns -1 if the element is not found. This makes sense if you consider being in a large hardware store, like Home Depot or Loew's. You need to find 1/2 inch bolts that are 8 inches long. You see a clerk and ask. "Do you have 8-inch long, 1/2-inch diameter bolts?" The clerk responds with yes and walks away. That is little help. You know the items are in the store, but not at all where they are. For that reason the search procedures that follows returns the index of the target number.

Linear Search Pseudo-Code

```
PROCEDURE linearSearch (list, target)
{
    n ← LENGTH (list)
    index ← 1
    REPEAT n TIMES
    {
        IF (numbers[index] = target)
        {
            RETURN index
        }
        ELSE
        {
            index ← index + 1
        }
    }
    RETURN -1
}
```

Sorting is not necessary for the linear search. You start at one end or you start at the top. Then you search sequentially from one item to the next. This is precisely the search you make when you need a specific document in a large pike of disorganized documents.

The College Board does not require that you do *formal* algorithmic analysis, but some simple analysis seems reasonable. Can you answer the following questions about a *linear search* used on a list of n elements?

- What is the best case search scenario?
- What is the worst case search scenario?
- What is the average case search scenario?
- If the list changes from n elements to 5n elements, how will that impact the search time?

Do these answers make sense?
- The best case search scenario is one comparison. The target is the first element.
- The worst case search scenario is n comparisons. The target is the last element.
- The average case search scenario is n/2 comparisons.
- The best case is still one comparison, but average and worst-case is now 5 times as long.

The *linear search* is effective. It is simple and it is slow. Is that problem for a small list? Not at all. With today's fast computers there is no problem searching small lists. How about searching through IRS records of millions of people? That is a different story. How about using the logic of the binary search algorithm?

Imagine a world before computers. The IRS has giant warehouse with incredibly long tables that are 1/4 mile long. Table after table have IRS tax returns. Young energetic teenagers are hired to race on their roller skates finding requested records.

The records are ordered. It could be ordered alphabetically by name or it could be ordered numerically by social security number. It does not matter. These skaters will not start on one end and slowly move along using a *linear search* algorithm.

No, they use the *binary search* algorithm, which goes as follows:

- The skaters race to the middle and check the record.
- There are three possibilities:
  - ➤ The record is found. Great. The skater races to the requester with the record.
  - ➤ They went too far. The record is to the left.
  - ➤ They did not go far enough. The record is to the right.
- Half the records can now be ignored. (Compare that to the linear search)
- Our young IRS worker now goes to the middle of the smaller section and the process is repeated, each time cutting the section in half until the record is found.

Computing the worst-case search scenario for linear search is simple. You have a very large list, like IRS records. If you search through 100,000,000 records, the worst case is 100 million. Now consider the binary search. After each comparison the remaining records are reduced by half. Let do this with 100 million and see what we get.

Comparison 00:	100,000,000 records	Comparison 15:	12,207 records
Comparison 01:	50,000,000 records	Comparison 16:	6,103
Comparison 02:	25,000,000 records	Comparison 17:	3,051
Comparison 03:	12,500,000 records	Comparison 18:	1,525
Comparison 04:	6,250,000 records	Comparison 19:	762
Comparison 05:	3,125,000 records	Comparison 20:	381
Comparison 06:	1,562,500 records	Comparison 21:	190
Comparison 09:	781,250 records	Comparison 22:	95
Comparison 10:	390,625 records	Comparison 23:	46
Comparison 11:	195,312 records	Comparison 24:	23
Comparison 12:	95,656 records	Comparison 25:	11
Comparison 13	48,828 records	Comparison 26:	5
Comparison 14:	24,414 records	Comparison 27:	2
			1 No comparison

Binary Search Pseudo-Code

The binary algorithm translates nicely into every programming language. Unlike the *linear search*, the index of the list is constantly working with a smaller list. This reality is nicely handled with a `lo` and `hi` index variable. These variables start on opposite ends and steadily work toward each other. After each comparison is made either `lo` gets larger or `hi` gets smaller. This continues until the target list item is found or when `lo` becomes larger than `hi`.

```
PROCEDURE binarySearch (list, target)
{
    n ← LENGTH (list)
    lo ← 1
    hi ← n
    REPEAT UNTIL (lo > hi)
    {
        mid ← (lo + hi) // 2
        IF (numbers[mid] = target)
        {
            RETURN mid
        }
        ELSE
        {
            IF (target > numbers[mid])
            {
                lo ← mid + 1
            }
            ELSE
            {
                hi ← mid - 1
            }
            index ← index + 1
        }
    }
    RETURN -1
}
```

The pitfalls and concerns for algorithm were shown in the first algorithm chapter. Those issues still apply. With sorting and searching a new component is introduced about selecting the appropriate algorithm. The binary search is far more efficient than the linear search for any large list of data, but the list must be ordered.

Concern #1: Know the difference between linear searching and binary searching.

Question01

Acme's database has a list 3000 employee records. The records are not ordered. What search algorithm will you use and what is the worst-case number of comparisons before the requested record is found or it is determined that the record does not exist?

    (A) Binary-Search   1

    (B) Binary-Search   12

    (C) Linear-Search   1500

    (D) Linear-Search   3000

Question02

Acme's database has a list 3000 employee records. The records are ordered according to employee's last name. What search algorithm will you use and what is the worst-case number of comparisons before the requested record is found or it is determined that the record does not exist?

    (A) Binary-Search   1

    (B) Binary-Search   12

    (C) Linear-Search   1500

    (D) Linear-Search   3000

Both questions have two parts. Which search do you use and what will be the maximum number of comparison necessary to find the target record? In *Question01* it is stated that the records are not sorted. That instantly eliminates the binary search. The linear search will need to start at the first elements and continue to the last element for a maximum of 3000 comparisons.

In *Question02* the list is ordered. The binary search is now an option. You need to look at the binary numbers 2, 4, 8, 16, 32, 64, etc. Find the smallest binary number that is larger than the number of elements in the list. 2^{11} equals 2048 and this binary number is smaller than 3000. The next binary is 2^{12}, which equals 4096 and it is larger than 3000. The exponent is the number of maximum comparisons.

Chapter 13 Questions
Sorting & Searching Algorithms

01.

Consider the adjacent procedure `partialSort`. It implements an incomplete sorting algorithm. What does executing `partialSort` accomplish at this stage?

(A) It checks if the number list is already sorted.

(B) It places the smallest number at index `n`.

(C) It places the largest number at index `1`.

(D) It places the largest number at index `n`.

```
PROCEDURE partialSort (nbrs)
{
    n ← LENGTH (nbrs)
    q ← 1
    REPEAT UNTIL (q = n)
    {
        IF (nbrs[q] > nbrs[q+1])
        {
            temp ← nbrs[q]
            nbrs[q] ← nbrs[q+1]
            nbrs[q+1] ← temp
        }
        q ← q + 1
    }
}
```

02.

Consider the adjacent `IF` statements. The top statement is from *Question01*. If the bottom statement replaces the original `IF` statement, what will be the result of executing the `partialSort` procedure?

(A) It checks if the number list is already sorted.

(B) It places the smallest number at index `n`.

(C) It places the largest number at index `1`.

(D) It places the largest number at index `n`.

```
IF (nbrs[q] > nbrs[q+1])

IF (nbrs[q] < nbrs[q+1])
```

03. Consider the four `sort` procedures below. Each one of the `sort` procedures includes the sorting code from *Question01*, placed inside a rectangle. The `partialSort` code segment places one element of `nbrs` in the correct location. An outer loop needs to repeat the `partialSort` code segment until `nbrs` is sorted. Which one of the procedures below will sort the elements in `nbrs` in ascending order? Keep in mind that the code segment inside the rectangular box is identical for each answer.

(A)
```
PROCEDURE sort (nbrs)
{
    n ← LENGTH (nbrs)
    REPEAT n-1 TIMES
    {
        q ← 1

        REPEAT UNTIL (q = n)
        {
            if (nbrs[q] > nbrs[q+1])
            {
                temp ← nbrs[q]
                nbrs[q] ← nbrs[q+1]
                nbrs[q+1] ← temp
            }
            q ← q + 1

        }
    }
}
```

(B)
```
PROCEDURE sort (nbrs)
{
    n ← LENGTH (nbrs)
    q ← 1
    REPEAT n-1 TIMES
    {
        REPEAT UNTIL (q = n)
        {
            if (nbrs[q] > nbrs[q+1])
            {
                temp ← nbrs[q]
                nbrs[q] ← nbrs[q+1]
                nbrs[q+1] ← temp
            }
            q ← q + 1
        }
    }
}
```

(C)
```
PROCEDURE sort (nbrs)
{
    n ← LENGTH (nbrs)
    REPEAT n-1 TIMES
    {
        q ← 0

        REPEAT UNTIL (q = n)
        {
            if (nbrs[q] > nbrs[q+1])
            {
                temp ← nbrs[q]
                nbrs[q] ← nbrs[q+1]
                nbrs[q+1] ← temp
            }
            q ← q + 1
        }

    }
}
```

(D)
```
PROCEDURE sort (nbrs)
{
    n ← LENGTH (nbrs)
    REPEAT n-2 TIMES
    {
        q ← 1

        REPEAT UNTIL (q = n)
        {
            if (nbrs[q] > nbrs[q+1])
            {
                temp ← nbrs[q]
                nbrs[q] ← nbrs[q+1]
                nbrs[q+1] ← temp
            }
            q ← q + 1
        }
    }
}
```

04.

Consider the adjacent code segment.
Look at the relationship between the value
of n and the output of `count` when
multiple executions are observed.

When the value of n is multiplied times 3
then the output of `count` is multiplied by

(A) 3

(B) 4

(C) 6

(D) 9

```
n ← <unknown positive integer>
count ← 0
REPEAT n TIMES
{
    REPEAT n TIMES
    {
        count ← count + 1
    }
}
DISPLAY (count)
```

05.

Consider the adjacent procedure `search`.
Does this procedure use a search algorithm
correctly so that it will determine if
`target` is in `numbers`?

(A) No, `search` will not find
`target` if it is the first element.

(B) No, `search` will not find
`target` if it is the last element.

(C) Yes, `search` works correctly.

(D) Yes, `search` will find `target`,
but it will not work properly
when `target` is not in `numbers`.

```
PROCEDURE search (numbers, target)
found ← false
FOR EACH nr IN numbers
{
    IF (nr = target)
    {
        found ← true
    }
    RETURN found
}
```

06. Look at the procedure from *Question05* again. The `search` procedure compared every element in the `numbers` list, even if `target` was found as the first element. Which of the following `search` procedures solves that inefficiency?

(A)

```
PROCEDURE search (numbers, target)
FOR EACH nr IN numbers
{
    IF (nr = target)
    {
        RETURN true
    }
    RETURN false
}
```

(B)

```
PROCEDURE search (numbers, target)
{
    k ← 1
    found ← false
    finished ← false
    n ← LENGTH (numbers)
    REPEAT UNTIL (finished)
    {
        IF (numbers[k] = target)
        {
            found ← true
        }
        finished ← (found OR k = n)
        k ← k + 1
    }
    RETURN found
}
```

(C)

```
PROCEDURE search (numbers, target)
{
    k ← 1
    found ← false
    REPEAT UNTIL (found OR k > n)
    {
        IF (numbers[k] = target)
        {
            found ← true
        }
        k ← k + 1
    }
    RETURN found
}
```

(D)

All three procedures in (A), (B) and (C) solve the inefficiency problem.

07. *Question06* addressed the inefficiency of the *linear search* implementation. Is there a second improvement that can be added? And if so, which of the following will improve the search procedures that were shown in *Question06*?

(A) The procedures in *Question06* can only be improved with a different algorithm.

(B) Knowing that some element exists is not sufficient. The procedure needs to return the location of the found element.

(C) The procedure should indicate if multiple targets exist in the `numbers` list.

(D) The *linear search* as it was shown is the most efficient implementation.

08.

Consider the adjacent `search` procedure, which is an implementation of the *binary search* algorithm. This algorithm and its implementation are considerably more complex than the linear search shown in previous questions. Why would somebody use a more complex algorithm like this?

(A) It is a matter of personal subjective taste.

(B) The *binary search* uses far less memory space than the *linear search.*

(C) The execution efficiency of the *binary search* far exceeds the efficiency of the *linear search* when the list becomes very large.

(D) It is not necessary to provide a sorted list for the *binary search.*

Note: // indicates integer division.

```
PROCEDURE search (numbers, target)
{
    lo ← 1
    hi ← LENGTH (numbers)
    REPEAT UNTIL (lo > hi)
    {
        mid = (lo + hi) // 2
        IF (numbers[mid] = target)
        {
            RETURN true
        }
        ELSE
        {
            IF (target > numbers[mid])
            {
                lo ← mid + 1
            }
            ELSE
            {
                hi ← mid - 1
            }
        }
    }
    RETURN false
}
```

09. Is the *linear search* ever better than the *binary search* and if so, when does this happen?

(A) The linear search is never better than the linear search.

(B) The *linear search* works correctly with a randomly ordered list.
The *binary search* requires an ordered list.

(C) The *linear search* is more efficient than the *binary search* for a very large list.

(D) The linear search is more efficient than the *binary search* for a very small list.

10. In a list of 2,000 elements what is the average number of comparisons made by a *linear search* to find the target element in an unordered list?

(A) Roughly 1000

(B) Exactly 2000

(C) Roughly 500

(D) Exactly 11

11. In a list of 2,000 elements what is the maximum number of comparisons made by a *binary search* to find the target element in an ordered list?

(A) Roughly 1000

(B) Roughly 500

(C) Exactly 11

(D) Exactly 13

12. In this question a flowchart is a way to visually represent an algorithm. The following chart shows the buildiong blocks used by the flowchart.

Block	Explanation
Oval	The start or end of an algorithm
Rectangle	One or more processing steps, such as a statement that assigns a value or variable
Diamond	A conditional or decision step, where execution proceeds to the side labeled `true` if the condition is true and to the side labeled `false` otherwise.
Parallelogram	Display a message

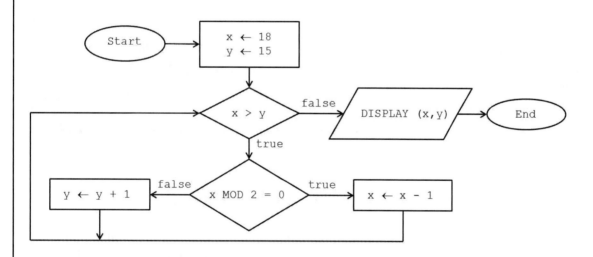

What is displayed as a result of executing the algorithm represented by the flowchart?

(A) 12 13

(B) 17 16

(C) 16 18

(D) 17 17

Chapter 14 Review
Types of Abstractions

The first chapter on abstraction focused on *bits & bases*. That chapter was only involved with data abstraction and specifically how numbers and characters are stored in a computer. If all data is represented ultimately in bits of 1 and 0 values then how does this all work? The chapter showed how to convert between the binary base-2, the decimal (for humans) base-10 and the hexadecimal base-16. The story of abstraction is mixed throughout the course.

APCS Examination Alert

Procedural Abstraction Is Very Important For Your AP Exam Score

Abstraction is one of the Big Ideas and its concepts will be tested on the very important End-Of-Course AP CSP Exam.

Additionally, students have to create two *performance tasks (PT)*. One PT, called *Create,* is a computer program. The intention and requirements are not important here and will be discussed in a separate chapter.

The connection is that the student-created program needs to demonstrate knowledge of abstraction. This knowledge includes demonstrating how to use existing abstractions and creating your own abstractions. In a program, such abstractions are mostly *procedural abstractions.*

A Computer Science Abstraction Case Study

A case study in computer science normally shows a sequence of program examples that help to explain a concept or multiple interacting concepts. The case study presented here will explain how a circle manages to appear on a monitor. This will be done with various drawings, programs, mathematics and hardware.

The goal of this case study is not to insure that you understand all the details of circle drawing. You will probably see various stages that you may not comprehend at all, but that actually is the whole point of abstraction. We are capable of using the tools at our disposal very nicely without knowing the details of how such tools do their job. This second abstraction chapter was intentionally separated quite a distance from the first chapter. An important aspect of abstraction in computer science is *procedural abstraction*. You have now learned more about programming and at this stage you will likely have used available procedures as well as created your own procedures. This case study looks heavily at procedural and other abstractions.

Case Study Step 01

The case study starts with a paint program. This paint program is created by Samantha Gant, a terrific 2017 computer science student at John Paul II High School, Plano, Texas. By using her program, I have access to the code that created the application, which makes the stages easier to explain. Look at the orange circle, which is more visible in the second image that blows up part of the paint selection menu.

Note: This is a multi-color display that will not look quite correct with shades of gray printed on paper. The colors are not significant for this case study.

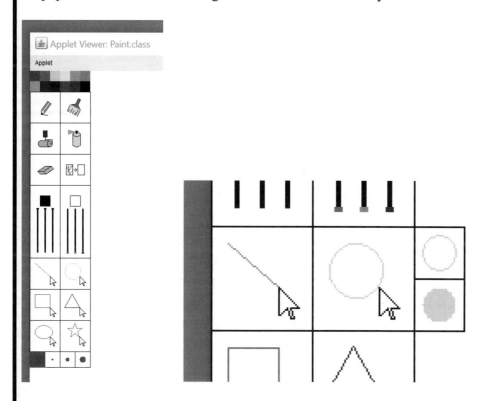

You are now looking at an example of abstraction. You see a circle and you have no idea how it appeared there. Furthermore, if you click on the circle, you can proceed to draw your very own circle. You really have no clue how this all manages to work. You are looking at a case of abstraction that I shall call *Application Abstraction*. You are using a program or an application, or an App that lets you perform some operation or function without providing any information how this functionality is performed.

Case Study Step 02

The next stage shows the `circleMenu` procedure. It is the procedure that displays the menu of the paint program to draw the different circles.

That means that in the creation of this procedure, called `circleMenu`, you will see that existing procedures `color`, `fillRect`, `drawRect`, `drawCircle` and `fillCircle` are used.

```
def circleMenu():
    color("white")
    fillRect(120,360,150,390)
    color("Black")
    drawRect(120,360,150,390)
    drawRect(120,390,150,420)
    color("Orange")
    drawCircle(135,385,20)
    fillCircle(135,405,20)
```

Case Study Step 03

The next layer of abstraction is mathematical. You have rather casually been using paint-type programs, drawing circles and curves, without saying thank you to our friendly mathematicians.

It is not the intention of this case study to explain how every stage works, but to show that these stages exist.

The code in the adjacent procedure will look quite intimidating to some students. Suddenly there are `sin`, `cos` and `radian` shown everywhere.

The mathematical functions `sin` and `cos` provide (`x`, `y`) coordinate values that form a circle. As the values are multiplied by a `radius` value (`r` in the program example), the circle changes in size.

```
def drawCircle(centerX,centerY,r):
    radian = 0.0
    x1 = cos(radian) * r + centerX
    y1 = sin(radian) * r + centerY
    while radian <= 2 * pi:
        radian = radian + 0.01
        x2 = cos(radian) * r + centerX
        y2 = sin(radian) * r + centerY
        drawLine(x1,y1,x2,y2)
        x1 = x2
        y1 = y2
```

Case Study Step 04

You have seen that with the help of mathematics it is possible to precisely determine the locations on the monitor where pixels need to be drawn to display a circle. If the circle needs to become larger, then an increase to the radius value multiplies the `sin` and `cos` values by a greater factor, which increases the size of the circle.

But how does a pixel end up at the monitor at the right location? Here we are facing yet another layer of abstraction. The next stage of the story revolves around the images shown below. You are looking at a *video card* and a *monitor*. This video card on the left has a VGA (Video Graphics Array) interface, which is an older interface that can still handle analog video resolution. DVI (Digital Visual Interface) and HDMI (High Definition Multimedia Interface) are the more modern interfaces used with HD televisions and monitors.

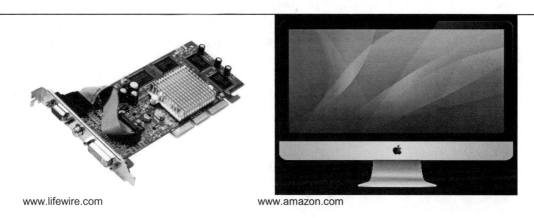

www.lifewire.com   www.amazon.com

The video card has its own memory known as video memory. Some older computers include the video memory on the mother board as part of the primary RAM (Random Access Memory). There is a one-to-one correspondence between the Video Memory and the Monitor's pixels. If the very first memory location in video memory indicates that the color is bright-red, then the top-left pixel on the monitor at coordinate location (0,0) becomes bright-red.

The video card determines the quantity and quality of the colors. Most video cards have a very large selection of colors based on RGB (Red, Green, Blue) values. Each color can have 256 shades with values 0 to 255. When we multiply the 256 possible shades for Red, Green and Blue we get 16,777,216 different shades of color. This means when you pick a location for a pixel, say at (250,325) and the color selected is bright-red, which is a (255,0,0) RGB color combination, then the color value is placed in the video memory, which corresponds to the (250, 325) location and presto there is a bright red pixel.

The case study ends here and yet the abstraction layers are not yet finished. The video card knows what needs to be done and the video card has an interface to the monitor. We are down to the computer knowing exactly which single little pixel must be displayed bright-red. Now comes an *electrical abstraction* layer. An electrical engineer will need to take over and explain how color and location information from the video card translates to some physics laws inside the monitor that control the display of the screen.

What is the big benefit of abstraction? It maintains sanity. It is good to discuss problems in general terms and explain processes in a sequence of steps without the complete knowledge of every possible detail that is used along the implementation highway. For individuals who do understand the working of all of these stages, it provides simplicity and allows focus on the job at hand. For people who do not have the computer science and/or the mathematical comprehension of this type of abstraction, it still makes it very possible to create circles in programs. Use the correct procedure, provide the correct parameter information and let the business behind the abstraction curtain do the rest.

Abstraction Simulations

You can expect questions about simulations, which is one of many component of the Abstraction Big Idea. Simulations can simplify much larger problems by modeling at a smaller scale, or a limited scale in a controlled environment. The picture below shows the only current ocean liner, and the largest ocean liner ever built, the Queen Mary 2, affectionately known as the QM2. She is 1132 feet long and can travel 35 mph. Do not confuse an ocean liner with a cruise ship. The QM2 makes scheduled Atlantic Ocean crossings not only in calm summer months, but also in the middle of the winter. The gigantic cruise ships built today would have a rough time handling the Atlantic in a December storm. For the QM2, it is part of a normal day's work.

How does the QM2 manage to cross the most volatile ocean on Earth with calm confidence? It is her amazing design and this design was made by numerous simulations in a very sophisticated, controlled environment.

Long before the current QM2 crossed the Atlantic, she started as a 15-foot model in a 600 meter water basin simulator in The Netherlands. For two years, ship models with different hull designs were exposed to every imaginable simulated ocean conditions. The ship's hull designs and its stabilizer designs were tested again and again until the performance was acceptable.

Consider the most expensive aircraft in the world, the Airbus A380, which costs close to half a billion dollars. How do you learn to fly such a plane or most other large, commercial planes for that matter? Student pilots get inside a flight simulator and never leave the ground. The ultra-sophisticated simulator is programmed for any type of weather or plane malfunction and can test a pilot response to any situation. This saves lots of money flying an expensive airplane and it eliminates the danger.

Some of the Main Benefits of Simulations

- Simulations can tests hypotheses in a controlled environment.
- Simulations help to refine more general hypotheses.
- Simulations can test in extreme environments without any danger.
- Simulations can test with models at a great cost reduction.

Abstraction is Good ... But

Does it matter if you know what is happening behind the curtain? Should the details of implementation always be hidden? Well, for some people, yes. If one person is going to use a circle procedure and not know how this procedure works, that is only possible if some other person understands the abstraction details, otherwise the procedure would not exist.

A lot of students do not like imaginary numbers in Algebra II. Like, who needs this dumb complex number stuff anyway? Do you enjoy your cell phone? Very likely you do and the design of the electronics in your cell phone requires knowledge of imaginary numbers. It is totally true that you can use a cell phone without ever learning Algebra, but somebody must have the knowledge to handle the mathematics of cell phone electronics.

Early GPS systems were not reliable. They were pretty good, but not accurate. The satellite worked correctly; everything worked correctly, but still the positioning was pretty good, but not totally accurate. The GPS developers then realized they had forgotten about Albert Einstein and his theories of relativity. Who needs that stuff? You guessed it, GPS designers. Satellites travel in space at speeds far exceeding anything on Earth. They also do not feel the same gravitational pull as objects on the Earth's surface. Einstein's theories show that both speed and gravity affect the passage of time. Once the GPS engineers applied Einstein equations, the GPS worked very accurately.

There are other issues. The electronic data in your world that stores images, movies and sound files has a wide variety of formats. Here is a list of some image formats that you see in the extension of a image file name:

JPG, PNG. TIF, GIF, PSD, BMP, PDF, EPS, AI, INDD, MOV, MTS, MP4, AVI, WAV, FLAC are seen in the media world and that list is not complete. These file formats are not at the same thing with a different extension. There are significant differences that impact the storage size and the quality of your data files.

Is there a need to know what is behind the abstraction curtain for students? You may be surprised. There are numbers, characters, images, movies and sounds that all needs to be stored on a computer and used on a computer. An earlier chapter talked about the need for data compression. Sometimes it is necessary to reduce the quality of the data file to allow faster transmission and require less storage space. It that an issue for high school students? Take a look at two examples that help to illustrate this significance.

Raster and Vector Images

There are two ways to create images. An image can be created with a series of pixels. This is true for the pictures you take with a camera. Both pictures show a sharp upper-case small **H**. The Vector image stays sharp as the size increases. The Raster image deteriorates and becomes fuzzy. The raster image is created with pixels. When the pixels are small, they are not visible. As an image enlarges so do the pixels and the picture loses quality. If you take a picture with a high resolution camera the pixels are smaller and the pixel enlargement is less visible.

Most people are more familiar with pixels and they know that photo enlargement may lose image quality. What is the secret of the vector image? This secret is used by a word processor. The characters that you display on an essay are not all the same size, created with pixels that become enlarged as you select a bigger font. Each character is created with a formula. The formula creates an original display based on its input parameters. That means that a vertical line in the letter **H** is longer as the characters gets larger, but it is drawn longer; it is not stretched.

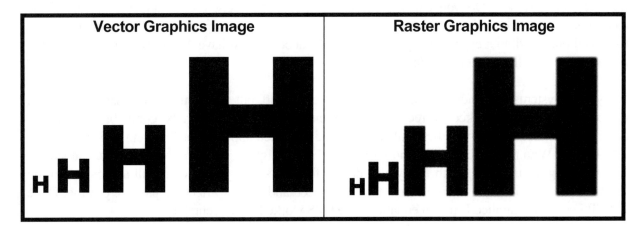

The images on this page will help to show the problem of using low resolution pictures. All images started with **Image 1**. **Image 2** is considerably reduced, but may still be acceptable at the size shown. **Image 3** is a considerable close-up of **Image 1** and shows good quality. **Image 4** is the same close-up, but uses **Image 2** and has very poor quality. It means that we need to be aware of the type of data files we store and how they are used.

It is not necessary to know the detail of each format. Having knowledge of some of the more popular formats is very useful. You do need to know that there is a compromise between data size for storage and data transmission that competes with data quality. A picture that looks great as a Facebook profile picture may be very low quality when blown up in a poster.

File Format	Media Type	Description
GIF	Image	Used for low resolution drawings. Color selection is only 256 and file size is drastically reduced. Enlargements become fuzzy very quickly.
JPG	Image	Uses lossy compression; used for high resolution photographs with good quality.
PNG	Image	Good quality for web pages; uses lossless compression; used for cartoons and line drawing images. Uses low resolution.
TIF	Image	Good format for quality graphics. Creates very large files.
AI	Image	Excellent Adobe file. Used for professional artwork. Uses vector graphics and allows enlarged images without quality loss.
MP4	Movie	Very popular file format that works on all platforms. Maintains good quality.
AVI	Movie	High quality format used a lot for legacy video files.
MOV	Movie	Apple QuickTime Movie file.
MTS	Movie	Popular HD camcorder file. Used for original archive movies.
WAV	Audio	Mostly Lossless format
FLAC	Audio	Lossless audio format
MP3	Audio	Lossy, but maintains quality from other file formats. Very popular audio file.
WMA	Audio	Similar to MP3. Meant for Windows systems and improves MP3 slightly.

Chapter 14 Questions
Abstraction II

---

01. Which of the following describes a *logic gate*?

    (A) It is a hardware abstraction that is modeled by Boolean logic.

    (B) It is a procedural abstraction that is modeled by Boolean logic

    (C) It is a high-level programming abstraction used in an application program.

    (D) It is a low-level programming abstraction used in an application program.

---

02. Abstraction occurs

    (A) in computer operations at the hardware, low-level only.

    (B) in computer operations at the application, high-level only.

    (C) primarily at the electrical hardware level.

    (D) at every level and stage of computer operations.

---

03. Before the world's largest ocean liner, the Queen Mary 2, started construction, a 15 foot model is used in a 600 meter water basin using sophisticated computer simulations. Which of the following is **not** a benefit of such simulations?

    (A) It assists in selecting the optimal hull design of the ship for all weather conditions.

    (B) It helps to determine the size of the crew necessary to manage all of the ship's needs.

    (C) It allows testing of dangerous water conditions without danger to people or ship.

    (D) It can save money by not using a faulty design that is very expensive to alter.

04. More than 10,000 trains are used in Germany per day. Many destinations require switching from one train to another. The optimal switching time very important. Which of the following is the best way to find it?

(A) A computer program uses data of passenger train use and runs simulation at many of the large train station to see how long it takes to move passengers.

(B) Thousands of observers measures train switching behavior and times at many different train stations.

(C) Surveys are mailed out asking passengers how much time they like to switch trains.

(D) A group of people are employed in a mock simulation to observe how they respond to switching between trains with different times available.

05. Characters are represented as numerical values initially using ASCII code. Later Unicode was introduced to represent characters. Why was Unicode necessary?

(A) ASCII used an older algorithm for its conversion. Unicode uses a faster algorithm

(B) Computer scientists realized that ASCII wasted memory. They switched to the smaller Unicode system for more efficient memory management.

(C) ASCII worked fine initially with western languages. Many middle east and eastern languages have more characters than ASCII can handle.

(D) The two systems are identical in purpose. It is pretty much a matter of personal preference as often is the case with chosen program languages.

06. Abstractions are not unique to computer technology. In everyday life, abstractions surround people. Which of the following is **not** an example of using an abstraction?

(A) Starting a car with a key or a start button

(B) Playing tennis

(C) Using an elevator

(D) None of the above. All three are examples of using one or more abstractions.

07. Procedural abstraction is used in many programs. Which of the following are benefits of using procedural abstraction?

    I.   It makes a program more readable by using self-identifying procedure names.

    II. It saves time and memory by writing the code once and using it many times.

    III. It allows programmers to use program functionalioty without understanding it.

    (A) I only

    (B) I and II only

    (C) II and III only

    (D) I, II and III

08. How can an analog image of colors become a digitized file of binary bits?

    (A) The image is stored as an array of pixels. Each pixel is an 8-bit sequence that stores the color value.

    (B) The image is stored as a two-dimensional array of pixels. Each pixel stores three 8-bit sequences for red, green and blue values.

    (C) The image is stored as a group of line colors. Each line uses an 8-bit sequence to store the color mix of RGB values.

    (D) An image is converted to a bitmap file where every small location of the image is a bit that is 1 or 0. If the bit value is 1 then the bit is assigned an RGB pixel triple that stores it color values.

09. What are good reasons for storing an image in a **PNG** format?

    I.   It is the best format for storing high-resolution picture images with a large file size.

    II. It uses a lossless compression file format.

    III. It is ideal format for storing line drawings with a small file size.

    (A) I only

    (B) I and II only

    (C) II and III only

    (D) I, II and III

10. What are good reasons for storing an image in a **JPG** format?

    I.   It is the best format for storing high-resolution picture images with a large file size.
    II. It maintains high quality even after using lossy data compression.
    III. It is ideal format for storing line drawings with a small file size.

    (A) I only

    (B) I and II only

    (C) II and III only

    (D) I, II and III

11. What are good reasons for storing an image in a **MP4** format?

    I.   It is one of the most popular file sharing formats on the web.
    II. It maintains high quality even after using lossy data compression.
    III. It is compatible with many platforms, PC and Mac

    (A) I only

    (B) I and II only

    (C) II and III only

    (D) I, II and III

12. What are good reasons for storing an audio file in a **MP3** format?

    I.   It is one of the most popular sound file formats in use today.
    II. It uses lossy data compression, but keeps acceptable sound quality for most files.
    III. It can convert lossless audio files, like **FLAC** into **MP3** without quality loss.

    (A) I only

    (B) I and II only

    (C) II and III only

    (D) I, II and III

Chapter 15 Review
The Internet

The Internet is a very big deal. The Internet is also extremely complex. The biggest player in providing customers with Internet capabilities is CISCO. This San Francisco based company sold 75% of the routers in 2017. Routers are special computers that help direct traffic on the Internet and find other requested computers.

Over two decades ago CISCO started an Academy to train people to become certified networking administrators. The textbook for the very first course is more than 1200 pages and that is for a CCNA or *Cisco Certified Network Associate*, Cisco's first level of Networking expertise. Good students can achieve this first certification in two semesters and when I taught these courses about 60% of my students passed the certification exam on the first try.

The Internet is one of 7 Big Ideas, but it is meant as a modest glimpse into what is going on, so do not try to go out and become a certified network administrator after you finish the AP CSP course. Remember that this is survey course that is designed to give you a good overview of the different fields in computer science and how they how they impact society. Looking at the Internet in its historical development helps to comprehend what we have today.

THE EARLY SNEAKER NET

Early computers were not networked. Figure 15.1 shows four computers. None of the computers are connected to another computer. None of the computers can communicate with any other computer. Computer-4 is connected to a printer. Users of Computers 1-3 need to store any data files on a diskette and physically walk to the Computer-4 computer to make printed copies.

Figure 15.1

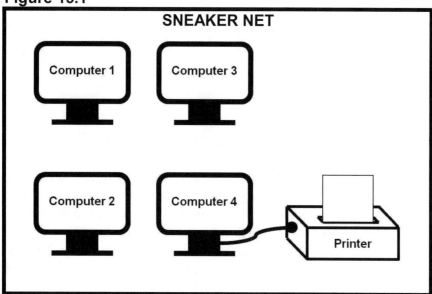

LOCAL AREA NETWORK (LAN)

The Internet, as we know it, is still in the future, but smart computer engineers are tired of running around to a printer computer with data files that need to be shared between members of the same department. You should not be required to run around with diskettes. A group of computers that share a common purpose are connected to a hub, shown in figure 15.2. Along with the computers the hub also has a printer attached. In this <u>Local</u> Area Network, communication is limited to those computers that are plugged into the same hub. The hub makes no judgment about where the traffic goes. Any information that arrives is shared with all connected devices.

Figure 15.2

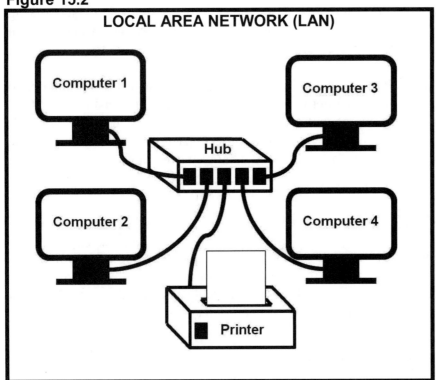

THE INTERNET

It is tempting, and a total over simplification, to call The Internet the sum total of all LANs that are interconnected. The Department of Defense must have outstanding communication with all its different units. Initially, this communication was in a hierarchical model, from top to bottom, as in from the Pentagon down to the smallest unit. This style of communication also means that Ft. Bragg in North Carolina could only communicate with Ft. Hood in Texas via the Pentagon. During the cold war it became clear that a well-aimed nuclear attack on the Pentagon would wipe out communication effectively throughout the entire armed forces of the United States. A new system was required that would keep the communication going, regardless of disruption anywhere in the Armed Forces grid.

Consider the imaginary small portion of the Internet shown in figure 15.3. Every letter represents a communication node on the Internet. It can be a town, an Army base, but whatever it is, it is a network center that passes data to other network centers. We are considering communication between Computer-1 and Computer-2. There exist many paths. A quick path is through nodes. **[F], [I]** and **[J].** Now imagine that the nodes that are gray are not functioning. There still is a path using nodes **[A], [M], [L]** and **[B].**

Figure 15.3

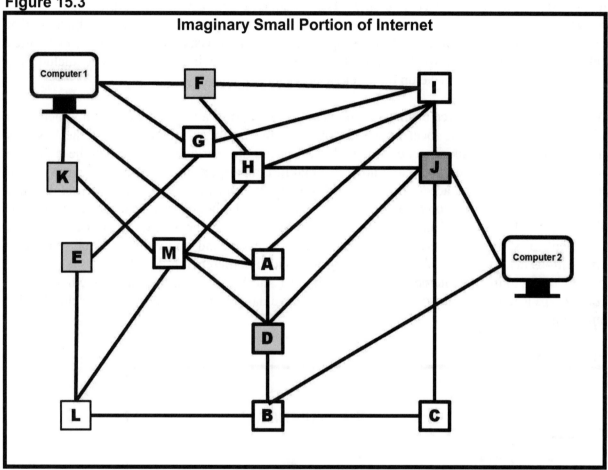

How does the communication manage to switch to a different path? What about the World Wide Web? Good questions; hang on that will be answered shortly. The World Wide Web or WWW needs to wait a little. It is not the same as The Internet and it was introduced at a later date using a then functional Internet.

INTERNET, INTRANET AND CLOUD

The Internet did not wake up one day and switch from a few Local Area Networks to a fully functional Internet. Businesses increased the sizes of their Local Area Networks. Multiple LANs in the same business became interconnected and became *Intranets*, which is like a really large LAN or a really small Internet. January 1, 1983 started the creation of a *network of networks* that became the Internet. Figure 15.4 illustrates a simple version of a modern Internet situation. At the top-left corner is a single person at home with one computer. The one computer is connected to an ISP or *Internet Service Provider*. The cloud is a popular way to draw where all the networks come together and are connected. Inside the Cloud you see a group of computers that manage large quantities of data and back up vital information. Using special data farms is often called *Cloud Computing*, which comes from the popular drawings of a cloud to include the connected networks that make up the Internet.

At the bottom you see three business computers that are part of a local network or Intranet when it becomes a network of local networks for the same business. Do notice that the business Intranet connects to a single node. This is the ISP or Internet Service Provider. On the right side is a traveling laptop that can be at a hotel in Frankfurt, an airport in Hong Kong or anywhere in the world where Internet access is provided. Cloud is not exactly a synonym for Internet. In early days all data files were stored locally and mostly within the boundaries of a business Intranet. To create high security data backup, accessible anywhere in the world, farms of computers designed to store data became available for businesses and individuals. Soon computer applications also were available online along with video conferencing, all of which was handled by devices within the Internet, accessible all over the world. This became known as *cloud computing*. It really seems you work online, you save data online as opposed to working locally and saving files locally.

Figure 15.4

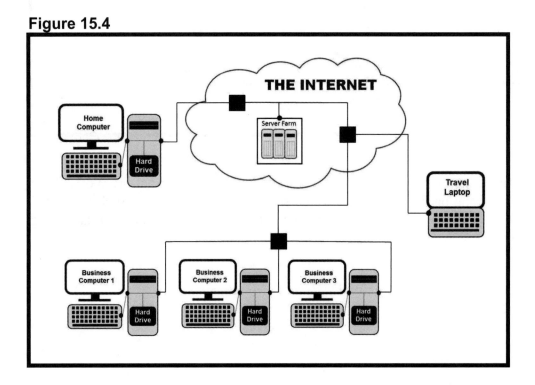

THE MAGIC ROUTER

It is challenging to do a quick network review in a few pages. Perhaps it seems easy enough to hook up more and more computers to a network and then create many networks of networks that grow and grow and grow. That is all great, but how does a data file get from Hong Kong to New York? This is a story of a very special computer, called a router.

Every computer connected to the Internet has an address. Long before the Internet became a reality, letters and packages were delivered around the world to the unique postal address of a recipient. Computers also have addresses and use an *Internet Protocol* address or *IP* address, something like 10.1.71.5.

Local computers and intranets have *gateway* servers, which have information for groups of computers attached to its responsibility. This is called a subnet. The router uses a combination of an IP address with a subnet mask, which identifies a subnet to find other computers.

The system is surprisingly simple. A router is connected to other routers. Each router has a table of subnets that it takes care of or at least knows about. Information comes its way looking for a specific IP address. Now there are two possibilities. If the router knows the address it will "route" (hence router) the data information to its destination. If not, the router sends information to all adjacent routers, the ones it is connected to, to see if any of those routers has knowledge of the requested IP address. This process continues until a message comes back that the location is found. There is a time limit and if too much time goes by the request times out.

ROUTERS AND PACKETS

Data files can be very large. This is cumbersome for networking traffic. Data is divided up into small *packets* of information. Individual packets travel along the Internet and at the destination router the packets are put back together. Packets do not necessarily all travel the same route as some paths may become unavailable or become very slow.

If you understand the concept that routers keep checking with other routers to find a path you should understand the genius of the Internet. Perhaps the fastest traffic from Dallas to Miami is via New Orleans. New Orleans is hit by a ferocious hurricane and all communication is down. Routers connected to New Orleans are now finding that traffic is no longer possible through New Orleans, but they get signals that Orlando can help get the packets to its final Miami destination. This means the Internet has no central command. This is route redundancy, which was the original intent of the Department of Defense.

Note: It is very possible that packets get lost or corrupted. If such is the case, the destination routers request a resending of the missing packets.

Recent growth of the Internet has created a newer system of IP addresses. The original IP address uses 4 groups of number from [1..255], and is running out of addresses. There now is an IPv6 system that uses 8 groups of 4-digit hexadecimal numbers to handle the increase in demand.

THE WORLD WIDE WEB (WWW)

This will come as a shock. There existed a time when you could not do a Google search to find the date of the Spanish Armada, 1588 in case you are curious. The early days of the Internet were not very colorful, but they were functional. Travel agents were able to make reservations online instead of looking up flight schedules in the OAG (Official Airline Guide) and special printers could print the tickets rather than hand writing each ticket. Email became popular and files could travel on the Internet using File Transfer Protocol (FTP).

In 1990, CERN, a European Organization for Nuclear Research, created the first web page. It started slowly, but grew very rapidly. First, you need to realize that there are website consumers and website providers. They have two totally different roles. When you look at a website you are seeing all the information and images that the website provider wants you to see.

The IP addresses from the Internet are still very much in play, but people are not interested in remembering numbers. They want to type in *www.aa.com* to access American Airlines or *www.johnpauliihs.org* to access John Paul II High School. You probably expect to find IBM at *www.IBM.com*. Today it is hard to have a website in your own name. You are a few decades late. I do have *www.schram.org*, but I reserved that name two decades ago.

Networking uses special computers called servers. Servers can be used for email. They can be used to identify proper users of a subnet in a business based on User ID and Password. They can be used for network printing or file sharing. With the arrival of the new World Wide Web a new server came into town called a *Domain Name Server (DNS)*.

If someone asks me how to get to my website, I could tell them to go to *64.251.200.135* and I would be very surprised if I could remember those numbers. In reality I would say that my web address is *www.schram.org*. Their next step is to go to their favorite web browser and type in the web address *www.schram.org*.

The Domain Name Servers behave in a manner that is similar to routers. When a packet arrives at a gateway server, the server seeks the IP address and tries to find a path to the final destination. If a domain name is involved, like www.ibm.com, the name is sent to the nearest domain name server. The domain name server is like a dictionary of domain names and a table of matching IP addresses. If an IP address is known, it is returned. If the DNS has no knowledge another DNS is found and this process continues until the IP address is returned.

In the old days before there were pretty windows and a mouse to navigate around the windows, computer users looked at a command prompt. Commands were entered on a black or green screen. There were no selections. You needed to know many *Disk Operating System* (DOS) commands. That DOS or command window, shown in figure 15.5, still exists today and allows access to some interesting computer tools.

Figure 15.5

```
[c:\] Command Prompt - tracert www.schram.org

Microsoft Windows [Version 10.0.16299.192]
(c) 2017 Microsoft Corporation. All rights reserved.

C:\Users\leonschram>tracert www.schram.org

Tracing route to www.schram.org [64.251.200.135]
over a maximum of 30 hops:
```

In the command prompt window of figure 15.5 the command **tracert www.schram.org** is typed. This command takes the domain name **schram.org** and looks up the IP address in a domain name server, which is **[64.251.200.135]**. You may have problems doing this at a high school computer lab. Security conscious computer techs at your school may have disabled the command prompt to prevent actions that could be harmful to the computer and/or school network. Many businesses do not like you to know their IP address and you may get some odd results there as well.

However, the point here is shown by figures 15.6 and figure 15.7. Both images show the top of the same website. Notice, at the top in the web address window, that the first image states **www.schram.org** and the second image shows **64.251.200.135**. Routers want IP addresses and you may use these nice domain names, but they get quickly translated to IP addresses by a *Domain Name Server* (DNS).

Figure 15.6

Figure 15.7

HTML AND THE WORLD WIDE WEB

Today you see pretty pictures on your computer and text in many colors and sizes. Everything you see is the result of web pages that were created behind the scene. Web page developers or anybody who understands something about web pages can create such pages.

You need to find a company that will store your web pages on The Internet. This will cost money. Do not have this illusion that use of the Internet is free. You may look at some web pages for free as you search the Web, but somebody is paying for your connection to the Internet and somebody else is paying to store the pages you are viewing.

For you to search and look at web pages requires a browser like Internet Explorer, Chrome or Safari, to name just a few. Creating a web page requires knowledge of a unique web page language called *Hyper Text Markup Language* (HTML). This is a language known to web browsers. The web browsers translate the HTML code into the web pages that are viewed by the general public. Figure 15.7 shows an example of a web page's HTML code, created by the provider.

HTML uses tags, which are placed between angle brackets, like **\<b\>Hello World\</b\>**. On a web page the text between the two B (for bold) tags will be displayed bold. Figure 15.8 shows what the web page users see on a web browser.

Figure 15.7

```
<html>
<head>
     <title>FormattingText01.html</title>
</head>


<body>
     <b>This statement will be Bold</b>
     <br><br>
     <i>This statement will be Italic</i>
     <br><br>
     <u>This statement will be Underlined</u>
     <br><br>
     <b><i><u>This statement shows all three features</u></i></b>
     <br><br>
     <i><u><b>This statement shows all three features again</b></u></i>
</body>
</html>
```

Figure 15.8

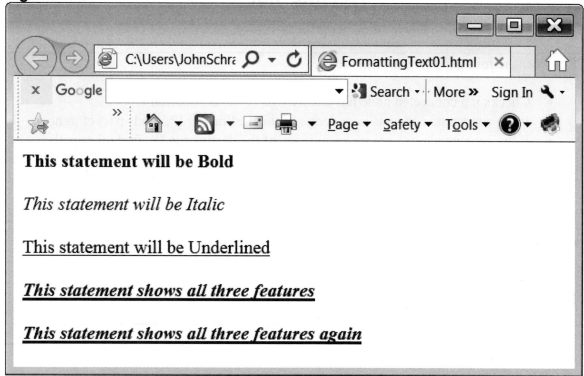

Many people find writing HTML code tedious and they use software, like Dreamweaver, to create web pages. The software is similar to using a word processor where you select font style and size and indicate bold, underline, etc. The software then creates the necessary HTML tags.

Using such software is convenient and it is certainly fast, but you do lose precise control over what happens to your web pages. If you have knowledge of HTML you have complete control and you can display anything you wish.

Web pages can be placed into two categories: static and dynamic. Static web pages are strictly for viewing. You look at information and at pictures. You can link from one web page to another web page.

Dynamic web pages are interactive. You can enter information. You can make online purchases. You can take online tests. You can reserve airline flights. You can pay your bills. HTML is not capable of handling this dynamic interaction. It requires a more sophisticated *scripting* program language that is embedded in the HTML. Remember HTML is the glue that holds the web pages together.

Chapter 15 Questions
The Internet

01. Consider the following Internet functions.

    - Checks if a connected node has knowledge of the destination IP.
    - If the connected node has knowledge of the destination IP, sends packet to node.
    - If the connected node has no knowledge of the destination IP, find other path.

    Which of the following is the Internet device that handles the above-mentioned actions?

    (A) Network interface card

    (B) Modem

    (C) Switch

    (D) Router

02. A routers transmits

    (A) data files on the Internet.

    (B) frames on the Internet.

    (C) packets on the Internet.

    (D) emails on a local intranet only.

03. If websites exist on the Internet at a specific IP addresses, like 229.150.17.45, How does some network request to a Domain Name, like *www.AAAPlumbing.com* manage to find the correct website on the Internet? Who or what handles the conversion from a name to a number?

    (A) Your local computer modem handles the conversions.

    (B) Your IPS (Internet Service Provider) converts all the names for its customers.

    (C) The gateway router, at the Internet entrance, converts the domain names.

    (D) A DNS (Domain Name System) server handles the conversions.

04. The Internet was designed to handle communication in such a way that if singular locations or entire regions are destroyed by natural disasters or war, the Internet can continue to communicate.

Which of the following are correct statements about Internet connectivity?

I.   The Internet is a large network of interconnected smaller networks. There is not one singular network that controls the communications for all the other networks.

II. Every device on the Internet has a unique IP (Internet Protocol) address.

III. Routers find paths between Internet devices and reroute traffic if any device or an entire large network on the Internet is no longer functional.

(A) I only

(B) I and II only

(C) II and III only

(D) I, II and III

---

05. A person at a home computer tries to browse several new locations on the Web. Initially, websites appear, like Google search and other commonly used websites, but there are difficulties reaching many other web sites?

What may explain this problem?

(A) The Internet is probably down. The reason you can see some websites is because your local computer's *cache memory* is storing frequently visited web sites.

(B) The Internet may be partially functional and some nodes are not available.

(C) This person may have a bad router that incorrectly tries to find connection and does not have an accurate table of its connections on the Internet.

(D) The local DNS server may be down and conversions from domain names to IP addresses are not possible for all requests.

06. The figure below represents two computers and a group of network nodes on the Internet. Each node has a router capable of passing files to another connected network node and also capable of finding an alternate route if a previous connection slows down or is no longer available.

The shaded network nodes, **Routers D, E, F, J** and **K**, are currently not capable of transmitting any packets to a connected network node.

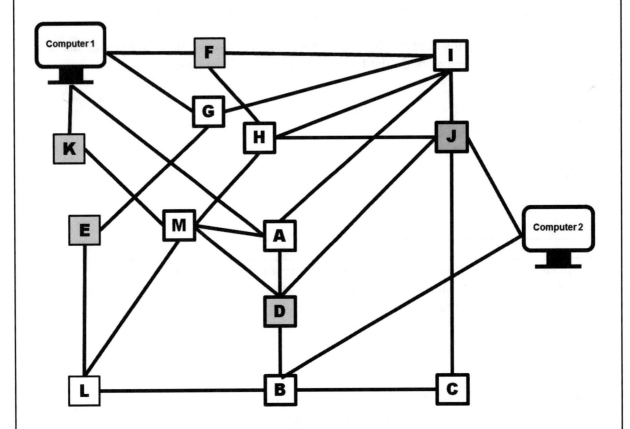

Considering the current status of this network, with five dysfunctional routers. What is the smallest number of routers necessary to connect **Computer 1** to **Computer 2**?

(A) 3 routers

(B) 4 routers

(C) 5 routers

(D) 6 routers

07. Look at the network of the previous question again. This time all the nodes are functional. Knowing that nodes can become dysfunctional, determine the minimum number of nodes that would prevent **Computer1** to communicate with **Computer2**?

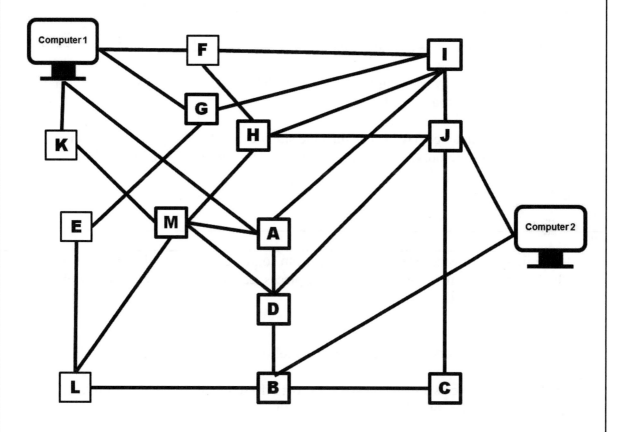

(A) 2 routers

(B) 3 routers

(C) 4 routers

(D) 5 routers

08. When two students sit close to each other they are surprised by the appearance of a website. Both students access the exact same webpage of the same web address, at the same time, and there are noticeable differences in appearance.

Which of the following might account for these differences?

(A) Different computers have different resolutions and window settings.

(B) The students may be using two different web browsers, which do not always handle web page information in the same way.

(C) On of the students may have visited the site previously. The pages visited may still be in his cache memory. It is possible that the web pages have been updated.

(D) All of the above

09. Large files are transmitted on the Internet from source computer to destination computer. The files are not sent whole, but in smaller pieces, called packets, by the router. What is true about the paths of the packets.

(A) The router selects a path and all packets follow that same path.

(B) The router selects a path and switches to a different path if the link is broken. The router may also switch to another path is the delay is too long.

(C) The router selects a path and then resends all the packets if the original path is broken before the transmission is complete.

(D) The router selects a path and then if the path is broken requests information from the destination when the link will be functional and then sends the remaining packet at that later time.

10. Which one of the following is a good analogy for the meaning of Internet bandwidth?

(A) The voltage required for an electric appliance

(B) The horse power of a car engine

(C) The number of lanes on a highway

(D) The number of pages in a book

11. You must decide between using a wireless connection or Ethernet cable to your home router. Which of the following is a reason to **<u>NOT</u>** select WIFI?

   (A) Multiple computers can have flexible locations.

   (B) Ethernet cable is more reliable than WIFI.

   (C) WIFI can have security issues.

   (D) Choices B and C

12. Which of the following provides the fastest Internet connection?

   (A) Wireless (radio frequency)

   (B) Wired cable (copper)

   (C) Personal messenger (bicycle)

   (D) Fiber optic cable (light)

Chapter 16 Review
Global Impact

The last chapter of the topical review and the last Big Idea, *Global Impact,* is really the essence of the AP Computer Science Principles course. You have probably already realized that many of the Big Ideas overlap and are not isolated. The previous Big Idea was The Internet. There are serious concerns about security and privacy related to using the Internet. Security and privacy are also major issues with this Big Idea of Global Impact. Right now, we are speaking specifically of the Global Impact of Computing. It is difficult to think of any computing innovation that has not had any global impact.

You may already have completed your *Explore Performance Task*. That performance task revolved around Global Impact. In a nutshell: Create a computational artifact that demonstrates the beneficial and harmful effects of a computing innovation. This project hardly is concerned with *at your home, in your neighborhood,* or *at your school.* Sure there is impact at all those places, but the real concern is global impact.

COMMUNICATION

Today's teenagers may wonder how long distance communication was possible away from homes or businesses. Telephones have been around for a long time now. Figure 16.1 shows Alexander Bell making the first long-distance phone call in 1892.

Figure 16.1

Bell on the telephone in New York (calling Chicago) in 1892

CREDIT: "Alexander Graham Bell at the opening of the long-distance line from New York to Chicago." 1892. Prints and Photographs Division, Library of Congress. Reproduction Number LC-G9-Z2-28608-B.

There is an irony in the proliferation of today's cell phones. They have managed to create their very own need. This sounds weird, but a young person may look around and think that a cell phone is now vital for emergencies. What if the car breaks down? How do you communicate?

They do not see what existed in the past. Every gas station, every drug store, every shopping area and at intervals on major highways, there were public telephones. Kids were reminded by their parents to always have the necessary dimes to make phone calls. Those public telephones disappeared when they were no longer necessary. Today many people have even stopped using a "landline" telephone at home.

The cellphone is one computing innovation that has rapidly spread around the world. Throughout the AP Computer Science Principles course it is stressed that computing innovations have both beneficial effects and harmful effects. Perhaps those people who are in love with their cell phone cannot think of any harmful effects. Let's check it out.

Cell Phone Beneficial Effects

- Communication is possible anywhere (if within cell tower reach)
- Cell goes beyond "old phone" communication. Texting, email, searching, GPS navigation are all now possible with mobile phone.
- Organize your life with calendars, wake-up call, reminders.
- Entertainment. Goodness yes there can be 30 seconds periods in your life that you are bored and the cell phone lets you play games.

Cell Phone Harmful Effects

- Cell phone use and driving should be at the top of the list. Many cities and now states forbid the use of cell phones, unless untouched and used with Bluetooth only.
- Job productivity loss. It is very common to see store employees busy with their cell phones while ignoring customers.
- Loss of humanity and civility.

The last item is a major concern to me. It should be a serious concern to everybody. I have been a computer science teacher for more than 30 years. I love computer science and most everything that it has done to enhance our lives. But I worry. A commercial comes to mind. It is a disturbing commercial to me. An anxious young man is about to propose to his girlfriend. He pulls the box out of his pocket and opens it. A gorgeous diamond ring appears. He looks at his girlfriend. She looks at her cell phone. She is oblivious to her surroundings. The boyfriend is getting impatient. She simply does not see what is happening. He takes out his cellphone and texts her to look up. She looks up as she sees the young man walk away with his engagement ring.

Yes, this is disturbing. Another example from my own personal life follows. At my school we have an annual grandparent breakfast. Several years ago I walked in the breakfast room and could not believe my eyes. I saw hundreds of students and hundreds of grandparents. Then I saw that every single student had a cellphone - face up - next to the plate. I know students. I care for teenagers deeply. That is why I am a high school teacher. The disturbing part to me was not that teenagers had their cell phone out. What disturbed me was that the presence of the cell phone had become so important and so normal that probably none of the teenagers realized the silent message, which said: "Grandma, grandpa, you do understand that you are second banana at this table. My cell phone comes first." I talked to my students. Nobody wanted to offend their grandparents. That was not their intention, but it happened nevertheless.

Email may not seem like a big deal and most young people prefer texting over emails. Lots of people are impatient. Imagine? Some have to wait a couple of minutes to get a text response. How do you handle such time delay? Old sailing boats took one year to travel from New York to San Francisco. Then the clipper ships arrived in 1850 and managed to do the voyage in 3 months. Translation: You mail a letter in 1850 and the quickest response was 6 months later. We have come a long way with computing technology.

Communication does not stop there. We have video conferencing today. Dozens of people at multiple locations around the globe watch large projections and conference with colleagues anywhere in the world. The projection can zoom in on the current speaker and notes presented by the speaker can go in a special window on the projection. This saves tremendous time and money and in the case of weather issues, collaboration is possible that otherwise would not exist.

IS THERE EQUITY GLOBALLY?

Access to technology in all its forms is not equally distributed around the world. This is an important concern. Modern businesses rely on the communication capabilities of modern technology. Advancements in all areas of science rely on communication, collaboration and distribution of the latest advances. Education is more and more dependent on access to resources that are available on the Internet. It is easy to say that once again the poorer areas of the world are lagging behind. Perhaps yes, but there are some very nice areas where technology has emerged where there was nothing before.

Many areas in the world have been too poor, too underdeveloped, too far from major cities to have the kind of infrastructure of communication that is normal to much of the world. There are many villages where there is absolutely no telephone communication. But curiously enough, it is far cheaper and far easier to establish cell phone communication than land line communication. This is now becoming reality in many remote, underdeveloped areas.

With the satellite technology rural villages now have access to both the Internet and television that was not possible before. At the same time, schools in poor areas that cannot afford expensive printed books, or even the expense of shipping for donated books, can download eBooks from educational sites for their students.

In the area of medicine, Internet communication and video conferencing have enabled rural areas without doctors to communicate about treatment for patients with local nurses.

It is exciting to see what technology can do for poor areas, but we must not get comfortable and consider the problem solved. Realize that the same technology that may help rural uneducated people can also cause problems with jobs. One example I noticed on a documentary was about the *last iron expert* in the village. It showed the story of a man who had followed the profession of his ancestors for ages. He finds iron ore in the nearby mountain areas. He heats the ore in a special, primitive oven that separates the iron from other substances. He then proceeds to make tools, utensils and other iron needs for the village. Today villagers can purchase such items cheaper from traveling merchants. This is a story that easily can precede the modern technology world, but as technology grows, and more and more jobs are performed by computers and robots, there is still a need for many to work. But these new workers must design, create, sell, maintain and enhance the robots and computing innovations of today and the future. This requires a shift in education that is not present in many parts of the world.

SOCIAL MEDIA

As a grandparent I absolutely love Facebook. On a daily or weekly basis I see posts of my family. My daughter posts short videos of our two grandsons getting base hits with their baseball team. Other family members show nice pictures of travels, outings, fun events and accomplishments. We see pictures of the future spouse of one of my children before we even meet her personally. At the same time as my sweet wife and I travel in the summer, our family and friends get daily updates. They know we are all right and there is a daily picture with information of the current location where we travel.

That is Facebook at its best. I have seen it quite bad, especially during the 2016 election year. Complete strangers called me a moron and thing far worse, simply because I disagreed with their opinion. I rapidly removed many "friends" that I acquired before I understood Facebook and just stayed away from politics on social media.

Something must be understood about communication. In face-to-face communication you see the person. You see the body language. You see the facial expressions. You see the reactions to your statements. You hear the words that are spoken. You hear the tone of those words. Much of that communication is not present with social media.

If you make a joke or statement in person, you notice ... OOPS somebody is visibly upset by your statements. You can clarify. You can say it was meant at a joke. You can say it was not meant to offend. You can do something. Sadly on social media you can make a post and suddenly you are bombarded by many people you don't even know for your lack of sensitivity. Sometimes it can be an honest mistake. You can leave out a critical word in a post. There is quite a difference in saying *I am in agreement with the 1st amendment* or *I am not in agreement with the 1st amendment.*

Politicians or anybody who feels strongly about somebody else can communicate in such a manner that the person looks good or bad. In politics this is called *spin*. This makes the event seem to be in a manner that is most advantageous to a person or an organization. This spin stuff has existed for centuries, but now with computing technology and social media the "information" can spread in minutes to amazing proportions.

The problem with spin is that people, a post, an email, a text can be 100% correct, but by omitting certain parts of the complete story, the truth of what actually happened can be completely distorted. Here is an example that happened to me way back in 1980 when I was teaching Advanced Life Saving at a summer camp to a group of teenage girls. A week after the summer camp there were rumors circulating that *Leon Schram had told a group of teenage girls to take of their clothes.* And yes I did say that, but here is the complete story of what I said.

> *Ladies this morning's lesson is the saving of a drowning victim who is underwater at the bottom of a pool, lake or river. You saw the person go down. You are not a lifeguard sitting at a pool in a bathing suit. You are a person wearing jeans, a sweatshirt and shoes, which you are wearing now on top of your bathing suit. If you jump in and swim with jeans,*

sweatshirt and shoes, you may become so exhausted dragging your clothes, shoes and victim that you both may drown. It is vital that you remove the heavy outer clothes and shoes before you jump in and try to save the person. When I blow the whistle, you have 20 seconds and then Ladies remove your clothes and shoes and jump in the water to bring your victim to safety.

This story I just told you spread rapidly and almost made it to the front page of the local newspaper. People who had zero knowledge of the event spread the information to other people. It spread slowly and the damage could be prevented before it became printed news.

That is not the case with social media. In the past a person reached a few people in person or by telephone. Now a quick post can be made and then it spreads rapidly. Imagine now that a politician does this and then uses technology in such a manner that a brief audio clip is created. Nothing is altered. Nothing is changed. The clip is an accurate, authentic piece of Leon Schram communication. However, the audio clip only states *"Ladies remove your clothes"*.

My point is this. In this world of technology you have a responsibility. Do not start a post unless it is known to be accurate and accurate in its description, not just a few incrimination words. If you see a post, do not blindly share the post. Sometimes, a bold heading on a post with a compelling picture gets your sympathy and you do not read the text below the picture. You can be surprised what you have just shared along with your like.

NAVIGATION WITH GPS

I have an excellent sense of direction and I am a good map reader. Anywhere on the world I can find my way. Long after Global Positioning Satellite (GPS) came on the scene I continued doing it my way. Now I am pretty much required to use GPS. Like the earlier pay phones that disappeared with the arrival of cell phones, maps are tough to find now that there is GPS. Big city maps are still available, but I used to drive into a small city and could get a local city map at any gas station. That is past tense.

I must admit that I really do like the modern GPS now. My eyes are not that great anymore and especially after dark it is difficult for me to read the street signs. Map reading is good, but you need to be able to read *Orleans Court* on the sign to know to turn there.

GPS is also an area where more rural areas and low-Income areas have benefitted. Creating multiple street signs at regular intervals and all over the place is extremely expensive. Local people may know the way, but traveling merchants and visitors surely benefit from the handy application of GPS on a cell phone or car navigation system.

SMART COMMERCIALS AND COOKIES

There are many pop-up windows that people dislike around the globe in any language. An unfortunate side effect of the Internet is a bombardment of many commercials. Yes, the Internet is not free. Facebook is not free. You may be under the illusion that it is free, but how do you suppose all the CEOs of companies like Facebook and Google manage to become billionaires. It is not from charity donations. They sell commercials and they sell huge amounts of them. Now many commercials are not wanted and many are annoying, but the commercials are getting smarter as businesses use more and more computing innovations to target the right audience with the right message.

For instance, I enjoy reading. I do this on my Kindle. It is great for my "reading glasses" eyes who like things bright. I can make the text large and I have a bright background for easy reading. Trust me my young readers, bright and large text is nicer with older eyes. This is yet another computer innovation, and big beneficial effect, for older people.

One of my favorite authors is Ken Follett. I have purchased every one of his books and mostly online to read on my Kindle. The last four books, written by Ken Follett, I purchased per Amazon's suggestion. Amazon sends me a pop up window, and trust me I never get a pop-up window with the latest music hit of any kind. Amazon knows that I have never bought or downloaded any music online. They do know that there are roughly five authors that I like and I buy all their books.

This means that I get two kinds of popups from Amazon. First, new releases of any of the authors whose books I may wish to purchase. Two, suggestions of books written by other authors that write a similar genre to the kind of books I like. Truth be told, I like this kind of *smart advertising*. It also gets results as I have purchased over 300 books from Amazon in the last 10 years. Since I have an account with Amazon, they can see my purchases and draw conclusions. This information is used for smart advertising to send me the correct commercial. Note I said they have an account and they know who I am and what I like. There is also smart advertising that happens when you have no account at all. It is done with *cookies*.

Cookies are a pretty neat computational innovation. A cookie is a small data file and this file is placed somewhere in your computer memory or on your computer's hard drive. You do not place the cookies; Businesses do this for you. Cookies do many things and this includes security.

For instance, the banks with which I do business are very security conscious. They want to know that the computer that is using a Chase account is an actual customer and not a fraud trying to steal their customer's identity. They do this with computer recognition. Suppose I use a new computer for the first time and I try to access my Chase account. Chase responds my saying that they do not recognize my computer and will send an authentication code to my email address or cell number that is on file with my account. The assumption is that only the actual customer will get this code. Half a minute later the code arrives. I enter the code and I enter the password and I am in. The bank will not ask this again, because a cookie is created with my unique Media Access Control (MAC) computer address that is saved on my computer with a cookie.

Keep in mind that I did enable cookies on my computer. The next time I access Chase, they look in my computer for Chase cookies and find that data stored matches a verified Chase customer. That is how Chase and many other banks use cookies, but cookies also determine pop-up windows. You may visit various companies and even make purchases online. For reasons that are not important you do not have a personal account with some company. You are basically an anonymous browser looking at products. You have looked at a Dillard's website and browsed information about lady winter jackets. Dillard's cannot store this information in their own database. They have no name and no address. Remember you are anonymous. They can create a "winter jacket" cookie and save it on your computer inside their own little Dillard's folder and recognize the information the next time you visit their website.

So should you enable cookies? Is it a nuisance? You decide. Personally, I like cookies. I log on to American Airlines and they know that DFW is my home airport. They know my seating preferences. Hertz's also knows that I like to rent medium size cars, but I do not want any of the extra insurance or GPS. I park my car with Park 'N Fly and they automatically go the DFW, which is where I park the car. In other words I save time with cookies. I do get good cookie commercials and I get some "who cares" commercials. Once again, you decide.

It is easy to ramble on and on about Global Impact, but it is tough to come to a close. This review will close with security. Security fits with the Internet. It fits with Data and Information and it also fits with Global Impact. I selected the last and I am finishing with security.

You have already read a few personal accounts in this chapter. Allow me one more story for the last chapter of the topical reviews. This is a story, in figure 16.2, from the early Seventies. Computers did exist, but not at the personal computer level. The Internet is still a decade away and the World Wide Web is even further in the future. I live in Garrett Park, Maryland.

Figure 16.2

The phone rings. I pick up. A man, who identifies himself as the manager of the Silver Spring Holiday Inn ask if I am Leon Schram. "Yes, I am," I respond. "Mr. Schram," the manager continues, "we have a situation here. There is a customer at our desk who gave us your number. The man has arrived in town to start a job at Holy Cross Church in Garrett Park. He has lost his wallet and called Father Bazan at the church and explained his problem. Father Bazan told him your name and gave your number. Do you know Father Bazan?" I am quite perplexed, where is this going? "What is my involvement," I ask. The manager continues. "I require a credit card for hotel registration. Father Bazan explained that the church does not allow priests to have credit cards. He suggested that you are a well known member of the church, and Scoutmaster, and would be able to assist. He also said that Father Bazan would cover all expenses in a couple of days." Everything seemed reasonable. I provided my credit card and the man was registered without any complications.

The following day I call Father Bazan. Father Bazan knows nothing; at least nothing about this man's situation or story. I drive to the Hotel. The man is enjoying a very lavish room-service breakfast, on my credit card I might add. I tell the manager he is not legit. The manager understands. He also explains that I gave my credit card number and consent for the man's expenses. He shows me the church bulletin he found in the hotel room. I had been hoodwinked by the "Church Bulletin Scam." Scam artists visit churches and pick up bulletins. The bulletins show names of the priests as well as active church members, such as ushers and scoutmasters.

The story you just read was a modest financial setback for me. In today's money it costs me around $400.00. It is a kind of scam that exists today and it is known as *Social Engineering*. Social engineering does not involve any kind of technology. A clever situation is presented that sounds plausible and it heavily presented with names and events that are known to the victim of the scam artist. I did not think for a minute that somebody tried to take advantage of me.

SECURITY

Social engineering needs to be heavily considered, because it is often combined with technical sophistication. The technology is used to obtain the information for a plausible story. In this section various techniques will be explained. The field of security is very large and today's students can major, and totally specialize in cyber security. Figure 16.3 is a Google definition of the very important and growing field of *Cyber Security*.

Figure 16.3

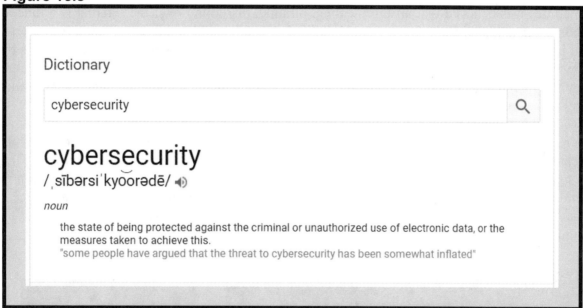

So let us talk about security issues, which are as old as mankind. There have always been people, organizations and governments who find it perfectly acceptable to take from others what is not theirs. Long ago homes and buildings acquired locks. Trunks, boxes and safes appeared with padlocks. People made efforts to hold on to their own property.

In our modern world the attitude of certain people has not changed. You have property; they want that property and many tricks are employed to change ownership of desirable property. In our modern days there is little profit to steal a purse or a wallet. Holding up store clerks is equally void of profits as most organizations employ a system where cash is constantly removed from registers and placed in vaults that cannot be accessed by employees.

Back in the sixties I was a young teenager and my first American job was working for a convenience store, called High's. Such stores with late hours are vulnerable to quick hold-ups. Every High's store back then used a simple system. Whenever there was $200 in the cash register, the cash was counted, bundled, placed in a paper sack and taped closed. The employee's name, date and time was recorded on the money packet and then it went into the safe. The safe had a one-way deposit opening, like a mailbox. Nobody in the store, including the manager had a key to open the safe. Every day people from a security company entered the store, opened the safe and retrieved the deposits.

There are still occasions of cash that is stolen from people, stores and there may be some bank holdups, but that is not where the real money is stolen by today's criminals. We have computers today. Computers let you word-process essays quicker. They let you create and alter financial balance sheets efficiently. Computers make reservations worldwide for travel and computers let you access any and all information you may be curious about. Sadly computers also allow the efficient stealing of money, property and this includes intellectual property.

Sometimes it is believed that all this stealing, pirating, disrupting over the Internet is a function of computer nerds with unique computer skills that can hack into any computer anywhere and steal information at will as well as transfer money as they see fit. It is not all computer skills that allow this criminal activity to take place. There exist many schemes that are not high-tech at all. They take advantage of computer users who do not recognize the tell-tale signs of fraudulent email and attempts to steal identity, such as the *Church Bulletin* scam explained earlier.

The real culprit in security is identity theft. This creates a problem that is not easily solved with a quick call to the bank. Billions of dollars are stolen each year with fraudulent tax returns. These are tax returns created by people who have stolen someone's identity. This problem is so common and so severe that the IRS has a special branch dealing with this problem. The image, in figure 16.4, taken from a government website, tries to educate people about identity theft and fraudulent tax returns.

Figure 16.4

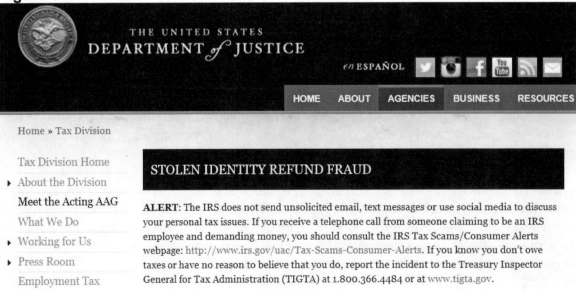

PHISHING, A VERY COMMON ATTEMPT TO GET YOUR IDENTITY

This review book has at its primary purpose a large set of questions that students can use to practice for the End-Of-Course AP CSP Exam. A secondary purpose is to make teachers and students aware of the scope of topics within this course. It is quite immense and a close look at the Course Description shows how many topics are actually included. This review hopes to also motivate students to go out and learn more about the many topics. It is precisely because of modern computing innovations, especially the World Wide Web with search engines, that acquiring information is easier than ever. Cyber security is a fascinating field and there is so much to investigate; so much to learn. For now I want to finish with the topic of phishing, because as an individual you will probably encounter this personally. Start with the figure 16.5 which provides Google's phishing definition.

Phishing is an attempt to acquire your personal information by using emails that appear to be originated with actual business companies and especially companies that you use. Most phishing emails will work hard on using the brand of the company by using appropriate logos, font style and color schemes that people recognize as used by their company.

Figure 16.5

I want you to do an exercise now and look at the first four *Phishing* emails. Every email you look at is an actual email. The first four emails are fraudulent and attempt to get identity information. Your mission is to look at these four emails and identify red flags that indicate that the emails are not legitimate companies. The emails do include the names of the actual people that were addressed, which adds to the legitimate look and feel of the email.

After Phishing04 stop and discuss with your group class or perhaps yourself and make conclusions. There are red flags that should alert you to not respond. Do you see them? They are plural. Write this down and check later in the chapter with the answers.

Phishing01

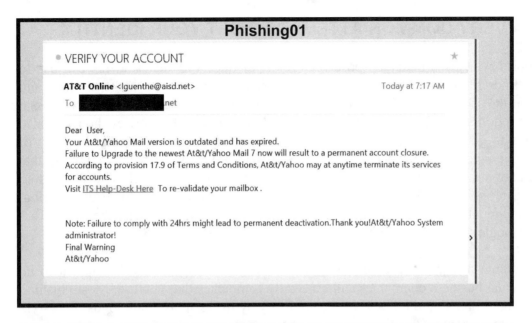

• VERIFY YOUR ACCOUNT ★

AT&T Online <lguenthe@aisd.net>   Today at 7:17 AM

To ███████████.net

Dear User,
Your At&t/Yahoo Mail version is outdated and has expired.
Failure to Upgrade to the newest At&t/Yahoo Mail 7 now will result to a permanent account closure.
According to provision 17.9 of Terms and Conditions, At&t/Yahoo may at anytime terminate its services for accounts.
Visit ITS Help-Desk Here To re-validate your mailbox .

Note: Failure to comply with 24hrs might lead to permanent deactivation.Thank you!At&t/Yahoo System administrator!
Final Warning
At&t/Yahoo

Phishing02

• Chase Online Deposit Statement

Chase <wyatt.mitchell@ttu.edu>

To ███████████ .net

CHASE ◊

Confirm ($USD) $340.00 deposit Transaction

Your online account has been suspended (Reason: the violation of terms of service).

Update and Restore your online account Now

Log On

Thank you for using Chase Bank .

Phishing03

• Chase Online Banking Benefit Log-On ★

Chase Bank Inc. <ibrim18@wooster.edu>   Today at 6:04 PM

To ███████ .net

CHASE ◊

Dear ███████████.net

This message confirms deposit of $3,850 has been made to your account as compensation and has been received on 09/03/2017 click below to claim and receive it in your account in 24hrs

Log On

Thanks for choosing Chase Bank
Please do not reply to this email directly. To ensure a prompt and secure response, sign on to email us.
© 2017 Chase Bank Plc.

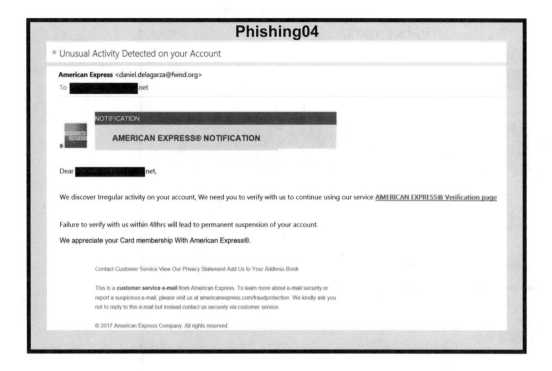

Phishing04

• Unusual Activity Detected on your Account

American Express <daniel.delagarza@fwisd.org>

To ███████████.net

NOTIFICATION

AMERICAN EXPRESS® NOTIFICATION

Dear ████████.net,

We discover Irregular activity on your account, We need you to verify with us to continue using our service AMERICAN EXPRESS® Verification page

Failure to verify with us within 48hrs will lead to permanent suspension of your account.

We appreciate your Card membership With American Express®.

Contact Customer Service View Our Privacy Statement Add Us to Your Address Book

This is a **customer service e-mail** from American Express. To learn more about e-mail security or report a suspicious e-mail, please visit us at americanexpress.com/fraudprotection. We kindly ask you not to reply to this e-mail but instead contact us securely via customer service.

© 2017 American Express Company. All rights reserved.

Before you are told what the red flags were, continue with the next four examples. Remember that these - all eight of them - are actual email communications that were used both in a complete legitimate manner or and they were completely bogus. Once you have your own bank accounts and credit card accounts you can expect to get phishing emails. Be alert!! The answers will be at the very end of the chapter.

There are red flags, such as the ones that existed in the previous four phishing images. There are also green flags that help you to identify legitimate emails from your online business communications. Look at the next four images, Phishing05 - Phishing08 and see if you can identify two common traits that are solid indicators of legitimate communication.

Phishing05

Citi® / AAdvantage® Card <Citicards@info6.citi.com>   Today

To ████████

Summary of your recent Citi Online session.

🔒 CONFIRMATION

citi | **AAdvantage** American Airlines

Cardmember since 2012
Account ending in 7239

Phishing06

Citi® / AAdvantage® Card <Citicards@info6.citi.com> Today

To ████████████

Summary of your recent Citi Online session.

⊘ CONFIRMATION

Citi | American Airlines **AAdvantage** ✈

Cardmember since 2012
Account ending in 7239

Phishing07

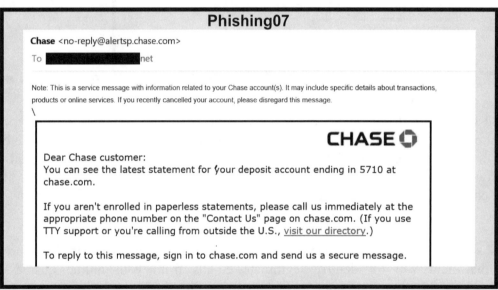

Chase <no-reply@alertsp.chase.com>

To ████████████ net

Note: This is a service message with information related to your Chase account(s). It may include specific details about transactions, products or online services. If you recently cancelled your account, please disregard this message.

\

CHASE ⬡

Dear Chase customer:
You can see the latest statement for ýour deposit account ending in 5710 at chase.com.

If you aren't enrolled in paperless statements, please call us immediately at the appropriate phone number on the "Contact Us" page on chase.com. (If you use TTY support or you're calling from outside the U.S., visit our directory.)

To reply to this message, sign in to chase.com and send us a secure message.

Phishing08

• Your American Express Forgotten User ID

American Express <AmericanExpress@welcome.aexp.com>

To ████████████ .net

Confirmation

Verify Your Request

Your Account Number Ending: -93000

Dear ████████

Did you recently verify your User ID or reset the password that you use to manage your American Express® Card account online?

Chapter 16 Questions
Global Impact

---

01. What is true about computing innovations?

(A) They have a beneficial impact on human life.

(B) They have a harmful impact on human life.

(C) They have both a beneficial and harmful impact on human life.

(D) They have little or no impact on human life.

---

02. What concerns have arisen with the proliferation of technical information such as browsing history, cookies, geolocation and survey request?

(A) They raise concerns about security.

(B) They raise concerns about privacy.

(C) They raise concerns about insufficient bandwidth on Internet connections.

(D) Both choices (A) and (B)

---

03. What are some of the harmful effects of social media?

(A) Reduction of personal, human interaction

(B) Cyber bullying

(C) Job productivity loss

(D) All of the above

---

04. What are some of the beneficial effects of social media?

(A) Updates about family events and accomplishments

(B) Efficient global communication family and friends while traveling

(C) Promote new or existing business ventures

(D) All of the above

---

05. What does Moore's law, from 1965, say about the chip technology?

(A) Moore predicted that computing would increase in power and simultaneously decrease in relative cost at a linear pace.

(B) Moore predicted that computing would increase in power and simultaneously decrease in relative cost at an exponential pace.

(C) Moore predicted that in 2030 a $1000 computer would exceed the computing power of the human brain.

(D) Moore predicted that by 2020 by the chip in a watch-sized computer would out perform the super computers of 2000.

06. Pope Francis had a meeting with Apple's CEO Tim Cook in 2016. Later Tim talked at the MIT graduation of 2017 and talked about his meeting with Pope Francis and a concern that they both shared.

What was the concern about the future of technology that Tim Cook told MIT students?

(A) Tim Cook said: *On the subject of artificial intelligence we are not as concerned that computers will become more like human beings, but that human beings will become more like computers.*

(B) Tim Cook said: *On the subject of artificial intelligence we are concerned that human beings will make significant decisions based more on the information provided by computers than by human beings.*

(C) Tim Cook said: *On the subject of artificial intelligence we are concerned that human beings will lose their ability to think and to create more and more as they rely on computers to provide them with answers.*

(D) Tim Cook said: *On the subject of artificial intelligence we are concerned that human being will lose the fundamental skill of problem solving as every aspect of life involves the assistance of a computer.*

07. Reliance on computers, tablets and cell phones have reached concerns about how people can function if such devices are forgotten, lost, stolen or do not work. Consider such tasks as navigation with a GPS or calling for help in a medical emergency. Why is this a problem? What is the biggest reason why people cannot do things the "old way" when cell phones and/or GPS is not available?

(A) People are not as good with map reading or using a public telephone.

(B) People do not know phone number, because they are stored in the phone system.

(C) Public phones have pretty much disappeared from highways, gas stations and stores. Maps are less and less available at gas stations and convenience stores.

(D) It is not really a problem. Today, you can wait until somebody stop and lets you use their cell phone.

08. Computers are a great help to people. In which of the following areas are computers better today than human beings?

I. Computer and perform calculations faster and more accurately than people.

II. Computers can store and retrieve information better than people.

III. Computers are more creative than people.

IV. Computers are better problem solvers than people. (Note: problem solving and problem recognition are not the same)

(A) I and II only

(B) III and IV only

(C) I, II and III

(D) I, II, III and IV

09. Collaborating with team members of a project is very productive. Today's large multi-nation corporations are spread globally. Which of the following computing innovations has helped collaboration significantly?

(A) Cloud computing

(B) Multiple local meetings with management

(C) Video conferencing

(D) Both choices (A) and (C)

10. Pirating software and other intellectual property rights are challenging issues with a technological world. Which of the following are techniques that companies use to prevent software pirating?

    I.   Sell software and software activation keys separately.

    II. Require online software verification, before software is activated.

    III. Sell cloud-based software applications that require "rental" fees for usage.

    (A) I only

    (B) I & III only

    (C) II & III only

    (D) I, II & III

11. How does modern technology benefit underdeveloped third-world countries?

    (A) Cell phones can be used in areas that have no land line telephone capabilities.
    (B) Access to educational materials, such as books, online encyclopedias and many other resources are far cheaper to deliver using the Internet than printed materials.
    (C) Nurses at remote areas can communicate with doctors about treatment by sending test results and health information to medical centers.
    (D) All of the above

12. Plagiarism is far easier with today's technology search tools. What has been done to catch acts of plagiarism?

    (A) Students projects are stored in a national database and compared to each other.

    (B) Students projects are compared to existing publications of the same topic.

    (C) Student projects are entered in software that searching for similar phrases.

    (D) Student projects are compared to sample of previous student writing.

Chapter 16 Security Phishing Answers

Phishing Fraud Red Flags

- Suspicious email addresses. Legitimate companies use email addresses that include the name of the company. This is especially true after the @ character.

- Legitimate companies always include the last 4 or 5 digits of your account number in any communication. Seeing these numbers is a green flag. If the numbers are not present, watch out.

- Email links that are present on the email. The email link normally links you to a site where you must log in. This is never done by a legitimate company. They will tell you to contact the company by phone or by login, but not provide a link to assist.

Phishing Legitimate Green Flags

- Email address. Legitimate companies use email addresses that include the name of the company. This is especially true after the @ character, such as @chase.com.

- Account number. Legitimate companies include the last four or five digits of your account number.

Look at this image. You see an American Express logo and you see the image of an actual credit card with the Centurion image. Anybody can copy that. Look for the email address and your account number. That tells the legitimate story.

Chapter 17 Review
Explore Performance Task

This chapter will be very different from the other chapters. This is not a chapter that explains computer numbers systems, some topic in a pseudo-code language or a discussion about data management and data representation. This chapter helps to clarify what is required to satisfy the free-response part of the AP CSP Examination.

The first AP Computer Science course started in 1983. It had the typical AP Exam division of Multiple-Choice questions and Free-Response questions. Free-Response was back then, and still is today, a test of the student's ability to hand-write program code to solve a provided problem.

The new AP Computer Science Principles course uses a very different Free-Response approach that very much uses computer technology. Students create computer science projects, called *computational artifacts* that are uploaded into a College Board dropbox for grading. It is a system somewhat similar to the one used in an AP Studio Art course where students upload a portfolio of the art they have created.

The nature of these performance tasks is that students need to use technology to be creative, but technological skills alone are not sufficient. There are very precise requirements and deadlines that must be followed.

AP COMPUTER SCIENCE PRINCIPLES ALERT!

At the start of the first performance task a student does not truly realize the amount of work that needs to be completed and the time that is required to do everything. This is quite common.

Procrastination is bad news with this assignment. The last couple of days of uploading projects to the College Board Digital Portfolio in 2017 was very slow due to extremely high volume. And the upload site actual crashed for two hours due to the high volume.

Due to high submission volumes, the Digital Portfolio was unavailable for two hours on Friday, April 28th.

Do your performance tasks early. Stay on task. Do not procrastinate.

College Board Resources for Performance Tasks

The College Board has placed a lot of information about the requirements and the logistics of the new AP CSP course on their website. This chapter does not so much explain how to complete the Explore Performance Task, as it guides you to the many resources that are available from The College Board. It takes quite some time to appreciate the totality of the AP Computer Science Principles Course. A tremendous effort, research and many pilot years went into creating this course. Grasping the intent, the content, the scope, the flexibility and the scoring of the new course is far more complex than it was for its cousin, the AP Computer Science (A) course.

The College Board and the AP Test Development Committee certainly realized this complexity and have made many resources available in the form of PDF documents, webinar videos and sample student artifacts with commentary based on the latest scoring format. Figure 17.1 and figure 17.2 show the sources for the AP CSP course available on the AP Central website. The file name shown is the College Board file name and a sequence number I added in front. These files were the most up-to-date files available at the download date, which is mostly **1/15/2018.**

Figure 17.1

Name	Date modified
01-ap-computer-science-principles-course-and-exam-description.pdf	10/19/2017 7:44 AM
02-computer-science-principles-digital-portfolio-teacher-guide.pdf	1/15/2018 3:14 PM
03-computer-science-principles-digital-portfolio-student-guide.pdf	1/15/2018 3:13 PM
04-ap-csp-student-task-directions.pdf	1/15/2018 3:10 PM
05-Explore Template.dotx	1/15/2018 3:12 PM
06-Create Template.dotx	1/15/2018 3:30 PM
07-Collegeboard_14SEP17_FIN.mp4	1/15/2018 3:49 PM
08-ap-computer-science-principles-practice-exam-2016.pdf	11/5/2017 3:29 PM

Using and Distributing College Board Resources

Although many College Board resources can be publically accessed, such as the Course Description, it is not appropriate to provide these documents with this publication. Some documents are public and many others are only available to registered AP professionals, which normally occurs after the AP Audit process is completed and authorized.

Figure 17.2

College Board AP Computer Science Principles Resources Explanation

01 - Course and Exam Description
The definitive authority for any AP Course. Make sure to download the latest version and check each year for updates to the course requirements.

02 - Digital Portfolio Teacher Guide
This is the starting document for an AP CSP teacher to set up digital portfolio classes. There are step-by-step screenshots included of the required processes.

03 - Digital Portfolio Student Guide
This is the starting document for AP CSP students to set up their digital portfolio boxes. There are step-by-step screenshots included of the required processes.

04 - Student Task Directions
The course description can be intimidating to students. A separate document has been lifted from the course description that strictly focuses on the performance task requirements for students. This file also provides an appendix with a detailed rubric for grading the Explore Performance Task and the Create Performance Task.

05 - Explore Written Response Template
This is a template that students can use to write the EXPLORE written responses. It provides students with the details of required responses right where they are entered.

06 - Create Written Response Template
This is a template that students can use to write the CREATE written responses. It provides students with the details of required responses right where they are entered.

07 - Recording of a College Board Sep14-2017 Webinar
This one-hour video records a webinar for AP CSP teachers that explains the current scoring system that will be used for the 2018 AP CSP performance tasks.

08 - AP Computer Science Principle Practice Exam
This is a special file that can only be downloaded by AP Computer Science Principles teachers who have completed the required AP Audit process for the course.

09 - Sample Responses to Performance Tasks
This is not a single file, like the 9 files listed above. There is a matrix on the College Board website with sample performance tasks that can be viewed, along with scoring criteria and provided commentary.

Use the Latest College Board Resources

All AP courses evolve and change over time. Some change slowly and other change quickly. AP Computer Science Principles is a new course with only one complete year of experience on record. That first year already identified necessary changes that were required, especially in the scoring area. It is therefore extremely important to look at the College Board resources that are available for the current school year and proper AP Exam date.

AP COMPUTER SCIENCE PRINCIPLES ALERT!

AP Courses change.
Change can be in curriculum and change can be in scoring criteria.
Always look for the latest resources by checking its effective date.

Figure 17.3, figure 17.4 and figure 17.5 demonstrate three different College Board resources that help to identify the intended school year and examination date. Usually, it is shown on the cover of the document, but sometimes the dates show up in the footer only.

Figure 17.3

The Most Important AP Course Document:
The Course Description

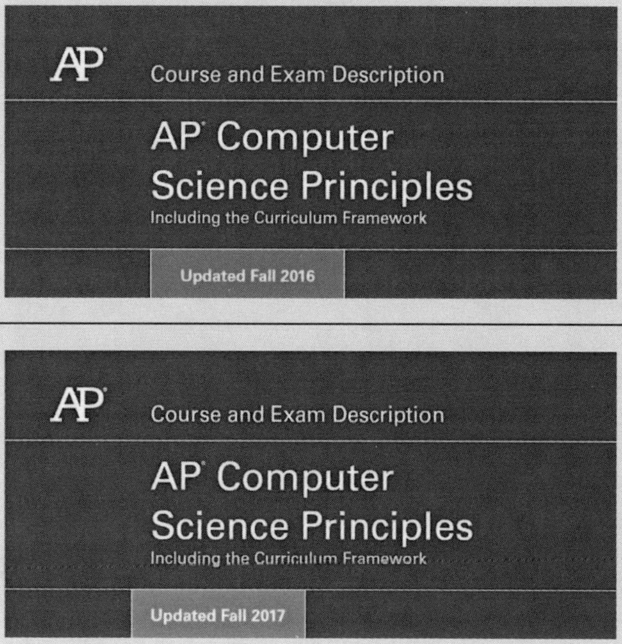

AP Course and Exam Description

AP Computer Science Principles
Including the Curriculum Framework

Updated Fall 2016

AP Course and Exam Description

AP Computer Science Principles
Including the Curriculum Framework

Updated Fall 2017

Figure 17.4

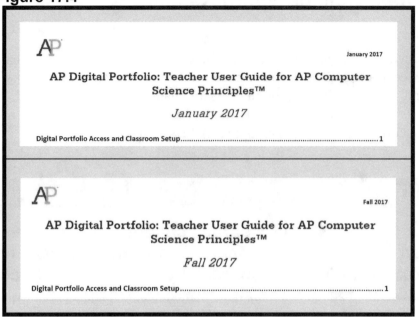

Figure 17.5

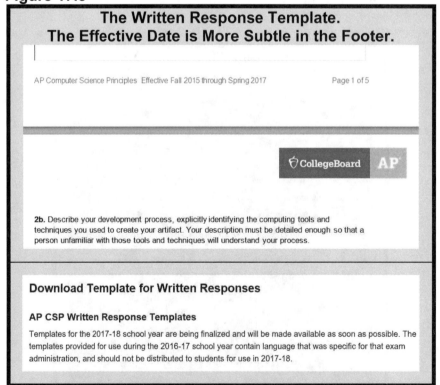

AP Prep Reality Check

The College Board resources are the definitive resource for teaching and preparing for any AP Exam. AP Prep books, such as this one, provide teachers with a brief topical review of each important topic in the curriculum, a large set of practice questions and some notes from the (hopefully) wisdom of the author/teacher.

AP Computer Science Principles is a remarkable course and its very large scope and flexibility create a natural complexity in curriculum planning and student preparation. The specific requirements are very well outlined in the College Board documents that were shown earlier. These documents are intentionally numbered in the sequence of their natural introduction.

The teacher certainly should read the course description multiple times. This is especially true for a new teacher. Do not be alarmed by the first reading OMG feeling. That is natural. With successive readings the curriculum will make excellent sense and you will be quite excited to be part of teaching this new course. Students can certainly read the course description, but special documents have been created just for their specific needs.

In this Explore Performance Task and the following Create Performance Task I want to add a few comments based on personal experiences and those shared by AP CSP teachers I have met around the United States. I do at least 12 Saturday Student Sessions (SSS) per year and I meet many teachers in addition to those I see at AP Summer Institutes. The course is new and our experiences cannot equal that of the existing AP Computer Science (A) course. Nevertheless, much has already been learned in such this short starting period.

Be Clear With the College Board Terminology

Forty percent of the AP Score is based on the creation of *Computational Artifacts*. There is no shortage of interesting terminology. Besides *computational artifacts*, you will also see *computing innovations* and *performance tasks*. This terminology will show up in many documents and web pages. We will start with explaining the *computational artifact*, which in turn requires an understanding of *artifact* first. Google says in figure 17.6 that it is an object made by a human being. It is often used in connection with history and archeology.

Figure 17.6

artifact Definition *(Google Dictionary)*

ar·ti·fact
/ˈärdəfakt/ ◀))

noun

1. an object made by a human being, typically an item of cultural or historical interest.
   "gold and silver artifacts"
   synonyms: relic, article; handiwork
   "hundreds of unidentified artifacts are stored in numerous rooms beneath the museum"

The College Board course description provides a specific explanation of a *computational artifact* in figure 17.7. It is still created by a human, but it is very important to note that is says: *by a human using a computer.* The explanation continues and indicates examples, such as a program, image, audio, video, presentation or web page file. This is a good start, but in any language thorough understanding of a word or phrase requires seeing it used in the context of various sentences and explanations. Right now it is extremely important to realize the phrase *a human using a computer.*

Figure 17.7

Computational Artifact *(College Board)*

A **computational artifact** is anything created by a human using a computer. An **artifact** can be, but is not limited to, a program, image, audio, video, presentation, or web page file. Aug 31, 2015

When you read the *College Board Course Description* multiple times or you read the condensed version for students, you will see both the Computational Artifact and Computing Innovation mentioned many, many times and soon you will really comprehend what this is all about. Figure 17.8 explains the Computing Innovation very well. A clear understanding is a must. Students earn many points with their written responses to multiple questions and the majority of the questions are about the *Computing Innovation* that the students select for their Explore Performance task.

Figure 17.8

Computing Innovation *(College Board)*

When completing the Explore – Impacts of Computing Innovations performance task, you will be expected to conduct investigations on a computing innovation. A computing innovation is an innovation that includes a computer or program code as an integral part of its functionality.

Even at this early start of a new course it is clear that many students struggle where to start with their performance tasks. What exactly is expected? There is certainly a lot of information provided by the College Board and students can read and hear the same information repeatedly, but starting is tough for many.

It really helps if the teacher uses the directions of the *Digital Portfolio Teacher Guide* first. This sets up the AP CSP class or classes. Students can do very little until this first step is done. Now it is the student's turn to use the *Digital Portfolio Student Guide*. They have to do a variety of steps to properly setup the College Board dropbox system that lets students upload required documents. This stage is pretty much a back and forth between the teacher and the students. Teachers keep in mind that students need to have a College Board account to be able to set up their AP CSP Digital Portfolio.

Teachers and students please note. It is frequently the case that students struggle to get to their Digital Portfolio. They followed directions step-by-step and properly created the account. Now time goes by and it is time to upload the files of their performance tasks. Suddenly some students cannot get into the Digital Portfolio. The problem is that they use the web address (URL) that is used by students to get access to the College Board website. That will not work. In their instructions of the Digital Portfolio Student Guide you see figure 17.9. The main point to remember is that the web address includes **digitalportfolio**.

Figure 17.9

Login For Your Digital Portfolio

DIGITAL PORTFOLIO ACCESS AND CLASS ENROLLMENT

Log in Using Your College Board Username and Password

- Go to **digitalportfolio.collegeboard.org** and log in using your College Board username and password.
  - ○ You may already have an account if you have taken an AP Capstone course or AP with WE Service course in a prior year, viewed AP® scores, or registered for the SAT® online.
    - ▪ If you do not remember your account credentials, you can request your username or reset your password.

Now back to the Explore Performance Task. The object is to create an artifact about the impact of a computing innovation using technology. How much technology? Let's take a look at two samples that were submitted in my class for Spring 2017. Both samples were videos, but my point can still be made by looking at static screen shots.

Both samples used movie-making computer software to create the videos. The first sample, *Computational Artifact*, shown in figure 17.10, is about the *GPS Computing Innovation*. The student draws different images on the white board that are impacted by the use of GPS. Only a few screenshots are shown, but the student draws pictures of a boat, a tablet, a car and other examples to illustrate where this computing innovation is used.

The drawing process is done on a white board and captured with a cell phone video. Even though the point about GPS is clear and even if the written responses are correct, the reality is that hand drawing is not using computer technology. Now there is technology used to create the final video, but for roughly the 60 seconds allowed in the video, the viewer observes an actual student hand drawing pictures. This is not really the intention of a computational artifact. Yes, there are students who used this approach and they did pass the AP Exam, but there are many other areas on the exam that add towards the total score. I personally graded my student performance tasks. Using the scoring criteria provided by the College Board, I did not award the first point for *Did the student create a Computational Artifact.*

Figure 17.10

In the next sample, shown by figure 17.11, the *Computational Artifact* is about the *Email Computing Innovation*. The student used software, called *GoAnimate*. There is an illusion that she rapidly draws on some background, but in reality everything is drawn by the software. It gives a very nice technical appearance and she added pleasant music with the presentation as well. For this second presentation I did award the point for *Did the student create a Computational Artifact* without any hesitation.

Figure 17.11

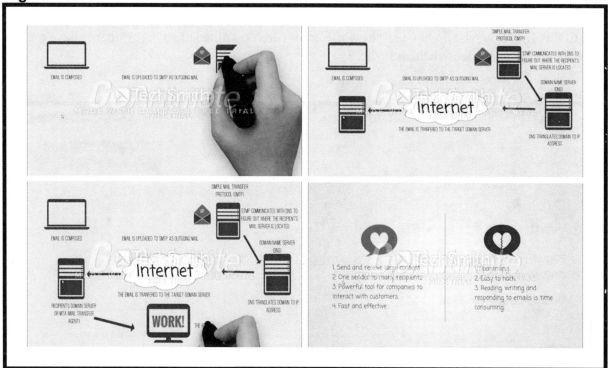

AP COMPUTER SCIENCE PRINCIPLES ALERT!

The Explore Performance Task has many requirements. So be aware, it is very possible that the provided video clearly shows beneficial and harmful effects of the selected *Computing Innovation*. That is great, but unless these effects are explained properly in the written reponses for that topic, the points are not awarded. In other words do not think that the computational artifacts takes care of all of the requirements. Make a nice video and then follow this up with well written responses to the many questions about your performance task.

Explore Performance Task Written Responses

The College Board has provided templates for submitting the required written responses for both the Explore Performance Task and the Create Performance Task. The Computer Artifact (CA) is considered item 1 and the written response is item 2. In Item 2, the written response has four separate questions. In figure 17.11 you see the top of the Explore Template provided by the College Board. Teachers from last year do not be surprised that the template looks different from last year. The questions numbers are there along with the expanding answer box, but the actual questions are available in the **ap-csp-student-task-directions.pdf** file. The template provides a link to this file. It is wise to have all these different files downloaded so that students have a clear overview what is needed when and where.

Figure 17.11

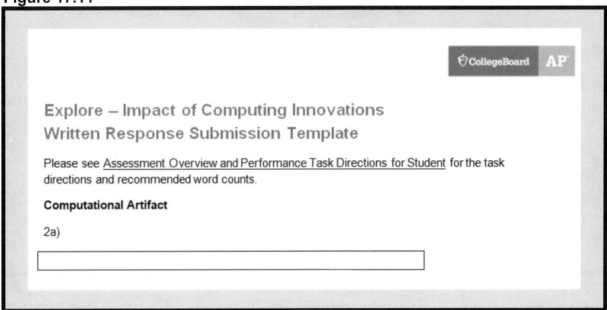

AP COMPUTER SCIENCE PRINCIPLES SCORING ALERT!

Both the Explore PT and the Create PT have a scoring sheet. The sheet is divided into eight rows. Each row explains the scoring criteria for the point on that row. It is binary. true or false; yes or no. Your teacher may not tell you if you answered the question properly, but you can personally look at the scoring sheet and score yourself. Be realistic. Be objective.

The very useful *Student Task Directions* document spells out clearly what all the requirements are for completing the artifact and written responses before they are ready for uploading. Carefully check every row and ask yourself: *Did I do that as specified?*

PERFORMANCE TASK SUBMISSION CONCERNS

Your teacher will guide you through the requirements of each performance task, but your teacher cannot tell you if you satisfied the requirements. Your teacher can make sure you do the logistics correctly. Watch out for the following issues!!

- Are your Explore files uploaded in Explore columns?
- Did you upload an Explore movie or a history essay?
- Is the audio of your file loud enough and clear enough?
- Is the movie the correct, less than 1 minute, length?
- Is the file the correct format?
- Is the file no greater than 30 MB?
- Did you answer the question in the correct question box?
- Have you compared your responses with the scoring criteria?
- Did you properly identify the data used by your computing innovation? (This is an area of confusion for many students.)

Chapter 18 Review
Create Performance Task

This chapter will be very different from the other chapters. This is not a chapter that explains computer numbers systems, some topic in a pseudo-code language or a discussion about data management and data representation. This chapter helps to clarify what is required to satisfy the free-response part of the AP CSP Examination. The first AP Computer Science course started in 1983. It had the typical AP Exam division of Multiple-Choice questions and Free-Response questions. Free-Response was back then, and still is today, a test of the student's ability to hand-write program code to solve a provided problem.

The new AP Computer Science Principles course uses a very different Free-Response approach that very much uses computer technology. Students create computer science projects, called *computational artifacts* that are uploaded into a College Board dropbox for grading. It is a system somewhat similar to the one used in an AP Studio Art course where students upload a portfolio of the art they have created.

The nature of these performance tasks is that students need to use technology to be creative, but technological skills alone are not sufficient. There are very precise requirements and deadlines that must be followed.

AP COMPUTER SCIENCE PRINCIPLES ALERT!

At the start of the first performance task a student does not truly realize the amount of work that needs to be completed and the time that is required to do everything. This is quite common.

Procrastination is bad news with this assignment. The last couple of days of uploading projects to the College Board Digital Portfolio in 2017 was very slow due to extremely high volume. And the upload site actual crashed for two hours due to the high volume.

> Due to high submission volumes, the Digital Portfolio was unavailable for two hours on Friday, April 28th.

Do your performance tasks early. Stay on task. Do not procrastinate.

Do not be concerned if this chapter seems identical to the Explore Chapter. Some students may do the Create Performance Task before the Explore Performance task and need this initial information that applies to both tasks you will complete. The second parts of the two chapters are different.

College Board Resources for Performance Tasks

The College Board has placed a lot of information about the requirements and the logistics of the new AP CSP course on their website. This chapter does not so much explain how to complete the Explore Performance Task, as it guides you to the many resources that are available from The College Board. It takes quite some time to appreciate the totality of the AP Computer Science Principles Course. A tremendous effort, research and many pilot years went into creating this course. Grasping the intent, the content, the scope, the flexibility and the scoring of the new course is far more complex than it was for its cousin, the AP Computer Science (A) course.

The College Board and the AP Test Development Committee certainly realized this complexity and have made many resources available in the form of PDF documents, webinar videos and sample student artifacts with commentary based on the latest scoring format. Figure 18.1 and figure 18.2 show the sources for the AP CSP course available on the AP Central website. The file name shown is the College Board file name and a sequence number I added in front. These files were the most up-to-date files available at the download date, which is mostly **1/15/2018.**

Figure 18.1

Name	Date modified
01-ap-computer-science-principles-course-and-exam-description.pdf	10/19/2017 7:44 AM
02-computer-science-principles-digital-portfolio-teacher-guide.pdf	1/15/2018 3:14 PM
03-computer-science-principles-digital-portfolio-student-guide.pdf	1/15/2018 3:13 PM
04-ap-csp-student-task-directions.pdf	1/15/2018 3:10 PM
05-Explore Template.dotx	1/15/2018 3:12 PM
06-Create Template.dotx	1/15/2018 3:30 PM
07-Collegeboard_14SEP17_FIN.mp4	1/15/2018 3:49 PM
08-ap-computer-science-principles-practice-exam-2016.pdf	11/5/2017 3:29 PM

Using and Distributing College Board Resources

Although many College Board resources can be publically accessed, such as the Course Description, it is not appropriate to provide these documents with this publication. Some documents are public and many others are only available to registered AP professionals, which normally occurs after the AP Audit process is completed and authorized.

Figure 18.2

College Board AP Computer Science Principles Resources Explanation

01 - Course and Exam Description
The definitive authority for any AP Course. Make sure to download the latest version and check each year for updates to the course requirements.

02 - Digital Portfolio Teacher Guide
This is the starting document for an AP CSP teacher to set up digital portfolio classes. There are step-by-step screenshots included of the required processes.

03 - Digital Portfolio Student Guide
This is the starting document for AP CSP students to set up their digital portfolio boxes. There are step-by-step screenshots included of the required processes.

04 - Student Task Directions
The course description can be intimidating to students. A separate document has been lifted from the course description that strictly focuses on the performance task requirements for students. This file also provides an appendix with a detailed rubric for grading the Explore Performance Task and the Create Performance Task.

05 - Explore Written Response Template
This is a template that students can use to write the EXPLORE written responses. It provides students with the details of required responses right where they are entered.

06 - Create Written Response Template
This is a template that students can use to write the CREATE written responses. It provides students with the details of required responses right where they are entered.

07 - Recording of a College Board Sep14-2017 Webinar
This one-hour video records a webinar for AP CSP teachers that explains the current scoring system that will be used for the 2018 AP CSP performance tasks.

08 - AP Computer Science Principle Practice Exam
This is a special file that can only be downloaded by AP Computer Science Principles teachers who have completed the required AP Audit process for the course.

09 - Sample Responses to Performance Tasks
This is not a single file, like the 9 files listed above. There is a matrix on the College Board website with sample performance tasks that can be viewed, along with scoring criteria and provided commentary.

Use the Latest College Board Resources

All AP courses evolve and change over time. Some change slowly and other change quickly. AP Computer Science Principles is a new course with only one complete year of experience on record. That first year already identified necessary changes that were required, especially in the scoring area. It is therefore extremely important to look at the College Board resources that are available for the current school year and proper AP Exam date.

AP COMPUTER SCIENCE PRINCIPLES ALERT!

AP Courses change.
Change can be in curriculum and change can be in scoring criteria.
Always look for the latest resources by checking its effective date.

Figure 18.3, figure 18.4 and figure 18.5 demonstrate three different College Board resources that help to identify the intended school year and examination date. Usually, it is shown on the cover of the document, but sometimes the dates show up in the footer only.

Figure 18.3

The Most Important AP Course Document:
The Course Description

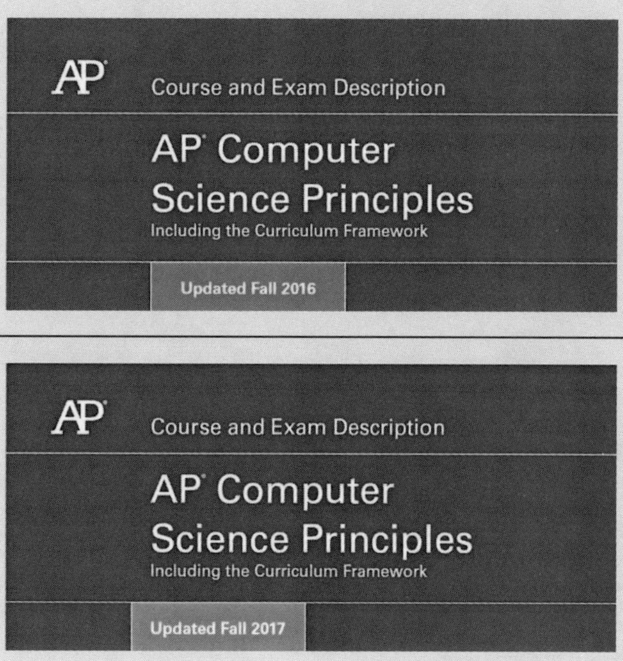

AP® Course and Exam Description

AP® Computer Science Principles
Including the Curriculum Framework

Updated Fall 2016

AP® Course and Exam Description

AP® Computer Science Principles
Including the Curriculum Framework

Updated Fall 2017

Figure 18.4

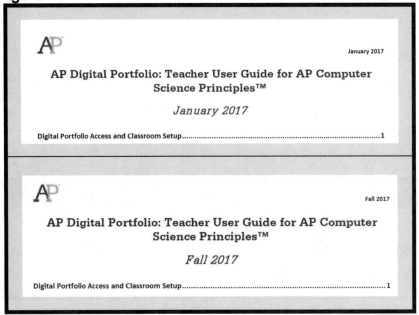

Figure 18.5

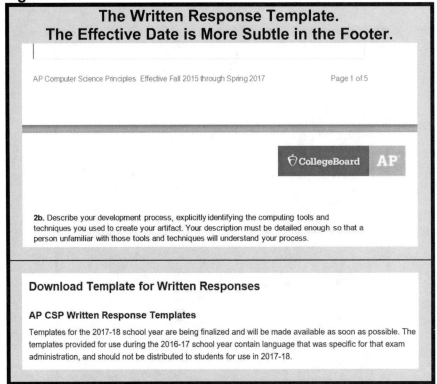

It really helps if the teacher uses the directions of the *Digital Portfolio Teacher Guide* first. This sets up the AP CSP class or classes. Students can do very little until this first step is done. Now it is the student's turn to use the *Digital Portfolio Student Guide*. They have to do a variety of steps to properly setup the College Board dropbox system that lets students upload required documents. This stage is pretty much a back and forth between the teacher and the students. Teachers keep in mind that students need to have a College Board account to be able to set up their AP CSP Digital Portfolio.

Teachers and students please note. It is frequently the case that students struggle to get to their Digital Portfolio. They followed directions step-by-step and properly created the account. Now time goes by and it is time to upload the files of their performance tasks. Suddenly some students cannot get into the Digital Portfolio. The problem is that they use the web address (URL) that is used by students to get access to the College Board website. That will not work. In their instructions of the Digital Portfolio Student Guide you see figure 18.6. The main point to remember is that the web address includes **digitalportfolio**.

Figure 18.6

<table>
<tr><td>

Login For Your Digital Portfolio

DIGITAL PORTFOLIO ACCESS AND CLASS ENROLLMENT

Log in Using Your College Board Username and Password

- Go to **digitalportfolio.collegeboard.org** and log in using your College Board username and password.

  o You may already have an account if you have taken an AP Capstone course or AP with WE Service course in a prior year, viewed AP® scores, or registered for the SAT® online.

    ▪ If you do not remember your account credentials, you can request your username or reset your password.

</td></tr>
</table>

AP Prep Reality Check

The College Board resources are the definitive resource for teaching and preparing for any AP Exam. AP Prep books, such as this one, provide teachers with a brief topical review of each important topic in the curriculum, a large set of practice questions and some notes from the (hopefully) wisdom of the author/teacher.

AP Computer Science Principles is a remarkable course and its very large scope and flexibility create a natural complexity in curriculum planning and student preparation. The specific requirements are very well outlined in the College Board documents that were shown earlier. These documents are intentionally numbered in the sequence of their natural introduction.

The teacher certainly should read the course description multiple times. This is especially true for a new teacher. Do not be alarmed by the first reading OMG feeling. That is natural. With successive readings the curriculum will make excellent sense and you will be quite excited to be part of teaching this new course. Students can certainly read the course description, but special documents have been created just for their specific needs.

Be Very Clear On the Program's Requirements.

It is easy to understand that your Create Performance Task is a program. It is also easy to understand that the program language is flexible as long as it is capable of satisfying the requirements. The list of requirements for the Create PT artifact is certainly greater than it is for the Explore PT artifact. Many students get confused with the WOW factor. Such students create large, complex programs with impressive capabilities. It might even be a video game. Do check the scoring criteria, because there are no points for a WOW type of program. The program requirements are itemized in figure 18.6

Figure 18.6

Create Performance Task
Program Requirements

- The program needs to demonstrate capabilities of the programming language features that include iteration and decision making.
  (This means that the program must make decisions based on various conditions. The program must also repeat certain processes)

- Use mathematical and logical concepts
  (This means that the program uses mathematical expressions with variables using arithmetic operators and/or Boolean operators)

- Implement an algorithm that integrates two or more algorithms.
  (This does mean algorithms that are mathematical and/or logical in nature.)

- Develop and use abstractions to manage the complexity of your program.
  (Do not get confused here. A program language provides many procedures to draw a circle, to compute the square root and many others. If any program language procedure is used it demonstrates that you know how to use an abstraction. Development means that create your very own procedure which can then be used without knowing the implementation.)

- Answer all the questions on required for Written Response.
  (The first four bullets concentrated on the actual program requirements. Besides the program itself there are questions about difficulties solved, collaboration used, etc.)

- Make sure turn in your program code file in pdf format and mark your algorithm and abstraction.
  (This means that the program code must be captured and turned into a PDF file. An oval is used to mark the algorithm that you created and a rectangle is used to mark the abstraction that you created. A common mistake is to confuse the two. There is also a problem with students marking the use of program language abstractions. Both the algorithm and the abstraction are your personal development and implementation.)

- Include comments of acknowledgement.
  (If any program code has been provided by somebody else, this must be clearly indicated in your program code file.)

- *Nowhere can your name appear. Neither the program video file name itself, nor the written response PDF file name nor the Program code file name can include your name. Furthermore, your name may not appear anywhere inside any file that is uploaded.*

AP COMPUTER SCIENCE PRINCIPLES SCORING ALERT!

Both the Explore PT and the Create PT have a scoring sheet. The sheet is divided into eight rows. Each row explains the scoring criteria for the point on that row. It is binary. true or false; yes or no. Your teacher may not tell you if you answered the question properly, but you can personally look at the scoring sheet and score yourself. Be realistic. Be objective.

AP Computer Science Principles
Sample Exam I

1. Consider the following code segment, which uses the variables x, y, z.

    ```
    x ← 5
    y ← 7
    z ← x - y
    x ← y - z
    y ← z - x
    DISPLAY (z)
    DISPLAY (x)
    ```

    What is displayed as a result of running the code segment?

    (A) -2 9

    (B) -11 -9

    (C) 9 -2

    (D) -11 2

2. Which of the following is a true statement about program documentation?

    (A) Program documentation is not started until a program is written, tested and complete.

    (B) Writing all the program documentation is the first step in creating any new program.

    (C) Program documentation should be added with the corresponding program code as it is developed.

    (D) Program documentation is only necessary for large professional programs.

3. Which of the following is a true statement about the use of an IP addresses?

(A) An IP address is a unique address only used to identify an individual device on the Internet.

(B) An IP address is a unique address only used to identify a network on the Internet.

(C) An IP address is used to identify the domain name of a website.

(D) An IP address is a unique address used to identify an individual device and a network on the Internet.

---

4. Consider the following code segment.

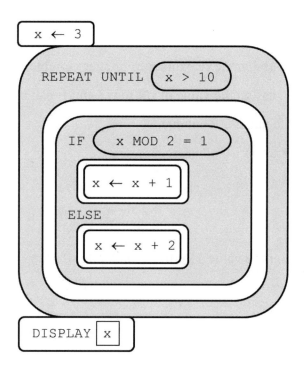

What is displayed as a result of running the code segment?

(A) 10

(B) 11

(C) 12

(D) 13

---

5. An algorithm is created to generate a random integer in a specified range. Which of the following programming structures must be added to the existing algorithm to generate a specified quantity of random numbers?

(A) Selection

(B) Iteration

(C) Searching

(D) Sorting

6. Consider the algorithm below, which processes two integer variables n1 and n2 and returns integer variable n3.

Step 1: Divide n1 by n2 and assign the remainder to integer variable rem.

Step 2: If rem has the value 0, assign the value of n2 to n3 and finish by returning the value of n3.

Step 3: If rem does not have the value 0, continue.

Step 4: Assign the value of n2 to n1

Step 5: Assign the value of rem to n2.

Step 6: Go to Step 1.

If the algorithm is tested by assigning value 120 to n1 and value 108 to n2, what value is returned by n3?

(A) 1

(B) 12

(C) 24

(D) 108

7. Which of the following income-tax return activities poses the least personal security risk?

(A) Using an online tax-return program and transmitting the tax documents online.

(B) Using a CD provided tax-return software application, printing the tax documents and mailing the return by placing it in the curbside mailbox.

(C) Going to a tax-return company, who prepares your tax documents and transmits them online.

(D) Using a CD tax-return software application, printing the tax documents and sending them to the IRS with a company like   FedEx or UPS.

---

8. `list` is a data structure with a large number of integers. Assume that the order of the `list` elements is unknown. Which of the following algorithms has the shortest execution time in a *worst-case* scenario?

(A) Finding a specified element in `list` with a *linear search* algorithm.

(B) Finding a specified element in `list` with a *binary search* algorithm.

(C) Arranging the elements in ascending order with a very fast algorithm, like the *merge sort*.

(C) Finding the median number in `list` by returning the middle element after first using a *sorting* algorithm.

9. Consider procedure `mystery` below.

```
PROCEDURE mystery (list)
{
    n ← LENGTH (list) - 1
    k ← 1
    REPEAT UNTIL (k > n)
    {
        if (list[k] > list[k+1])
        {
            temp = list[k]
            list[k] = list[k+1]
            list[k+1] = temp
        }
        k ← k + 1
    }
}
```

Assume that procedure `mystery` is always called with a non-empty parameter `list`, which contains positive integers. Which of the following best describes the contents of `list` after procedure `mystery` finishes executing?

(A) The integers in `list` are sorted in *ascending* order.

(B) The integers in `list` are sorted in *descending* order.

(C) The order of the integers in `list` is unknown, but the smallest integer is the last element in `list`.

(D) The order of the integers in `list` is unknown, but the largest integer is the last element in `list`.

10. Which of the following is the proper, ethical, use of software with the purchase of a single CD or single download file to install software?

(A) The software can only ethically be installed and used on one computer.

(B) The software can be installed on multiple computers, such as both home and office, but there can only be one user at a time.

(C) The ethical use is based on the number of licenses that were granted with the purchase agreement, not the quantity of CDs or downloads.

(D) As long as the software is used for a non-profit purpose, such as education, the number of users is not limited.

11. Which of the following is MOST likely to indicate a phishing attack?

(A) A call from a Department of Motor Vehicles employee requesting personal information to help verify the new computer record updates.

(B) A call from a loan officer asking you to come to the bank office to verify loan information and sign the loan application.

(C) An email from a bank - with the last four digits of your debit card shown - stating that your debit card PIN must be reset on the online bank account.

(D) A call from a credit card fraud department investigating if three recent purchases were made by you.

12. Which of the following statements are true about comparing low-level programming languages with high-level programming languages?

I.   Low-level program languages are closer to computer machine language.

II. High-level program languages are closer to human language.

III. High-level program languages make programming simpler by including many procedural abstractions

(A) I only

(B) II only

(C) II & III only

(D) I, II & III

---

13. An Internet user enters a Web address in a browser's URL window. The user wants to download a data file from the website. Which of the following is true about manner in which the requested file travels from the webserver origin to the website user's computer?

(A) The entire data file is transmitted on the Internet by any available route from webserver to user computer.

(B) The data file is broken up into packets before transmission. Individual packets all travel by the same shortest available route and are reassembled at the destination computer.

(C) The data file is broken up into packets before transmission. Individual packets all travel by the same route or different available routes and are reassembled at the destination computer.

(D) The webserver checks for the shortest possible route and transmits the entire data file when the shortest route becomes available.

14. Many large data files are compressed to make Internet transmission more efficient. Which of the following statements is true about the *lossless* and *lossy* data compression techniques?

   I.   *Lossless* data compression techniques will reduce the number of bits that are actually transmitted, but after transmission every bit of the original data file can be restored.

   II.   *Lossy* data compression techniques will reduce the number of bits that are actually transmitted, but after transmission every bit of the original data file can be restored.

   III. Data compression does allow efficient Internet transmission of data, but it will always permanently reduce the data file, which can result in a quality loss of the video and audio data.

   (A) I only

   (B) II only

   (C) III only

   (D) I & II only

15. Consider the following code segment.

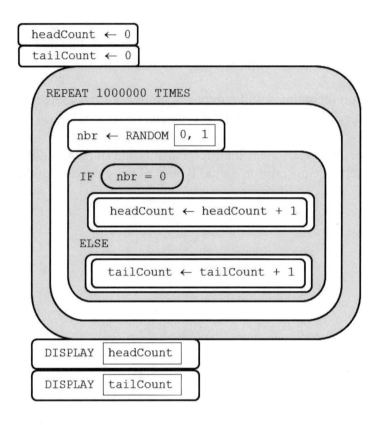

The code segment can be used for a practical computer programming purpose.
Which of the following statements is a plausible purpose for using this code segment?

(A) This code segment can be used to check if flipping a coin will create a distribution of exactly 50% heads and exactly 50% tails.

(B) This code segment can be used to check if the RANDOM function generates a proper distribution of random values based on the laws of probability.

(C) This code segment checks to see if the RANDOM function will only generate values of 0 and 1.

(D) All of the above

16. Consider the program below. The initial value of variable x is not known.

```
x ← <positive integer value>
IF (x > 500)
{
    IF (x < 200)
    {
        DISPLAY ("Austria")
    }
    ELSE
    {
        DISPLAY ("Liechtenstein")
    }
}
ELSE
{
    if (x > 600)
    {
        DISPLAY ("Croatia")
    }
    ELSE
    {
        DISPLAY ("Liechtenstein")
    }
}
```

What is displayed as a result of running the program, assuming x is a positive integer?

(A) The output cannot be determined without the value of x.

(B) Liechtenstein

(C) Croatia

(D) Austria or Croatia

17. The question below uses a robot in a grid of squares. The robot is represented as a triangle, which initially is located in the bottom-row, second square from the left and facing upward.

Starting Grid

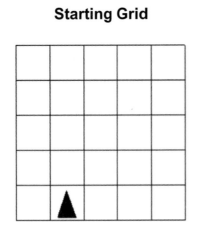

The following program code segment is used to move the robot within the grid.

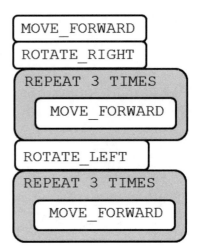

```
MOVE_FORWARD
ROTATE_RIGHT
REPEAT 3 TIMES
    MOVE_FORWARD
ROTATE_LEFT
REPEAT 3 TIMES
    MOVE_FORWARD
```

Which of the following grids shows the result of executing the program segment?

(A)

(B)

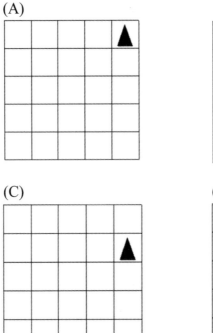

(C)

(D)

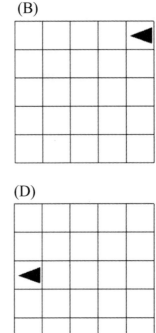

18. Consider the three code segments below. These segments are part of an employment program that screens for education and work experience. Prospective employees must have at least 12 years of education and they must also have 5 years of experience. Assume that all values for education and experience are non-negative.

Which of the three code segments will screen prospective employees correctly?	**CODE SEGMENT I**

(A) I only
 	
(B) II only
 	
(C) I and II
 	
(D) I and III
	<pre>IF(education ≥ 12)
	{
	    IF(experience ≥ 5)
	    {
	        DISPLAY("You're hired")
	    }
	    ELSE
	    {
	        DISPLAY("You're not qualified")
	    }
	}
	ELSE
	{
	    DISPLAY("You're not qualified")
	}</pre>

CODE SEGMENT II

```
IF(education >= 12 or experience >= 5)
{
    DISPLAY("You're hired")
}
ELSE
{
    DISPLAY("You're not qualified")
}
```

CODE SEGMENT III

```
IF(education >= 12 and experience >= 5)
{
    DISPLAY("You're hired")
}
ELSE
{
    DISPLAY("You're not qualified")
}
```

19. A large university with more than 50,000 students has a database of student records. The two most common database access operations are **one:** access to update student information, such as course registration, dropped courses, grades, etc. and **two:** access at graduation time to identify the class standing of students.

Which of the following sorting procedures will provide the university with the most efficient database access?

(A) Sort the database according to name or student ID for quick individual student access.

(B) Sort the database according to student initial enrollment date to identify student seniority status.

(C) Sort the database according to GPA for quick access of student ranking.

(D) Sort the database according to SAT score or other objective admission criteria.

---

20. The code segment below is expected to display `Divisible by 3 and 4`, if `nbr` is divisible by 3 and also by 4 and display `Not divisible by 3 and 4` otherwise.

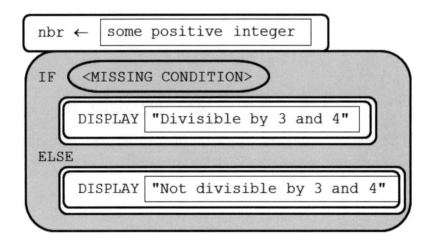

Which of the following can be used to replace < MISSING CONDITION > so that the code will work as intended?

(A) `(nbr MOD 3 = 0 OR nbr MOD 4 = 0)`

(B) `(nbr MOD 3 AND nbr MOD 4 = 0)`

(C) `(nbr MOD 3 = 0 AND nbr MOD 4 = 0)`

(D) `(nbr MOD 3 OR nbr MOD 4 = 0)`

21. The figure below represents two computers and a group of network nodes on the Internet. Each node has a router capable of passing files to another connected network node and also capable of finding an alternate route if a previous connection slows down or is no longer available.

The two shaded network nodes, **Router A** and **Router F**, are currently not capable of transmitting any packets to a connected network node.

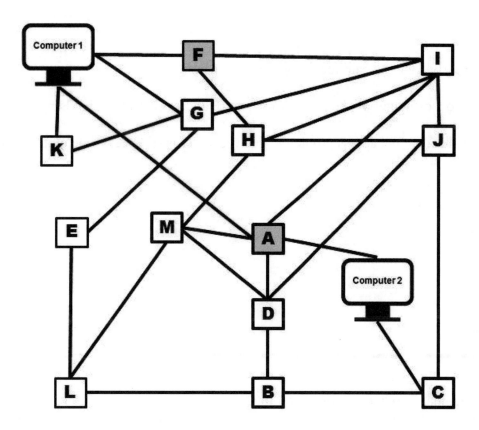

Considering the current status of this network, with two dysfunctional routers. What is the smallest number of routers necessary to connect **Computer 1** to **Computer 2**?

(A) 3 routers

(B) 4 routers

(C) 5 routers

(D) 6 routers

22. Hornet High School uses a webserver that is physically located within the intranet of the Hornet Independent School District. Teachers use the webserver for online quizzes and tests. Access to the school webserver is done with an IP address, like `10.3.74.17`.

The school does not use a domain name, like *www.hornetserver.org*. Using a domain name is easier to remember than four numbers, but the school still prefers to use an IP address.

Which of the following are valid reasons to continue using an IP address and not a domain name?

I. There is a yearly fee to be paid for using a domain name.

II. Connection to a computer on the intranet with an IP address is faster than using a domain name.

III. If the school has Internet access problems, the webserver is still accessible on the local intranet.

(A) II only

(B) I & II only

(C) II & III only

(D) I, II & III

---

23. The American Standard Code for Information Interchange - better known as ASCII - uses numerical values to encode characters. The decimal (base 10) value **97** represents **lower-case a**, **98** is **b**, **99** is **c** and this pattern continues and **lower-case z** has ASCII value **122**. Each one of the ASCII characters can be represented as a 7-bit number.

What ASCII character is represented by the binary (base 2) number `1101110`?

(A) h

(B) j

(C) n

(D) q

24. Consider the four pictures in the table below. **Picture 1** is the original picture taken with a high-resolution camera. This picture is uploaded to a social media website and is shown in **Picture 2**. **Picture 3** is the result of blowing up **Picture 1** to get a close-up of the central figure in the statue. **Picture 4** is the result of blowing up **Picture 2** after downloading it from the social media website.

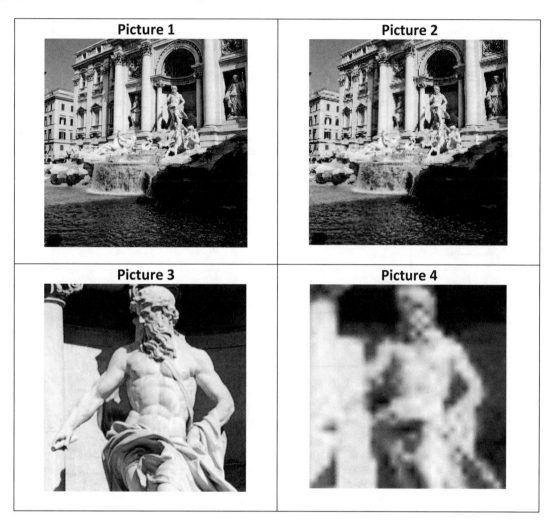

There is a major difference in the quality of **Picture 3** and **Picture 4**. Which of the following might be a reason for the deterioration in the picture quality?

(A) Picture quality deteriorates with time. It may have been some time since uploading the original picture.

(B) The social media website discourages downloading pictures and distorts the download file.

(C) The process of dividing files into packets for Internet transmission lowers data file quality.

(D) Many social media sites intentionally lower the resolution of posted media, because with lower resolution the files take up less memory and process quicker.

25. Algorithms can be visually represented by a flowchart, such as the one shown below. Building blocks used by the flowchart are explained in the table below.

Block	Explanation
Oval	The start or end of an algorithm
Rectangle	One or more processing steps, such as a statement that assigns a value or variable
Diamond	A conditional or decision step, where execution proceeds to the side labeled true if the condition is true and to the side labeled false otherwise.
Parallelogram	Display a message

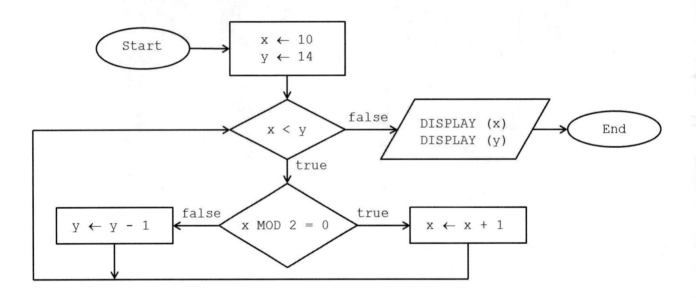

What is displayed as a result of executing the algorithm in the flowchart?

(A) 9 9

(B) 11 10

(C) 10 10

(D) 11 11

26. A school administration program stores information about students. The web-based software is updated when any teacher, administrator or counselor makes an entry. The following student information is stored in the central database. Information can be retrieved by school employees based on their individual access rights.

- Personal student information about address, birthdate, gender, family data and medical records
- Attendance and tardies
- Individual grades for teacher assignments along with grade cycle averages and semester averages
- Student class standing

Which of the following requests cannot be determined using the school's database?

(A) Absences for the students who rank in the top 10% of their class

(B) Seniors who are exempt from finals, because they have grade averages in every course greater than 85, no more than 3 absences, no more than 2 tardies and no detentions or suspensions

(C) Students who are failing one or more classes that have more than 5 absences per 9-week cycle

(D) Students who need to take daily medicine at school.

---

27. Consider the following numbers in three different number bases.

Binary numbers will be indicated as base-2, like `101100 (base-2)`.
Decimal numbers will be indicated with (base-10), like `6879 (base-10)`.
Hexadecimal numbers will be indicated with (base-16), like `a5f2bc (base-16)`.

Which of the following are in ascending order, from left-to-right?

(A) `100 (base-10)`   –   `1100100 (base-2)`   –   `64 (base-16)`

(B) `FF (base-16)`   –   `255 (base-10)`   –   `11111111 (base-2)`

(C) `139 (base-10)`   –   `10001011 (base -2)`   –   `8B (base-16)`

(D) None of the above

28. An integer is called *perfect number* when the sum of its factors - except for the number itself - add up to the number.

Examples are :

$$6 \;=\; 1+2+3$$
$$28 \;=\; 1+2+4+7+14$$
$$496 \;=\; 1+2+4+8+16+31+62+124+248$$

Consider procedure `perfect` below. The intention of procedure `perfect` is to check if parameter `nbr` is a *perfect* number and then return `true` or return `false` otherwise.

```
PROCEDURE perfect (nbr)
{
    count ← 1
    sum ← 0
    REPEAT UNTIL (count = nbr)
    {
        if (<MISSING CODE>)
        {
            sum = sum + count
        }
        count = count + 1
    }
    RETURN sum = nbr
}
```

Which of the following replacements for <MISSING CODE> results in procedure `perfect` correctly identifying *perfect* numbers?

(A) `(count MOD nbr = 0)`

(B) `(sum MOD count > 0)`

(C) `(nbr MOD count = 0)`

(D) `(nbr MOD count > 0)`

29. The question below uses a robot in a grid of squares. The robot is represented as a triangle, which initially is located in the bottom-left corner and facing toward the top of the grid. The robot is capable of moving into a white cell or a gray cell, it cannot move into a black cell. For this question only, you must keep in mind that the ROTATE_LEFT() command IS NOT available.

Starting Grid   **Ending Grid**

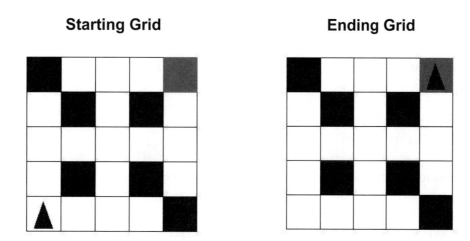

Which of the following code segments can be used to move the robot to the gray square?

(A)	(B)	(C)	(D)
| ```
MOVE_FORWARD()
MOVE_FORWARD()
ROTATE_RIGHT()
REPEAT 4 TIMES
{
    MOVE_FORWARD()
}
REPEAT 3 TIMES
{
    ROTATE_RIGHT()
}
MOVE_FORWARD()
MOVE_FORWARD()
``` | ```
MOVE_FORWARD()
MOVE_FORWARD()
ROTATE_RIGHT()
REPEAT 4 TIMES
{
    MOVE_FORWARD()
}
ROTATE_LEFT()
MOVE_FORWARD()
MOVE_FORWARD()
``` | ```
ROTATE_RIGHT()
REPEAT 4 TIMES
{
    MOVE_FORWARD()
}
REPEAT 3 TIMES
{
    ROTATE_RIGHT()
}
REPEAT 4 TIMES
{
    MOVE_FORWARD()
}
``` | ```
ROTATE_RIGHT()
MOVE_FORWARD()
MOVE_FORWARD()
REPEAT 3 TIMES
{
    ROTATE_RIGHT()
}
REPEAT 4 TIMES
{
    MOVE_FORWARD()
}
ROTATE_RIGHT()
REPEAT 3 TIMES
{
    MOVE_FORWARD()
}
``` |

30. Acme Inc. must decide on the nature of its data processing capabilities. The three most important goals for the Acme Inc. software are:

- Fast data processing
- Secure data storage
- All employees need to have access to the data created or altered by other employees.

Which of the following data processing management systems will best serve the needs of Acme Inc.?

(A) All data processing occurs with data stored on local computers and is backed up daily to a local server on the Acme Inc. Intranet.

(B) All data processing and data storage are managed by cloud computing.

(C) All data processing is managed with data stored on the local computer. All local data of Acme Inc. computers are synced with drop boxes on computers of Acme Inc. Intranet and also the Cloud.

(D) Individual employees of Acme Inc. may each decide how to manage their data processing.

---

31. Hornet High School has purchased new software for its computers that prevent access to inappropriate websites. The new software has been tested very thoroughly and is then installed on all school computers. Each computer receives a sticker to identify its proper installation to insure that no computer is forgotten.

After software installation and testing is complete all teachers are assembled in a faculty meeting for a demonstration of the new computer website-access software. The demonstration first checks if the computer shows the proper sticker and then starts by showing how a known, popular, but very inappropriate student website can no longer be accessed. To the demonstrator's dismay the offensive website appears as if the software had never been installed.

Which of the following might account for this problem, even after testing the software?

(A) The software must not have been tested at all.

(B) The software installers failed to empty the cache on the computers, or at least the demonstration computer.

(C) There are too many problem websites and it is not possible to protect all of them.

(D) The software was not installed on the demonstration computer.

32. Consider the following numbers in three different number bases.

- Binary   1001101 (base-2)
- Decimal   82 (base-10)
- Hexadecimal 5A (base-16)

Which of the following lists of numbers, are in ascending order, from left-to-right?

(A) 1001101 (base-2),   82 (base-10),   5A (base-16)

(B) 5A (base-16),   1001101 (base-2), 82 (base-10)

(C) 82 (base-10),   5A (base-16),   1001101 (base-2)

(D) 1001101 (base-2),   5A (base-16),   82 (base-10)

---

33. Many young people believe that use of the Internet is free. Is that true? Which of the following is a true statement about access and using the Internet?

(A) People at home pay money to an ISP (Internet Service Provider) to get access to the Internet.

(B) People at work use computers without cost, but the company pays an ISP.

(C) Many places provide free access to the Internet, like airports, but they are compensated by selling adds that will appear on the customer's computer.

(D) All of the above

34. Consider procedure `reverse` below. Parameter `x` is a list of integers.

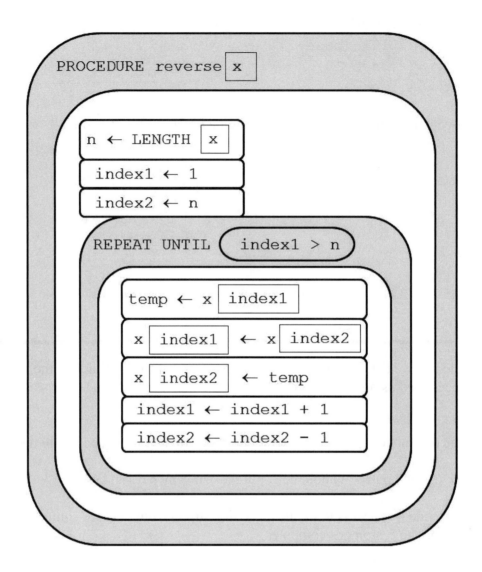

Assume that procedure `reverse` is called, with list x containing integers [11, 22, 33, 44, 55]. Which of the following shows the contents of list x after executing procedure `reverse`?

(A) [55, 44, 33, 22, 11]

(B) [55, 44, 33, 44, 55]

(C) [11, 22, 33, 22, 11]

(D) [11, 22, 33, 44, 55]

35.   Consider procedure isSorted below. The intention of procedure isSorted is to check if the
       elements of the list parameter are sorted in ascending order, which returns true and if not sorted in
       ascending order returns false.

```
PROCEDURE isSorted (list)
{
    sorted ← true
    n ← LENGTH(list) - 1
    k ← 1
    REPEAT UNTIL (k >= n)
    {
        IF (<MISSING CODE>)
        {
            sorted = false
        }
        k ← k + 1
    }
    RETURN sorted
}
```

Which of the following replacements for <MISSING CODE> results in procedure isSorted correctly
identifying a list sorted in ascending order?

(A) (list[1] < list[k])

(B) (list[k] < list[k+1]

(C) (list[k] > list[k+1])

(D) (list[1] > list[n])

36. Consider the adjacent code segment.
    What is the output of executing the code segment?

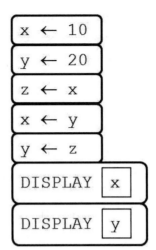

(A) 10 10

(B) 10 20

(C) 20 10

(D) 20 20

37. Customer bank transactions; which include deposits, withdrawals, loan payments, investments, etc.; must be accurate and stored securely to protect against natural disasters, terrorist attacks and electrical grid problems. Which of the following keeps the constantly changing data of the banks secure.

(A) All transaction are stored electronically locally where they were made and then paper copies are printed that are stored in vaults.

(B) Banks have branches around the country and all transactions are copied on the computers of the bank branches.

(C) Banks use one of the available cloud services to back up their data.

(D) Banks use gigantic, high-speed, mainframe computer centers, spread around the country that constantly mirror all the data that is stored and newly created.

38. A person is concerned about the access and/or loss of very important data information. The data needs to be safe, but also easily accessible from many locations. Which of the following is the ideal way to handle the data?

(A) Keep the data stored on several local computers only without Internet access to prevent hacking issues.

(B) Keep the data stored by a cloud service to insure permanent data storage and easy global access.

(C) Backup all the data on multiple external hard drives.

(D) There is no ideal solution. Internet cloud computing provides the most convenient access, but there can be issues with data breaches. Home computers without Internet and external hard drive backup are more secure, but have very poor access for a traveling person.

---

39. Consider the following famous *farmer-crossing-the-river* puzzle.

A farmer wants to cross a river and take with him a wolf, a goat, and a cabbage. There is a boat that can fit himself plus either the wolf, the goat, or the cabbage. If the wolf and the goat are alone on one shore, the wolf will eat the goat. If the goat is alone with the cabbage, the goat will eat the cabbage. How can the farmer get all three across?

The solution of this problem is an example of

(A) a computer program.

(B) a Boolean logic diagram.

(C) an algorithm.

(D) a selection control structure.

40. The famous German mathematician Gauss already made a name for himself in the 4th grade. His class was asked to add all the integers from 1 to 100. Gauss did this in less than one minute and produced the correct result of 5050.

Gauss created a clever algorithm that adds consecutive integers from 1 to n, with n being the largest number. Which of the following algorithms will correctly perform such a result without the tedious one-number-at-a-time addition?

(A) Step 1: Compute n plus 1
    Step 2: Divide the result of Step-1 by 2
    Step 3: Compute n minus 1
    Step 4: Multiply the results of Step-2 and Step-3.

(B) Step 1: Compute n divided by 2
    Step 2: Compute n plus 1
    Step 3: Multiply the results of Step-1 and Step-2.

(C) Step 1: Compute n divided by 2
    Step 2: Compute n minus 1
    Step 3: Multiply the results of Step-1 and Step-2.

(D) Step 1: Compute n divided by 2
    Step 2: Compute n plus 2
    Step 3: Multiply the results of Step-1 and Step-2.

41. Consider the following four binary numbers.

- 10101010
- 01111111
- 01010111
- 10100100

Which of the following displays the number in order from smallest to largest?

(A) 01010111   01111111   10100100   10101010

(B) 10101010   10100100   01111111   01010111

(C) 01010111   10101010   10100100   01111111

(D) 01111111   01010111   10101010   10100100

---

42. Consider the following code segment that initializes 5 variables.

```
a ← 10
b ← 15
c ← 20
d ← 25
e ← 30
```

Which of the following code segments does not correctly compute the mean of the 5 variables?

(A) ```
sum = a + b + c + d + e
meanA = sum / 5
```

(B) `meanB = a / 5 + b / 5 + c / 5 + d / 5 + e / 5`

(C) `meanC = (a + b + c + d + e) / 5`

(D) `meanD = a + b + c + d + e / 5`
```

43. An airline keeps data information on its frequent flyers passengers to determine the perks that they have earned, which include:

- Name and address
- Gender
- Age
- Job Status
- Total frequent flyers miles flown
- Available frequent flyer miles for free flights or upgrades
- Record of previous frequent flyer tickets awarded
- Upcoming ticketed flight reservations
- Elite status (Gold, Silver, Platinum)

Which of the following statistics cannot be determined with the database information shown above?

(A) The number of female flyers that have Elite status

(B) The most popular geographic destinations for frequent flyer award tickets

(C) The largest category of frequent flyers based on (Gender, Age, Location and Education)

(D) The average number of reserved future flights for Elite passengers

---

44. This question presents four scenarios that use a program to solve a problem. Which one of these scenarios is the most likely to involve the use of heuristics in its program?

(A) A group of boy scouts and parents climb Pikes Peak together. After hiking up the trail for several hours one of the parents uses GPS to see where they are in relation to the peak and about how long it will take to hike there.

(B) A young couple wants to go on the earliest possible retirement and uses a program to manage their financial investment and expenditures towards that goal.

(C) A land owner want to pay a farmer to bale hay on his land. The land owner uses a program that computes the number of bales that his land will yield along with the cost of baling. The goal of the land owner is to make a $25.00 profit per bale of hay.

(D) A student want to use a program to determine the total cost of becoming a medical doctor after high school to help decide on which medical school to attend and how much money needs to be saved or borrowed.

45. People receive many business emails, which include emails from their banks, credits card companies and insurance companies. Each one of these companies stores sensitive private information. A growing number of emails are sent out that look like legitimate business emails, but they are *phishing* attempts. Which one of the following helps to identify if the emails is in fact from your bank or your credit card company?

(A) The email contains the proper logos and appearance you expect,

(B) The email includes the last four digits of your account number.

(C) The email includes your name.

(D) The email is concerned about possible fraudulent action and wants verification about your account.

---

46. There is a difficult compromise between providing security for people in a country and at the same time respect their privacy. What can government agencies do to address these conflicting concerns?

(A) Check all electronic communication, including email, phone calls, text and social media to look for red flags that signal potential security problems.

(B) Check the metadata of communication, which does not include data that causes privacy invasion.

(C) Check all electronic communication, including email, phone calls, text and social media to look for red flags and ignore any communication that is of no security concern.

(D) Listen for keywords in all communication and only check the communication that is potentially a security concern.

47. A programmer uses the Java programming language. The programmer want to prevent memory overflow and use a large enough data type, but also not waste memory with a data type that is not necessary. He needs to work with integers in the `[1000..9999]` range. Java has four different data types to store integers that are shown below.

One bit is used for the sign. For instance, the `byte` data type uses 8 bits, which means 256 possible binary combinations, but only 7 bits are used for the actual number. This is true for each data type. Which data type should the programmer select?

- `byte`   8 bits of storage
- `short`   16 bits of storage
- `int`   32 bits of storage
- `long`   64 bits of storage

(A) `byte`

(B) `short`

(C) `int`

(D) `long`

48. Privacy concern and identity theft are a reality in a technological world. A wallet with driver's license and credit cards can be lost or stolen. A phishing attack on your email account can get lots of personal information. Which one of the following is actually not a serious problem when the information is compromised?

(A) Credit card number

(B) Social Security number

(C) Checking account number

(D) Bank routing number

49. Consider procedure `mystery` and the code segment that calls the procedure below. Note that **//** indicates integer division.

```
PROCEDURE mystery (x)
{
    n ← LENGTH (x)
    temp ← x[n]
    REPEAT UNTIL (n = 0)
    {
        x[n] ← x[n] // temp
        n ← n - 1
    }
}


list ← (55, 44, 33, 22, 11)
mystery (list)
FOR EACH item IN list
{
    DISPLAY (item)
}
```

What is displayed as a result of executing the code segment?

(A) 11 11 11 11 11

(B) 55 44 33 22 1

(C) 5 4 3 2 1

(D) 5 44 33 22 11

50. Social media communication has created problems that did not exist with face-to-face communication, such as

(A) The body language response of an insensitive comment is not available. With face-to-face communication a person can immediately improve the situation by clarifying what was meant.

(B) Social media does not handle simple mistakes well. A written statement like *I am not in favor of such a change* becomes totally different when *not* is left out. With face-to-face communication the omission of not can be instantly corrected.

(C) Social media rapidly brings in other people, some family and friends, but often total outsiders who agree or disagree and what was a simple discussion between two people rapidly can becomes an emotional blasting between two groups who took sides.

(D) All of the above

---

51. Consider the screenshot below displaying a set of files in a computer folder.

Name	Date modified	Type	Size	Length	Title	Contributing artists
Blue Danube.mp3	10/9/2017 8:49 AM	MP3 File	13,876 KB	00:07:38	The Blue Danube, Op. 314	André Rieu, Johann ..
C0023.MP4	9/23/2017 7:51 AM	MP4 File	490,464 KB	00:01:13		
C0024.MP4	9/23/2017 7:52 AM	MP4 File	29,573 KB	00:00:04		
Design01.java	6/5/2017 3:15 PM	jGRASP Java file	2 KB			
Design02.java	6/5/2017 3:15 PM	jGRASP Java file	2 KB			
DSC_0040.JPG	9/23/2017 8:25 PM	JPG File	3,565 KB			
DSC_0044.JPG	9/23/2017 8:25 PM	JPG File	4,187 KB			
Go.bat	5/6/2017 7:12 AM	Windows Batc...	1 KB			
Go.command	5/6/2017 7:13 AM	COMMAND File	1 KB			
Graphics01.py	5/6/2017 1:10 PM	PY File	1 KB			
Graphics02.py	5/6/2017 1:11 PM	PY File	1 KB			
Green Berets.mp3	10/9/2017 8:49 AM	MP3 File	4,730 KB	00:02:26	The Ballad Of The Green Berets	SSgt. Barry Sadler
Lab07a.docx	8/12/2017 6:53 AM	Microsoft Wor...	163 KB			
Lara's Theme.mp3	10/9/2017 8:49 AM	MP3 File	5,806 KB	00:03:17	Lara's Theme (From "Doctor ...	The City Of Prague ...
Methods.docx	6/5/2017 2:05 PM	Microsoft Wor...	1,094 KB			
Quiz07.01-05.pptx	6/5/2017 4:55 PM	Microsoft Pow...	131 KB			
Quiz07.06-12.pptx	6/5/2017 4:56 PM	Microsoft Pow...	177 KB			
The Prayer.mp3	10/9/2017 8:49 AM	MP3 File	8,297 KB	00:04:27	The Prayer [feat. Céline Dion]	Andrea Bocelli

Without opening a single file and only looking at the screenshot what information is being supplied?

(A) Compressed data

(B) Only media information

(C) Data representation

(D) Metadata

52. Consider the `mystery` procedure below, which uses three integer parameters.

```
PROCEDURE mystery (a, b, c)
{
    temp ← a
    IF (b > temp)
    {
        temp ← b
    }
    IF (c > temp)
    {
        temp ← c
    }
    RETURN temp
}
```

What value is returned by the procedure as a result of calling `mystery`?

(A) The mean of parameters a, b and c

(B) The median of parameters a, b and c

(C) The value of the largest parameter

(D) The value of the smallest parameter

---

53. For many decades computer CPUs have increased in processing speed. In the last decade there has been less increase in processing speed, but more increase in the number of processors, called multi-core which uses multiple processors at the same time. What is a likely explanation for this trend?

(A) Single processors had reached the mathematical limits of physics and could not go faster.

(B) It is simple to create and use faster single processors, but marketing with multi-core sells better.

(C) The electrical consumption and heat problems have grown to a problematic point and the same processing power can be created more efficiently with multi-core processors.

(D) It is a personal choice really. A single, fast CPU or a multi-core unit is about the same cost and efficiency.

54. The question below present two grids. In each grid is a robot represented as a triangle, which initially is located in the bottom-left corner and facing right. The robot is capable of moving into a white cell or a gray cell, but it cannot move into a black cell.

Robot Grid A

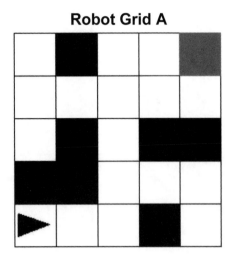

Robot Grid B

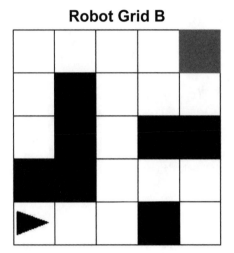

Now consider the adjacent program. The same program is meant to move the robot from its starting position to the gray cell in both grids. The program uses the procedure GOAL_REACHED(), which returns true if the robot is inside the gray cell or returns false otherwise.

Using the same program, for which grid does the program reach the gray cell correctly?

```
REPEAT UNTIL (GOAL_REACHED())
{
    IF (CAN_MOVE ("forward"))
    {
        MOVE_FORWARD ()
    }
    ELSE IF (CAN_MOVE ("left"))
    {
        ROTATE_LEFT ()
        MOVE_FORWARD ()
    }
    ELSE IF (CAN_MOVE ("right"))
    {
        ROTATE_RIGHT ()
        MOVE_FORWARD ()
    }
}
```

(A) Robot Grid A only

(B) Robot Grid B only

(C) Both Robot Grid A and Robot Grid B

(D) Neither Robot Grid A nor Robot Grid B

55. The median of a set of numbers is the exact middle number in an odd-sized list and it is the mean of the two middle numbers in an even-sized list. Consider incomplete procedure GET_MEDIAN below. Parameter list is an ordered sequence of integers that can be odd-sized or even-sized.

Note that **//** indicates integer division.

```
PROCEDURE GET_MEDIAN (list)
{
    n ← LENGTH (list)
    IF (n MOD 2 = 0)
    {
        mid1 = n // 2
        mid2 = mid1 + 1
        < Missing Code 1 >
    }
    ELSE
    {
        mid = (n + 1) // 2
        < Missing Code 2 >
    }
}
```

Which of the following program statements must replace the < Missing Code 1 & 2 > statements for the procedure to return the correct median? (Top statement is for < Missing Code 1 > & bottom statement is for < Missing Code 2 >)

A)	(B)
RETURN (list[mid1] + list[mid2]) / 2	RETURN list[mid]
RETURN list[mid]	RETURN (list[mid1] + list[mid2]) / 2
C)	(D)
RETURN (list[mid1] + list[mid2]) / 2	RETURN (list[mid1] - list[mid2]) / 2
RETURN list[mid + 1]	RETURN list[mid - 1]

56. A program assigns two positive integers to two variables. The two integers are added and stored in a third variable. When the value of the variable is displayed the answer is not mathematically correct.

Which of the following can explain this type of program error?

(A) The program probably contains one or more syntax errors.

(B) This is likely a roundoff error.

(C) The program must contain a logic error and assigned the sum to the wrong data type.

(D) It is probably a memory overflow error, caused by using a data type that does not have sufficient storage to handle the size of the number

---

57. The diagram below represents a circuit with multiple logic gates with the Boolean operator AND or OR label. Every gate has two inputs and one output. The final output must be `false`.

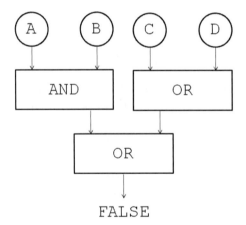

The following inputs are known:
Input A is `true`   Input B is `false`   Input C is `false`   Input D is unknown

If the final output must be `false`, what must be the input value of D?

(A) true

(B) false

(C) true or false

(D) Cannot be determined

---

58. The identity theft threat is not just a technical computer hacking problem. It can also be social engineering, such as a phishing attack, which is not a special program designed to steal data, but an attempt to deceive an individual into thinking that they are communicating with a legitimate bank or other company. Most of the phishing attacks occur using email. Which of the following helps an email reader to identify phishing attacks?

(A) The computer screen look legitimate, including company logos, but the email address has no part of the company name in it.

(B) The sentences used in the email seem to be written with grammatical error and English usage that is not the norm of US companies communicating with their customers.

(C) The email implies that information needs to be updated, including sensitive private information like social security numbers.

(D) All of the above

---

59. Many online companies request permission to use cookies, which can be turned off. Are there any benefits in letting a company use cookies?

(A) Cookies are strictly a company benefit. There is no consumer benefit.

(B) Cookies store consumer information on the consumer's computer. This helps company to direct customers more efficiently. For instance, Amazon may suggest newly published novels by an author that the cookies indicate the customer has purchased in the past.

(C) Cookies should never be used. It slows down computer operations considerably.

(D) Cookies are fine for business making purchases online, but not for individual online shopping.

60. A school district considers the purchase of a new gradebook software package for student, teacher and administrative purposes. The software is actually stored on one of the companies servers it so can be accessed from school or home. Teachers have the ability to enter grades. Students can look up their own grades. Administrators can see everyone's grades. The demonstrations of the software capabilities appear to be very impressive and the software is purchased. To the surprise of administrators and teachers the software frequently slows down considerably during the school year.

What might account for this unexpected problem?

(A) The demonstration software showed features that were known to be efficient and avoided slow operations.

(B) The demonstration software was used in a local intranet environment, which operates must faster.

(C) The demonstration was conducted with a few people accessing the software. During the school year there were hundreds of students, parents, teachers and administrators accessing the online software at the same time.

(D) The Internet does not always operate at the same speed. During the demonstration it may have been using exceptionally fast connections that are not always present during the school year.

61. Lower-level program languages are harder to program than the more convenient higher-level languages. Why would any programmer be interested in using a more difficult language.

(A) The greater convenience of a high-level language goes at a cost as programmers lose much of the computer control that is available at lower levels.

(B) For professional programmer a tough language is a challenge to overcome like a long-distance run for a runner.

(C) The only reason programmer are still using low-level languages is to maintain old programs that were written at a time when only low-level language were available.

(D) Professional programmers can code in low-level machine code as easily as a high-level drop-and-drag language. Such programmers use whatever language works best for the situation.

62. A *linear search* can be used with any kind of list, randomly arranged or sorted. A *binary search* requires that a list is   sorted. Can a linear search also benefit from a sorted list?

(A) Searching with a linear search is identical in efficiency and not depended on any type of order.

(B) A linear search is slightly faster searching a sorted list, but not enough to make this a concern.

(C) In the event that a search item is not present during a *linear search*. A search algorithm can benefit considerably from a sorted list and can stop searching.

(D) It is not really an issue, because all modern data is always sorted.

---

63. Consider the code segment below.

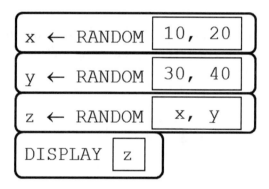

What is the range of possible integers displayed by executing the program?

(A) [10..40]

(B) [40..60]

(C) [10..60]

(D) [10..20 or 30..40]

64. The question below uses a robot in a grid of squares. The robot is represented as a triangle and located at the   starting position before program execution. The code segment below is used to move the robot during program   execution within the grid, and possibly outside the grid.

Starting Grid

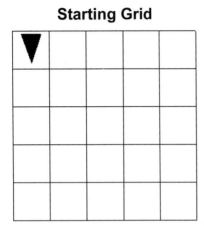

```
REPEAT 3 TIMES
{
    n ← RANDOM (1, 5)
    IF (n MOD 2 = 0)
    {
        MOVE_FORWARD ()
        MOVE_FORWARD ()
        ROTATE_LEFT ()
    }
    ELSE
    {
        MOVE_FORWARD ()
        ROTATE_LEFT ()
        MOVE_FORWARD ()
    }
}
```

The robot moves randomly and finishes at an unknown location after each execution. Which one of the four grids below represents a robot path that is not possible as a consequence of executing the program?

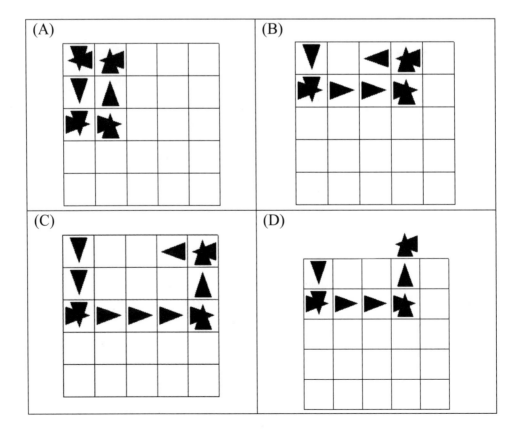

65. A modern computer image is displayed with pixels that use RGB values. A bright-red pixel is (255,0,0), bright-green is (0,255,0) and bright-blue is (0,0,255). A medium-gray pixel is (100,100,100). A computer program can alter a color image to a black-and-white or gray-scale image.

Incomplete procedure `convert`, below, is meant to change a single color pixel list parameter and return it as a grayscale pixel list.

```
PROCEDURE convert (colorPixel)
{
    r ← colorPixel[0]
    g ← colorPixel[1]
    b ← colorPixel[2]
    < Missing Code >
    RETURN grayPixel
}
```

Which of the following four code segments can be used in place of <Missing Code> make procedure `convert` accept a list of color pixel values and return a list of grayscale pixel values properly? Note that **//** indicates integer division.

(A)	(B)

`gray ← r + g + b // 3`
`grayPixel ← [gray,gray,gray]`
	`gray ← (r + g + b) // 3`
	`grayPixel ←`
	`[r+gray,g+gray,b+gray]`

(C)	(D)
`gray ← r + g + b` `grayPixel ← [gray,gray,gray]`	`gray ← (r + g + b) // 3` `grayPixel ← [gray,gray,gray]`

66. What is the only variable that can be represented by one binary digit?

(A) A single character

(B) A single-digit integer

(C) A Boolean variable

(D) There is not any variable that can be represented by only one binary digit.

Directions: For each of the remaining questions, <u>two</u> of the suggested answers will be correct. You must select both correct answer choices to earn credit. No partial credit will be earned if only one correct choice is selected. Select the two that are best in each case and then enter both of the appropriate letters in the corresponding space on the answer sheet.

---

67. Consider the following Boolean expressions.

```
x ← true
y ← false
result1 ← NOT (x AND y)
result2 ← NOT (x OR y)
result3 ← NOT (x) OR NOT (y)
result4 ← NOT (x) AND NOT (y)
```

Which results are `true`?

Select <u>two</u> answers.

(A) `result1`

(B) `result2`

(C) `result3`

(D) `result4`

---

68. The decimal number `125` is equivalent to which one of the following numbers?

Select <u>two</u> answers.

(A) `d7` (Base-16)

(B) `111101` (Base-2)

(C) `7d` (Base-16)

(D) `1111101` (Base-2)

---

69. The use of simulations is increasing in our technologic world. Which of the following are examples of simulations?

Select two answers.

(A) Using a GPS in a car to assist in finding an address.

(B) Training future pilots in a mockup plane how to fly.

(C) Observing the behavior of a ship model in a 600 meter pool before construction of the ship starts.

(D) Playing poker on a computer in a casino.

70. Consider the adjacent procedure `mystery`. Assume that mystery is called using an initial value of n equals 3.

Which of the code segments below will execute with the same output as procedure `mystery`?

Select two answers.

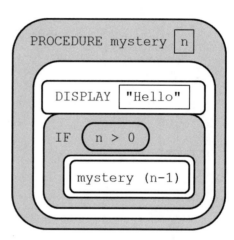

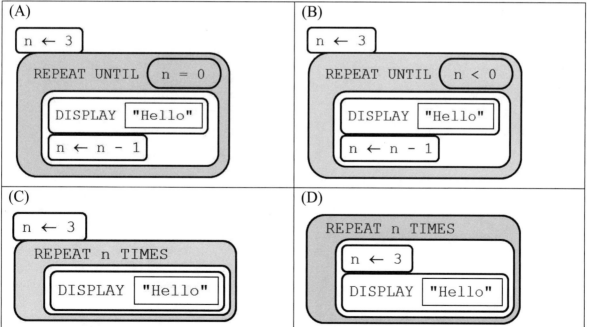

71. The question uses a robot in a grid of cells. The robot is represented as a triangle, which initially is located in the top-left corner and facing down. The robot is capable of moving into a white cell or a gray cell, but it cannot move into a black cell.

Which of the following program code segments will move the robot into the gray cell as a result of running the program?

Select <u>two</u> answers.

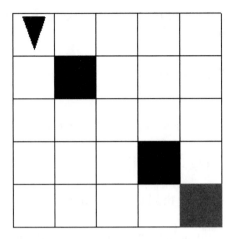

(A)	(B)
| ```
REPEAT 2 TIMES
{
    MOVE_FORWARD()
    MOVE_FORWARD()
    ROTATE_LEFT()
    MOVE_FORWARD()
    ROTATE_RIGHT()
}
MOVE_FORWARD()
MOVE_FORWARD()
``` | ```
REPEAT 2 TIMES
{
    MOVE_FORWARD()
    MOVE_FORWARD()
    ROTATE_LEFT()
    MOVE_FORWARD()
    ROTATE_RIGHT()
}
ROTATE_LEFT()
MOVE_FORWARD()
MOVE_FORWARD()
``` |
| (C) | (D) |
| ```
ROTATE_LEFT()
REPEAT 2 TIMES
{
    REPEAT 4 TIMES
    {
        MOVE_FORWARD()
    }
    ROTATE_RIGHT()
}
``` | ```
ROTATE_LEFT()
REPEAT 2 TIMES
{
    MOVE_FORWARD()
    MOVE_FORWARD()
    ROTATE_RIGHT()
    MOVE_FORWARD()
    MOVE_FORWARD()
    ROTATE_LEFT()
}
``` |

72. A polling company wants to test the random number generator of various program languages. For this test the random number generator needs to generate integers in the [1..10] range. The program generates 1,000,000 random integers and checks for their randomness. Which of the four program segments below gives useful information to help determine correct randomness?

Select <u>two</u> answers.

(A)
``
rndList ← (0,0,0,0,0,0,0,0,0,0)
REPEAT 1000000 TIMES
{
    rnd ← RANDOM (1, 10)
    rndList[rnd] ← rndList[rnd] + 1
}
FOR EACH item IN rndList
{
    DISPLAY (item)
}
``
	(B)
	``
	REPEAT 1000000 TIMES
	{
	    sum ← 0
	    rnd ← RANDOM (1, 10)
	    sum ← sum + rnd
	}
	mean ← sum / 1000000
	DISPLAY (mean)
	``

(C)
``
rndList ← (0,0,0,0,0,0,0,0,0,0)
REPEAT 1000000 TIMES
{
    rnd ← RANDOM (1, 10)
    rndList[rnd] ← rnd
}
FOR EACH item IN rndList
{
    DISPLAY (item)
}
``
	(D)
	``
	sum ← 0
	REPEAT 1000000 TIMES
	{
	    rnd ← RANDOM (1, 10)
	    sum ← sum + rnd
	}
	mean ← sum / 1000000
	DISPLAY (mean)
	``

73. Cloud computing seems very desirable for global access of data and inexpensive use of software that is easily updated. This may not apply to everybody. Which two groups of people will be least likely to use it?

Select <u>two</u> answers.

(A) People in remote areas where fast Internet is not available and cloud computing is too slow.

(B) High school students

(C) Retired people who do not use computers in multiple locations and generate very little data.

(D) People who have several external hard drives for backup security

---

74. What are the two principal functions of an IP address?

Select <u>two</u> answers.

(A) It identifies the individual host or computer.

(B) It identifies the location of the host on the network.

(C) It matches an Internet address with a physical address.

(D) It identifies an individual website, such as WWW.IBM.COM

AP Computer Science Principles
Sample Exam II

1. The diagram below represents a circuit with multiple logic gates with the Boolean operator AND or OR label. Every gate has two inputs and one output. The final output must be `true`.

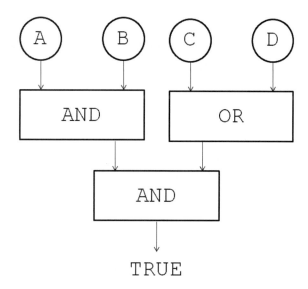

The following inputs are known:

Input A is `true`
Input B is `unknown`
Input C is `false`
Input D is `true`

If the final output must be `true`, what must be the input value of B?

(A) `true`

(B) `false`

(C) `true` or `false`

(D) Cannot be determined

2. Acme Inc. has a group of employees working on a common project. The employees are scattered at many different locations. Collaboration on the project is key and every member needs to know about when other members make any changes or finish important stages in the project.

Which one of the following communication scenarios will work well for Acme Inc.?

(A) Every time a team member finishes a stage, a group email is sent to all members with attachments of the latest completions.

(B) Acme can use the Cloud with local drop boxes that are synced to the Cloud and to every member of the team. When any team member saves a change on the project, it will be automatically updated for everybody.

(C) Whenever a member finishes a stage he/she calls for a video conference to communicate with everybody.

(D) Whenever an update is required, members use a high-speed electronic fax system to inform everybody.

---

3. Consider the code segment below.

```
x ← RANDOM  10, 20
y ← RANDOM  30, 40
z ← x + y
DISPLAY  z
```

What is the range of possible integers displayed by executing the program?

(A) [10..40]

(B) [40..60]

(C) [10..60]

(D) [10..20 or 30..40]

4. Many online companies use cookies with their customers. Which of the following explains the benefit of cookies?

(A) Cookies store personal data information on a computer for easy access and use by the computer user.

(B) Cookies store web pages that are frequently used to avoid loading long, complicated web pages.

(C) Cookies store information on a person's computer that online companies find beneficial for future promotions and interactions with the customer.

(D) Cookies are used in modern computers to turn on computers quicker.

5. A school district upgrades all its computer and educational software to the newest versions available to improve technology capabilities and assist education. After the software is installed, the performance of the new software seems slower than the previous software versions. What might be an explanation for this problem?

(A) The new software may not have been thoroughly tested and will require improvements to work properly.

(B) The district purchased new software, but still uses old computers, which cannot handle the computing power required to run the more demanding, new software efficiently.

(C) Very likely the new software must be re-installed with proper settings for maximum performance.

(D) The slow performance might be misleading, because many teachers and educators are not yet familiar with operating the new software.

6. This question uses a robot in a grid of squares. The robot is represented as a triangle and starts at the top-left cell on the adjacent grid.

    The goal of a program segment for this question is to finish in the gray cell, shown in the adjacent grid image.

    Which of the program segments below will make the robot move correctly to the gray cell?

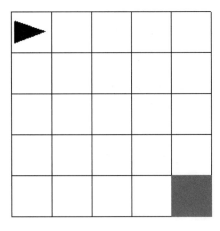

(A) REPEAT 4 TIMES
    {
        MOVE_FORWARD ()
        ROTATE_RIGHT ()
        MOVE_FORWARD ()
        ROTATE_RIGHT ()
    }

(B) REPEAT 4 TIMES
    {
        MOVE_FORWARD ()
    }
    ROTATE_RIGHT ()
    REPEAT 4 TIMES
    {
        MOVE_FORWARD ()
    }

(C) REPEAT 2 TIMES
    {
        REPEAT 4 TIMES
        {
            MOVE_FORWARD ()
        }
        ROTATE_RIGHT ()
    }

(D) All of the above

7. Modern programming languages have many features of reliability and convenience that were not available with older languages. Why is there still a need to learn and use older programming languages?

(A) Legacy program languages have been used on thousands of programs that are running today. Such programs require maintenance by people familiar with these languages.

(B) Older languages are simpler and very good to use for introductory computer science courses.

(C) Modern languages are very expensive. Older languages are cheap and save a lot of money.

(D) All of the above

---

8. Consider a list of data of roughly 10,000 records that is sorted numerically according to an account number.

Is it ever possible for a *linear search* to find a desired record with fewer comparisons than a *binary search*?

(A) No, it is not possible. The *binary search* will always be faster than the *linear search*.

(B) Yes, it is possible. Actually, the *linear search* will be faster than the *binary search* for 50% of the searches.

(C) Yes, it is occasionally possible when the target record is located at the front of the list.

(D) Yes, it is occasionally possible when the target record is located at the end of the list.

9. A modern computer image is displayed with pixels that use RGB values. A bright-red pixel is (255,0,0), bright-green is (0,255,0) and bright-blue is (0,0,255). A company decides to save memory for its image storage and create software that reduces the number of color combinations by using 4 bits for each color rather than 8 bits.

What will be the impact of the number of color selections for this type of software?

(A) There will be 1/2 the available colors.

(B) There will be 1/4 the available colors.

(C) There will be 1/8 the available colors.

(D) There will be less than 1% of the previous color selection.

---

10. For this question procedure SUBSTRING(str, a, b) is available. This procedure returns a substring of the str parameter. The index of str starts at 1 for the first character. Parameter a is the starting character index of the substring and parameter b is the index following the last character of the substring.

Consider the following code segment.

```
s1 = "Aardvark"
k = 1
REPEAT 5 TIMES
{
    s2 = SUBSTRING (s1, k, 7)
    k = k + 1
}
DISPLAY (s2)
```

What is output as a result of executing the code segment?

(A) var

(B) va

(C) ard

(D) dva

---

11. Which of the following is a good reason for including program documentation in a program?

    (A) Enhancing a program in the future becomes simpler when the original logic of the program is forgotten.

    (B) The program may require maintenance by individuals who did not write the original code.

    (C) Inexperienced programmers can learn better from existing programs with well-written documentation at key locations in the program.

    (D) All of the above

---

12. Consider the following code segment, which uses the variables a, b, c, d.

```
a ← 10
b ← 15
c ← 20
d ← a
a ← b
b ← c
c ← d
DISPLAY (a, b, c, d)
```

What is displayed as a result of running the code segment?

    (A) 15 20 10 15

    (B) 10 10 10 10

    (C) 15 20 10 10

    (D) 10 10 15 20

13. An Internet address of a website can be accessed with an *IP address* or a *domain name*. Is there a difference in the website access speed between using an IP address or a domain name?

(A) The access speed is rough the same.

(B) Using a domain name is slower, because the domain name requires going to a Domain Name System (DNS) server, which then translates the domain name into an IP address.

(C) Using an IP address is slower, because the IP address requires going to a Domain Name System (DNS) server first, which then translates the IP address into a domain name.

(D) Using domain names is faster for international access, but IP addresses are faster for domestic access

---

14. Consider the following code segment.

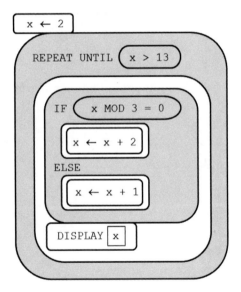

What is displayed as a result of running the code segment?

(A) 11

(B) 12

(C) 13

(D) 14

---

15. Consider the following Boolean expressions.

```
a = < unknown Boolean value >
b = < unknown Boolean value >
result1 = NOT (a OR b)
result2 = NOT (a) AND NOT (b)
```

Without knowing the initial values of Boolean variables a and b, what can be stated correctly about Boolean variables `result1` and `result2`?

(A) Both `result1` and `result2` will always be the same.

(B) Both `result1` and `result2` will always be different.

(C) Both `result1` and `result2` will always be `true`.

(D) Both `result1` and `result2` will always be `false`.

---

16. A loan application requires the inclusion of your social security number. You are very concerned about identity theft. Which of the following is the most secure method of transmission to get the application to the loan officer?

(A) You personally hand-carry the loan application and hand it to the loan officer.

(B) You mail the loan application using the regular postal delivery service.

(C) You email the loan application as an attachment.

(D) You fill out an online application provided by the loan officer.

17. The following information about variables that be understood before looking at the later algorithm steps.

- n1, n2 and n3 are the numerators of three fractions.

- d1, d2, and d3 are the denominators of the same fractions.

- getGCF(a,b) function returns the greatest common factor (gcf) of a and b.

- getLCM(a,b) function returns the least common multiple (lcm) of a and b.

1. Compute the lcm of d1 and d2 using getLCM (d1,d2).

2. n1 becomes lcm divided by d1 times n1.

3. n2 becomes lcm divided by d2 times n2

4. d1, d2 and d3 become the lcm.

5. n3 becomes n1 plus n2.

6. Compute the gcf of n3 and d3 using getGCF (n3,d3).

7. n3 becomes n3 divided by the gcf.

8. d3 becomes d3 divided by the gcf.

Which of the following explains the purpose of this algorithm?

(A) The algorithm reduces fractions n1/d1, n2/d2 and n3/d3

(B) The algorithm assigns the *sum* of fractions n1/d1 and n2/d2 to n3/d3 and then reduces fraction n3/d3.

(C) The algorithm assigns the *product* of fractions n1/d1 and n2/d2 to n3/d3 and then reduces n3/d3.

(D) The algorithm assigns the *quotient* of fractions n1/d1 and n2/d2 to n3/d3 and then reduces n3/d3.

18. A *linear search* is used for finding information in a large list of records. Assume that the average search time for a list of n records takes k micro seconds.

If the list grows and there are now 3n records, what will become the expected search time?

(A) 9k

(B) 6k

(C) 3k

(C) Slightly greater than k

---

19. Consider procedure mystery below.

```
list1 ← (5, 4, 3, 2, 1)
list2 ← list1
REMOVE (list2, 1)
n ← LENGTH(list1)
DISPLAY (list1[n])
DISPLAY (list2[n])
```

What is output as a result of executing the code segment?

(A) 2 1

(B) 1 1

(C) 2 2

(D) 1 index out of range error

20. Some years ago Borland introduced Turbo Pascal with a *no nonsense copyright license*. The company explained the purchase and use of their software was the same as purchasing a printed book.

Which of the following explains the proper, ethical use of the Turbo Pascal software?

(A) It can only be installed and used on a single computer only.

(B) It can be installed and used on a home computer and a business computer simultaneously. It really is a double license.

(C) It can be installed and used on many computers simultaneously, just like a book can be read by many people.

(D) It can be installed on multiple computers, but it can only be used by one person at a time, just like a book can be used by many people, but only one person at a time can read the book.

---

21. For experienced, professional programmers, a modern high-level programming language with drop-and-drag features can be tedious and lacking the control that professional programmers require. If such is the case why are the drop-and-drag languages popular?

(A) Drop and drag languages look flashy and allow considerable capabilities with little knowledge and effort.

(B) Drop and drag languages are terrific for early grade introduction of coding with something like Lego Robots or create simple video games.

(C) Drop and drag languages do introduce many program concepts like control structures and procedures in a clear visual manner that help to teach students new to computer science.

(D) All of the above

22. In the Fifties and Sixties, Morse Code and encryption were very popular for Boy Scout indoor winter activities. The symbols below represent a secret message that is encoded in one of the popular encryption schemes of that time. Initially, there would be no hints of any kind and scouts were busy trying to determine the message.

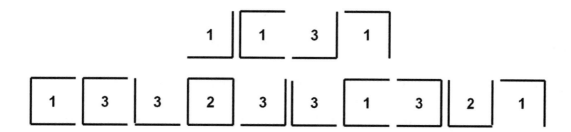

After some time if scouts struggled, they were given the adjacent key to solve the puzzle.

Using this key, which of the following is the English version of the message?

(A) WORD PROCESSING

(B) APCS PRINCIPLES

(C) HARD ENCRYPTION

(D) WARM CORNFLAKES

ABC	DEF	GHI
JKL	MNO	PQR
STU	VWX	YZ

23. The pixel coloring system that assigns Red, Green and Blue values to individual pixels have millions of color combinations. This system quickly indicates the dominant color, such as (200,100,50) where red dominates. If the RGB values are the same, such as (150,150,150) or (75,75,75) there is no dominant color. What does a color triple of the same three values indicate?

(A) It indicates a grayscale value with 0 totally black and 255 totally white.

(B) It indicates a grayscale value with 0 totally white and 255 totally back.

(C) It indicates the intensity of gray with 0 a being light-gray and 255 a dark gray

(D) When triples have the same three values it indicates black or white. RGB triples from 0 to 127 will appear black and triples from 128..255 will be totally white.

---

24. When files are sent over the Internet they are broken up into packets that travel individually to their final destination. What happens when individual packets do not arrive at the final destination?

(A) This is one reason for the existence of corrupt files. The file will arrive at its destination incomplete and may not function properly.

(B) A message is sent to the destination computer to resend the entire file.

(C) The recipient of the file needs to check if the file is acceptable, and if not request another copy of the entire file.

(D) A check is performed at the destination. Any packet that does not arrive triggers a request for to resend that individual packet.

25. A city manager wants to determine the average value of homes in the city. The city has some homes that are very low priced and likewise there exist some homes that are very expensive. These homes are a small number, but they can distort the statistics.

A programmer is instructed to create a program that eliminates any homes less than $100,000 and any homes greater than $500,000 from the list used for the statistical survey.

Consider the adjacent incomplete purge procedure.

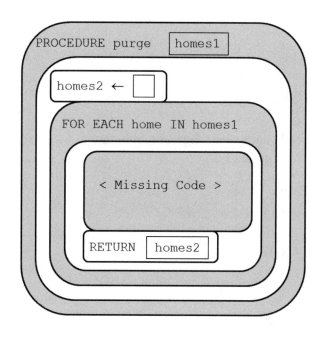

Procedure purge is expected to use a list parameter of all homes values in the city and then return a list without any homes below $100,000 and above $500,000.

Which of the code segments below can substitute the **<Missing Code >** and then make procedure purge execute correctly?

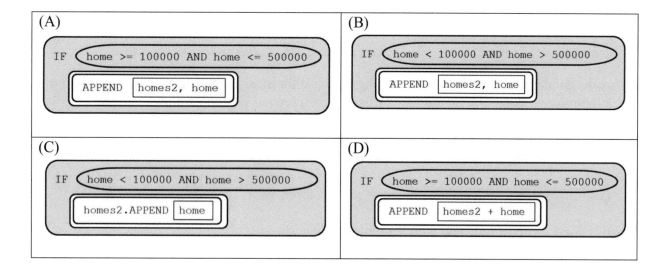

(A)

```
IF  home >= 100000 AND home <= 500000
        APPEND   homes2, home
```

(B)

```
IF  home < 100000 AND home > 500000
        APPEND   homes2, home
```

(C)

```
IF  home < 100000 AND home > 500000
        homes2.APPEND  home
```

(D)

```
IF  home >= 100000 AND home <= 500000
        APPEND   homes2 + home
```

26. Consider the program below.

```
a ← RANDOM (50,80)
b ← RANDOM (30,60)
c = a - b
DISPLAY (c)
```

What is the range of numbers that can be displayed as a result of executing the code segment?

(A) [30 .. 80]

(B) [-10 .. 20]

(C) [-10 .. 50]

(D) [20 .. 30]

27. A school keeps a database for all its students with a great variety of information. A small part of the database is shown below. Right now the concern is Senior finals exemptions. Seniors must have at least an 85 GPA. Additionally, they must have less than 3 tardies and 0 suspensions. Currently the program can only sort two of the categories in the database.

Name	Absences	Tardies	Grade	Suspensions	GPA
Tom Smith	4	1	12	0	92
Sue Jones	3	0	11	0	89
Meg Baker	5	3	12	0	74
Bob Griffin	2	4	12	1	67

A decision must be made how to sort the database for maximum efficiency in determining exemptions? What will be the first sort and which second sort will follow?

(A) First Sort by absences and then Second sort by tardies

(B) First sort by GPA and then Second sort by absences

(C) First sort by Grade and then Second sort by tardies

(D) First sort by GPA and then Second sort by Grade

28. The question below uses a robot in a grid of squares. The robot is represented as a triangle, which initially is located in the top-left square, facing right. For this question the robot needs to visit every gray cell on the adjacent grid. The sequence of gray cells is not important, but the robot must finish in the center.

Which of the following program segments will move the robot as required?

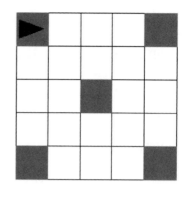

(A)
```
REPEAT 4 TIMES
{
    REPEAT 4 TIMES
    {
        MOVE_FORWARD
    }
    ROTATE_RIGHT()
}
REPEAT 2 TIMES ()
{
    ROTATE_RIGHT ()
    MOVE_FORWARD ()
    MOVE_FORWARD ()
}
```

(B)
```
REPEAT 4 TIMES
{
    REPEAT 4 TIMES
    {
        MOVE_FORWARD
    }
    ROTATE_RIGHT()
}
ROTATE_LEFT()
REPEAT 2 TIMES ()
{
    ROTATE_RIGHT ()
    MOVE_FORWARD ()
    MOVE_FORWARD ()
}
```

(C)
```
REPEAT 4 TIMES
{
    REPEAT 4 TIMES
    {
        MOVE_FORWARD ()
        ROTATE_RIGHT ()
    }
}
ROTATE_LEFT()
REPEAT 2 TIMES ()
{
    ROTATE_RIGHT ()
    MOVE_FORWARD ()
    MOVE_FORWARD ()
}
```

(D)
```
k ← 0
REPEAT 20 TIMES
{
    k ← k + 1
    if (k MOD 5 = 0)
    {
        ROTATE_RIGHT ()
    }
    ELSE
    {
        MOVE_FORWARD ()
    }
}
REPEAT 2 TIMES
{
    ROTATE_RIGHT ()
    MOVE_FORWARD ()
    MOVE_FORWARD ()
}
```

29. Applicants for a driver license must be at least 16 years old and not older than 95. A program is used to insure that applicants are the correct age. This question is limited to the small code segment in the program responsible for checking the applicant's age

Which one of the following code segments will **NOT** accurately identify the wrong age?

```
(A) IF (NOT (age ≥ 16 AND age ≤ 95))
    {
        DISPLAY ("You may not apply for a license")
    }
    ELSE
    {
        DISPLAY ("Proceed with the application")
    }
```

```
(B) IF (NOT (age ≥ 16) OR NOT (age ≤ 95))
    {
        DISPLAY ("You may not apply for a license")
    }
    ELSE
    {
        DISPLAY ("Proceed with the application")
    }
```

```
(C) IF (age < 16 OR age > 95)
    {
        DISPLAY ("You may not apply for a license")
    }
    ELSE
    {
        DISPLAY ("Proceed with the application")
    }
```

```
(D) IF (NOT (age ≥ 16) AND NOT (age ≤ 95))
    {
        DISPLAY ("You may not apply for a license")
    }
    ELSE
    {
        DISPLAY ("Proceed with the application")
    }
```

30. Consider the following code segment.

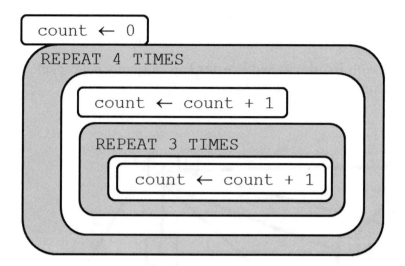

What is the value of `count` when the code segment has finished executing?

(A) 16

(B) 18

(C) 20

(D) 12

---

31. A large corporation requires network communication and sensitive data storage within its own facility with maximum security. What type of network is ideal for such a corporation?

(A) Everything should be handled by a Local Area Network or LAN

(B) An Intranet of combining LANs with effective firewalls for the exclusive access of the corporation

(C) Use a reliable cloud service company on the Internet

(D) It does not matter as long as there are proper firewalls in place.

32. The image below represents two computers and a group of network nodes on the Internet. Each node has a router capable of passing files to another connected network node and also capable of finding an alternate route if a previous connection slows down or is no longer available.

The two shaded network nodes with **Router D** and **Router I** are currently not capable of transmitting any packets to a connected network node.

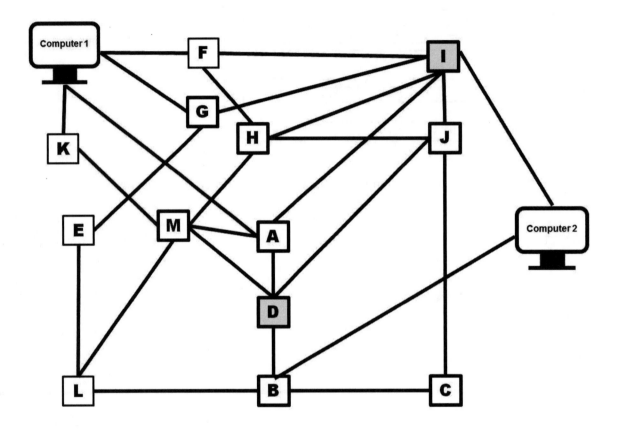

Considering the current status of this network, with two dysfunctional routers. What is the smallest number of routers necessary to connect **Computer 1** to **Computer 2**?

(A) 3 routers

(B) 4 routers

(C) 5 routers

(D) 6 routers

33. The American Standard Code for Information Interchange - better known as ASCII - uses numerical values to encode characters. The decimal (base 10) value 97 represents lower-case a, 98 is b, 99 is c and this pattern continues and lower-case z has ASCII value 122. Each one of the ASCII characters can be represented as a 7-bit number.

What is the hexadecimal value of ASCII character **k**?

(A) 107

(B) 6b

(C) 6f

(d) 113

---

34. Consider the adjacent image, which demonstrates an example of pixilation when individual pixels of an image become visible to the human eye.

What causes an image to show pixilation?

(A) It happens frequently when printed pictures are scanned into digital file format.

(B) It occurs when an image is printed on low quality paper.

(C) It only happens to pictures with low resolution.

(D) It happens to any picture, regardless of resolution, when sufficient zooming is applied.

35. Algorithms can be visually represented by a flowchart, such as the one shown below. Building blocks used by the flowchart are explained in the table below.

Block	Explanation
Oval	The start or end of an algorithm
Rectangle	One or more processing steps, such as a statement that assigns a value or variable
Diamond	A conditional or decision step, where execution proceeds to the side labeled `true` if the condition is true and to the side labeled `false` otherwise.
Parallelogram	Display a message

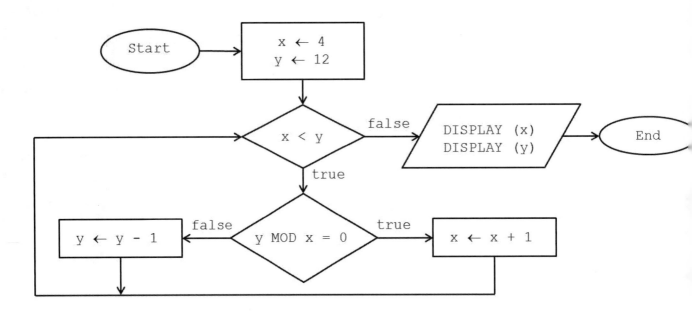

What is displayed as a result of executing the algorithm in the flowchart?

(A) 6 6

(B) 5 5

(C) 5 6

(D) 6 5

36. Companies give rights of access on a company intranet based on an employee position. It is the practice of one company to give somebody rights that are equal to the rights of a person because they have the same position in the company.

Is this a good practice or are there potential problems with such a network administration shortcut?

(A) It is no problem. The rights of the new employee are correct since they are the same as another employee of equal position and network access privileges.

(B) It can cause problems because such rights are only temporary and need to be renewed regularly.

(C) There can be serious problems. If an employee is promoted, new more exclusive rights are assigned. Unintentionally, other people, who were not promoted, now have those very same rights.

(D) There can be a serious problem, because the new employee now has access to the personal information of the other employee.

---

37. Consider the following numbers in three different number bases.

Binary numbers will be indicated as *base-2*, like `101100` (base-2).
Decimal numbers will be indicated with *(base-10)*, like `6879` (base-10).
Hexadecimal numbers will be indicated with *(base-16)*, like `a5f2bc` (base-10).

Which of the following are in ascending order, from left-to-right?

(A) `305` (base-10)   -   `11010100` (base-2)   -   F4 (base-16)

(B) F5 (base-16)   -   `275` (base-10)   -   `111111111` (base-2)

(C) `256` (base-10)   -   `110001011` (base -2)   -   8B (base-16)

(D) None of the above

38. A *Pythagorean triple* is a set of three positive integers (a, b, c)
    such that $a^2 + b^2 = c^2$.

    An example of a Pythagorean triple is (3, 4, 5).

    Consider incomplete procedure isPythagorean below. The intention of procedure
    isPythagorean is to check if parameters (a,b,c) are a Pythagorean triple and then
    return true or return false otherwise.

    ```
    PROCEDURE isPythagorean (a, b, c)
    {
        <MISSING CODE>
    }
    ```

    Which of the following code segments can replace **<Missing Code>** such that procedure
    isPythagorean will execute correctly?

    (A) RETURN c * c = a * a + b * b

    (B) temp = a * a + b * b
        IF (temp = c * c)
        {
            RETURN true
        }
        ELSE
        {
            RETURN false
        }

    (C) RETURN c * c ← a * a + b * b

    (D) Both choices (A) and (B)

39. This question uses a robot in a grid of squares. The robot is represented as a triangle, which initially is located in the bottom-center and facing up. The robot is capable of moving into a white cell or a gray cell, it cannot move into a black cell. The adjacent grid shows the grid at the start of executing the program code below.

```
REPEAT 4 TIMES
{
      MOVE_FORWARD()
}
ROTATE_LEFT()
MOVE_FORWARD()
MOVE_FORWARD()
ROTATE_RIGHT()
ROTATE_RIGHT()
REPEAT 4 TIMES
{
    MOVE_FORWARD()
}
```

Starting Grid

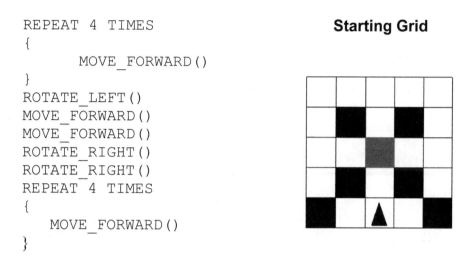

Which of the following grid images represents the grid after executing the code segment?

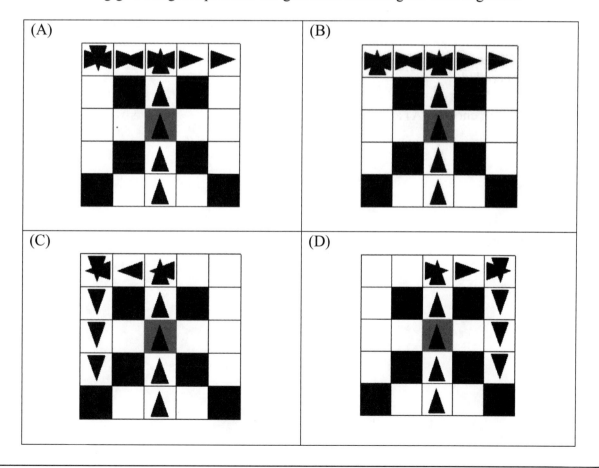

40. Acme Inc. must decide on the nature of its data compression policy. Acme transfers thousands of data files daily to its many branches and its customers. Some documents require strict *lossless* compression and others may be transmitted with *lossy* compressions. Which of the following data files cannot be sent with *lossy* compression?

(A) Employee profile pictures for record keeping

(B) Customer legal contracts

(C) Archived video files of video conference meetings

(D) Archived audio files of telephone recordings

---

41. *Caching* stores frequently visited web pages on a local computer for fast future access. One example is the login web page of a bank that may not change much. Which of the following are disadvantages of using cache memory for web page browsing?

(A) The web page may be old and does not reflect current company updates.

(B) Keeping web pages in cache can be quite expensive as the number of web pages grows.

(C) Cache can distort the web page access since customer visits to cached web pages is not recorded.

(D) Both choices (A) and (C)

42. Students use some online software for quiz and test taking. The software works fine, but the colors are not the same on all computers. It is not a difference in intensity or brilliance, but some colors are totally different. What might be the cause for this difference?

(A) Students have different color settings on their browsers that change colors.

(B) Some students have a Windows operating system and others use a Mac operating system. Not all operating systems handle colors in the same manner.

(C) Students are using different browsers. A web page created on one browser may be using non-standard HTML features unique to one browser that may not be recognized by another browser.

(D) Students may be using different monitors that do not all show colors in the same manner.

---

43. Consider the adjacent code segment.

What is the output of executing the code segment?

(A) 11 33 55

(B) 22 44 44 66

(C) 11 44 44 55

(D) 11 44 33 66 55

```
k ← 1
list ← (11,22,44,33,88,66,55)
REPEAT UNTIL (k = LENGTH (list))
{
    IF (list[k] % 2 = 0)
    {
        REMOVE (list, k)
    }
    k ← k + 1
}
FOR EACH item IN list
{
    DISPLAY (item)
}
```

44. A common Internet complaint is the slowness of satellite Internet. This confuses many people, because there appears no problem with satellite television reception outside bad weather reception problems.

Which of the following accounts for this discrepancy in satellite speed?

(A) Television is one-way communication. Television broadcasts and customer select a channel to receive the broadcast that is ongoing. Internet is two-way communication. You send a request and then get a response.

(B) Television handles thousands of customers at once with a single broadcast. The Internet has to deal with each person individually.

(C) Internet communication goes through many different nodes to find it final destination and then return over pretty much the same number of nodes. Television has a much simpler path from broadcast station to satellite and from satellite to customers.

(D) All of the above

45. Real computer programs use many different modules. There are procedures, functions, libraries and many separate files that all combine to run one large program. The three images below include two procedures and a block of program code that uses the procedures. Look at the three code modules to determine their purpose.

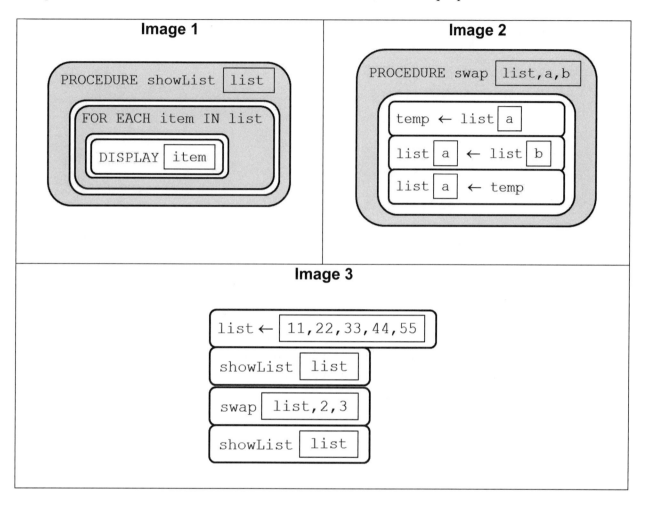

Program execution starts with Image 3. It simulates a code segment from a real program that calls the two procedures. What will be displayed as a result of executing the program segment?

(A) 11 22 33 44 55
    11 33 22 44 55

(B) 11 33 22 44 55
    11 22 33 44 55

(C) 11 22 33 44 55
    11 22 44 33 55

(D) 11 22 33 44 55
    55 44 33 22 11

46.   Consider procedure isSorted below. The intention of procedure isSorted is to
check if the elements of the list parameter are sorted in descending order, which
returns true and if not sorted in descending order returns false.

```
PROCEDURE isSorted (list)
{
    sorted ← true
    n ← LENGTH(list) - 1
    k ← 1
    REPEAT UNTIL (k >= n)
    {
        IF (<MISSING CODE>)
        {
            sorted = false
        }
        k ← k + 1
    }
    RETURN sorted
}
```

Which of the following replacements for <MISSING CODE> results in procedure
isSorted correctly identifying a list sorted in ascending order?

(A) (list[1] < list[k])

(B) (list[k] < list[k+1)

(C) (list[k] > list[k+1])

(D) (list[1] > list[n])

47. Consider the image below. It is an example of an image that many people see who use online companies. This type of image, which includes a *Personal Image* and a *Personal Phrase* follows the entry of one's *User ID* and *Password*.

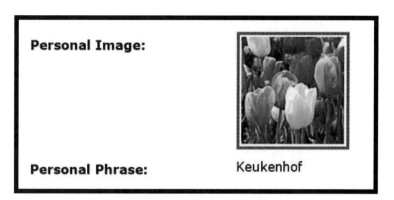

Why does a company add this type of information with the usual login requirements?

(A) It is a third level of security to identify the customer after the User ID and Password.

(B) It is meant as a pleasant greeting by showing something that is personal to the customer.

(C) It lets the customer know that the login screen is legitimate and not a *phishing* attempt. Phishing attacks can duplicate the appearance of business logins very closely, but they know nothing about a *Personal Image*.

(D) It is a new type of login that does not use password entries, but image and phrase recognition.

---

48. There are many Cloud Services that manage Internet storage and dropbox convenience, like *GoogleDrive, OneDrive* and *Dropbox*. These companies provides services for free. Why would somebody wish to pay money for Cloud Services when they are available free?

(A) The free services provide a rather limited amount of data storage that is often insufficient.

(B) Paid services often include sophisticated encryption of data that is more secure.

(C) Paid services include special advanced features that are not available for free.

(D) All of the above

49. Consider the following algorithm.

Consider the following information about variables that must be understood before looking at the algorithm steps.

- n1, n2 and n3 are the numerators of three fractions.

- d1, d2, and d3 are the denominators of the same fractions.

- getGCF(a,b) is a *Greatest Common Factor* function that returns the gcf of a and b.

1. Multiply n1 times d2 and assign the product to n3.
2. Multiply d1 times n2 and assign the product to d3.
3. Compute the gcf of n3 and d3 using the getGCF function.
4. Divide n3 by the gcf.
5. Divide d3 by the gcf.

Which of the following explains the purpose of this algorithm?

(A) The algorithm reduces fractions n1/d1, n2/d2 and n3/d3

(B) The algorithm computes n3/d3 as the *sum* of n1/d1 and n2/d2 and then reduces n3/d3.

(C) The algorithm computes n3/d3 as the *product* of n1/d1 and n2/d2 and then reduces n3/d3.

(D) The algorithm computes n3/d3 as the *quotient* of n1/d1 and n2/d2 and then reduces n3/d3.

50. Consider the following four hexadecimal numbers.

- `af603b`

- `f37de2`

- `1234567`

- `abcdef`

Which of the following displays the numbers in order from smallest to largest?

(A) `abcdef`   `af603b`   `f37de2`   `1234567`

(B) `1234567`   `abcdef`   `f37de2`   `af603b`

(C) `f37de2`   `af603b`   `abcdef`   `1234567`

(D) `af603b`   `f37de2`   `1234567`   `abcdef`

---

51. Consider the following algorithm which uses a list of consecutive integers [2 .. 100]

Step-1: Mark all numbers from 2 to 100 as True.

Step-2: Mark all multiples of 2 as False.

Step-3: Mark all multiples of 3 as False.

Step-4: Skip any number that is marked False.

Step-5: Continue, but only mark multiples of a number False, if the number is True.

Step-6: When you reach 100 you are finished.
            All numbers `2..100` should be marked True or False.

Look at the list of consecutive integers. What are the numbers that are marked True?

(A) They are multiples of a previous number.

(B) They are factors of a later number.

(C) They are prime numbers, which are only divisible by 1 and itself.

(D) They are perfect numbers, which are numbers, whose factors add up to the number.

52. Consider the following code segment and Boolean expression.

```
a ← true
b ← false
c ← < unknown Boolean value >
d ← false
e ← < unknown Boolean value >

result ← a OR ( NOT ((b AND c) OR (a AND e)) )
```

What can be correctly stated about the value of `result`?

(A) Nothing can be stated about `result` without knowing the values of c and e.

(B) The value of `result` equals `true`.

(C) The value of `result` equals `false`.

(D) The value of `result` equals `true` only if c equals `true` and e equals `false`.

53. The US Army keeps an extensive database on all its current and previous members, which includes:

- Personal information, such as name, birthdate, gender, marital status, etc.
- Detailed medical records, including check-ups and all medical procedures.
- Training completed and certificates earned, such as Paratrooper, Ranger, etc.
- History of promotions
- Medals earned
- Overseas deployments
- Observation reports of commanding officer

Which of the following statistics **cannot** be determined with the database information shown above?

(A) The lightest soldier to win a Medal of Honor

(B) The youngest 4-Star General.

(C) The soldier with the record for doing largest number of pushups

(D) The soldier who has been overseas the largest number of days

54. This question presents four scenarios that use a program based on an algorithm to solve a problem. Which one of these scenarios is the most likely to involve the use of heuristics in its algorithm?

(A) Parents who are home schooling their children want to have a program that tests proficiency in the main subject areas and measure improvement.

(B) A person wants to use a program to compute how much money must be saved per month to have one million dollars saved at age 65.

(C) A baseball coach wants to use a program to store baseball performance statistics for each player.

(D) A young man uses an online dating service, which includes a program that provides a list of potential dates that may result is a serious relationship.

---

55. Consider the adjacent code segment.

What is the range of integers that can be displaced by executing the code segment?

(A) [11 .. 90]

(B) [10 .. 91]

(C) [50 .. 51]

(D) Cannot be determined.
It is constantly changing.

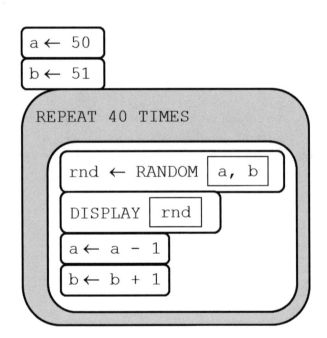

```
a ← 50
b ← 51

REPEAT 40 TIMES

    rnd ← RANDOM  a, b

    DISPLAY  rnd

    a ← a - 1
    b ← b + 1
```

56. There have been multiple incidents of large companies compromising millions of customer's personal data. What can a person do to help protect against fraudulent use of personal information?

(A) Acquire credit reports on a regular basis and check for any fraudulent activity.

(B) Close all credit accounts and pay with cash only.

(C) Place a lock with each one of the credit score companies that no new account may be opened without the account holder's approval.

(D) Close your account with the company that compromised your personal information.

---

57. Some program languages have both signed and unsigned numerical data types. This is done with a sign bit. For instance, if a `byte` data type store integers in an 8-bit sequence then 7 bits are used for the number and 1 bit is used for the sign. What percentage of the memory is lost for number use with a signed number?

(A) It is always 50% for an 8-bit number, but it increases with larger numbers differently.

(B) It is always a 50% reduction for any numerical data type.

(C) It is 50% with 8-bits, 25% with 16-bits, 12.5% with 32-bits and 6.25% with 64-bits

(D) It 6.25% with 8-bits, 12.5% with 16-bits, 25% with 32-bits and 50 % with 64-bits

---

58. Privacy concern and identity theft are a reality in a technological world. A wallet with driver's license and credit cards can be lost or stolen. A phishing attack on your email account can get lots of personal information. Which one of the following is the most serious problem when the information is compromised?

(A) Credit card number

(B) Social Security number

(C) Checking account number

(D) Bank routing number

59. Consider procedure `mystery` and the code segment that calls the procedure below. Note that *//* indicates integer division.

```
PROCEDURE mystery (x)
{
    n ← LENGTH (x)
    k ← 1
    REPEAT n TIMES
    {
        x[k] ← x[k] // x[1]
        k ← k + 1
    }
}

list ← (11, 22, 33, 44, 55)
mystery (list)
FOR EACH item IN list
{
    DISPLAY (item)
}
```

What is displayed as a result of executing the code segment?

(A) 11 11 11 11 11

(B) 1 22 33 44 55

(C) 1 2 3 4 5

(D) 11 22 33 44 1

60. Some people pirate software for profit and make illegal copies that are sold to others. Then there are people who casually pass a copy on to a friend, ask no money and think this is fine. This type of "casual" pirating is much harder now with a different approach to selling and protecting software.

Which of the following are tactics that companies use to prevent customers from making illegal copies of their software?

I. Software is no longer sold with enclosed activation keys, whether store purchased or company downloaded. The software activation is kept separate. After software installation, a second process activates the software, which is then recorded.

II. Many software companies allow 2 or 3 copies to be made to keep customers happy and avoid this small-scale pirate problem.

III. Some companies are totally getting away from selling software for local computer installation. Customers pay a monthly fee for cloud-based software that cannot be copied or used by somebody else.

(A) I only

(B) I & III only

(C) II & III only

(D) I, II & III

61. What is metadata?

(A) It is the final analysis of large quantities of random data.

(B) It is data that describes other data, such as an audio file, where the metadata specifies the file format, file size and title of the song.

(C) It describes the data that is required for accurate polling analysis.

(D) All of the above

---

62. Consider procedure `swap` and the code segment below.

Procedure swap that swaps list elements

```
PROCEDURE swap (list, a, b)
{
    temp ← list[a]
    list[a] ← list[b]
    list[b] ← temp
}
```

Code segment that swaps list elements

```
temp ← list[a]
list[a] ← list[b]
list[b] ← temp
```

The code segment actually has less program code than the procedure. What then is the advantage of using the procedure?

(A) The procedure is *self-documenting* and provides more clarity in understanding the program logic.

(B) If multiple swaps are necessary the code segment must be written multiple times; the procedure is written once and can then be used multiple times.

(C) Multiple procedures can be placed in libraries that allow convenient access without necessarily understanding how such procedures function.

(D) All of the above

63. A rental company keeps a database for all its rentals. Part of the database information is shown below.

Name	Tool	Date	Duration	Amount	Repair
Tom Smith	Posthole Digger	07-15-17	2	$89	Yes
Sue Jones	Rug Cleaner	07-17-17	1	$24	No
Meg Baker	Boom Lift	07-18-17	7	$987	No
Bob Griffin	Generator	07-20-17	14	$241	No
Bob Weisman	Power Washer	07-20-17	3	$157	Yes
John Eilers	Generator	07-21-17	7	175	No
Kirk Benton	Small Tractor	07-23-17	1	150	No
Nate Barry	Pickup Truck	07-23-17	1	50	No

The database provides lots of information. Which of the following is **NOT** information that can be determined?

(A) Repairs required for rental over 7 days

(B) Busiest days of the week for rentals

(C) Average repair cost based on number of rental days

(D) Average receipt per rental

64. Two mortgage programs provide the following information on a home mortgage loan.

- The mortgage loan amount

- Annual Percentage Rate

- Monthly payment

- Total amount to be paid in 30 years

- Total interest to be paid in 30 years

Two loan officers each used a different program to compute the same information.

The results were not identical on both programs, even if the differences were very small.

For both programs the monthly payments were the same.

Surprisingly, the total payments and total interest were different.

What might account for the difference?

(A) A computer used one or more data types that is too small and caused memory overflow.

(B) One computer used rounded monthly payments and interest payments. The other computer only rounded off after all computations were made.

(C) One of the computers could have a logic error in its program.

(D) The two programs used two different mortgage computation formulas.

65. The question below present two grids. In each grid is a robot represented as a triangle, which initially is located in in two different locations. The robot is capable of moving into a white cell or a gray cell, but it cannot move into a black cell.

Robot Grid A

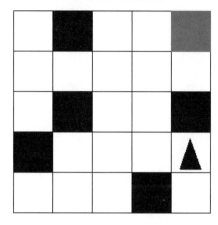

Robot Grid B

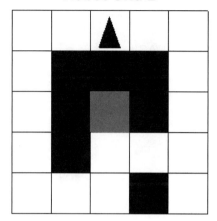

Now consider the adjacent program. The same program is meant to move the robot from its starting position to the gray cell in both grids. The program uses the procedure GOAL_REACHED(), which returns true if the robot is inside the gray cell or returns false otherwise.

Using the same program, for which grid does the program reach the gray cell correctly?

```
REPEAT UNTIL (GOAL_REACHED())
{
    IF (CAN_MOVE ("forward"))
    {
        MOVE_FORWARD ()
    }
    ELSE IF (CAN_MOVE ("left"))
    {
        ROTATE_LEFT ()
        MOVE_FORWARD ()
    }
    ELSE IF (CAN_MOVE ("right"))
    {
        ROTATE_RIGHT ()
        MOVE_FORWARD ()
    }
}
```

(A) Robot Grid A only

(B) Robot Grid B only

(C) Both Robot Grid A and Robot Grid B

(D) Neither Robot Grid A nor Robot Grid B

66. Consider incomplete procedure `purge` below.

Assume that `s1` is a character string stored in a list of characters.

Procedure `purge` returns only the alphabetical characters of `s1`.

```
PROCEDURE purge (s1)
{
    s2 = [ ]
    FOR EACH c IN s1
    {

        < Missing Code >

        s2 = s2 + [c]
    }
    RETURN s2
}
```

Which of the following program statements must replace the < Missing Code > for procedure `purge` to return the correct character string of alphabetical characters only?

(A) IF (c ≥ "A" AND c ≤ "Z") OR (c ≥ "a" AND c ≤ "z")

(B) IF (c ≥ "A" OR c ≤ "Z") AND (c ≥ "a" OR c ≤ "z")

(C) IF (c ≥ "A" OR c ≤ "Z" OR c ≥ "a" OR ≤ "z")

(D) IF (c ≥ "A" AND c ≤ "Z" AND c ≥ "a" AND c ≤ "z")

Directions: For each of the remaining questions, <u>two</u> of the suggested answers will be correct. You must select both correct answer choices to earn credit. No partial credit will be earned if only one correct choice is selected. Select the two that are best in each case and then enter both of the appropriate letters in the corresponding space on the answer sheet.

---

67. Consider the procedure `mystery` below.

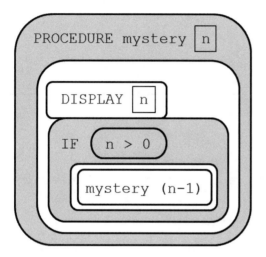

What will be output as a consequence of executing procedure `mystery`?

Select <u>two</u> answers.

(A) `0, 1, 2 .... n-1, n`

(B) `4, 3, 2, 1, 0` if n equals 4

(C) `0, 1, 2, 3, 4` if n equals 4

(D) `n, n-1, n-2, .... 2, 1, 0`

68. This question uses a robot in a grid of squares. The robot is represented as a triangle and starts at the top-left, gray cell on the grid, facing right.

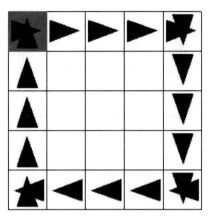

The goal of a program segment for this question is to make the robot move clockwise around the grid and finish at the same starting cell. The path of the robot is shown by the adjacent grid image.

Which of the program segments below will make the robot move in the required pattern?

Select <u>two</u> answers.

(A)	(B)
| ```
x ← 1
REPEAT 19 TIMES
{
    IF (x MOD 5 = 0)
    {
        ROTATE_RIGHT ()
    }
    MOVE_FORWARD()
    x ← x + 1
}
``` | ```
x ← 1
REPEAT 19 TIMES
{
    IF (x = 5 OR x = 10 OR x = 15)
    {
        ROTATE_RIGHT ()
    }
    MOVE_FORWARD()
    x ← x + 1
}
``` |
| (C) | (D) |
| ```
REPEAT 4 TIMES ()
{
    REPEAT 4 TIMES ()
    {
        MOVE_FORWARD ()
    }
    ROTATE_RIGHT ()
}
``` | ```
x ← 1
REPEAT 16 TIMES
{
    IF (x = 5 OR x = 9 OR x = 13)
    {
        ROTATE_RIGHT ()
    }
    MOVE_FORWARD()
    x ← x + 1
}
``` |

69. Frequently, people think that the *Internet* and the World Wide Web are one and the same. Which of the following are true statements about the Internet and the World Wide Web?

Select <u>two</u> answers.

(A) The Internet is an enormous network of networks.

(B) The Internet and the World Wide Web are synonymous.

(C) The World Wide Web is a group of more than one billion websites that are built on the Internet.

(D) Software, like Internet Explorer and Firefox are used by routers to manage the Internet.

---

70. There three measures of centrality, *mean, median, mode.*
Which of the following will compute the *mean* of a group of 5 numbers?

Select <u>two</u> answers.

(A) mean = (n1 + n2 + n3 + n4 + n5) / 5

(B) mean = n1/5 + n2/5 + n3/5 + n4/5 + n5/5

(C) mean = n1 + n2 + n3 + n4 + n5 / 5

(D) mean = (n1 + n2 + n3 + n4 + n5) / (5/2)

71. Cloud computing is very popular and heavily promoted. Everything seems possible with the Cloud. Are there any major issues with this popular Internet technology?

Select <u>two</u> answers.

(A) Using the Cloud does cost money. There is some free use, but that is very limited in data storage.

(B) Using the Cloud is quite complicated. It is much simpler to work with local applications and data storage.

(C) If all your applications and data are in the Cloud, you cannot function at all when the Internet is down.

(D) There is a security concern. Is your data really safe?

---

72. Consider the following Boolean Expressions

```
x ← < unknown Boolean value >
y ← < Unknown Boolean value >
result1 ← NOT (x AND y)
result2 ← NOT (x) OR NOT (y)
result3 ← result1 = result2

result4 ← NOT (x OR y)
result5 ← NOT (x) AND NOT (y)
result6 ← result4 = result5
```

Which Boolean variables will always be `true`?

Select <u>two</u> answers.

(A) `result2`

(B) `result5`

(C) `result3`

(D) `result6`

73. The binary number `11111110` is equivalent to which one of the following numbers?

Select two answers.

(A) `fe` (Base-16)

(B) `254` (Base-10)

(C) `1d4` (Base-16)

(D) `246` (Base-10)

74. A programmer is working on a graphics program in a language that includes many program commands for making graphics shapes, like lines, rectangle, circles and arcs.

Taking advantages of such program commands is a good example of using abstraction in programming. When the programmer uses a `drawCircle` command and only needs to know the (x,y) coordinate of the center of the circle and the radius of the circle at least two abstractions are being used.

Which of the following are the abstractions used to draw a circle?

Select two answers.

(A) Graphics abstraction

(B) Procedural abstraction

(C) Mathematical abstraction

(D) Boolean abstraction